ALL THE TROUBLE

IN THE WORLD

ALSO BY P. J. O'ROURKE

Modern Manners

The Bachelor Home Companion

Republican Party Reptile

Holidays in Hell

Parliament of Whores

Give War a Chance

*Age and Guile Beat Youth, Innocence,
and a Bad Haircut*

ALL THE TROUBLE
IN THE WORLD

The Lighter Side of Overpopulation,

Famine, Ecological Disaster,

Ethnic Hatred, Plague, and Poverty

P. J. O'ROURKE

THE ATLANTIC MONTHLY PRESS
NEW YORK

Printed in the United States of America

FIRST PAPERBACK EDITION

Library of Congress Cataloging-in-Publication Data

O'Rourke, P. J.
    All the trouble in the world: the lighter side of overpopulation,
    famine, ecological disaster, ethnic hatred, plague, and poverty / by
    P. J. O'Rourke.—1st ed.
    , I. Title.
PN6162.073   1994   818'.5402—dc20   94-21547
        ISBN 0-87113-611-2 (pbk.)

Design by Laura Hammond Hough

The Atlantic Monthly Press
841 Broadway
New York, NY 10003

10 9 8 7 6 5 4 3 2 1

For Ed and Myra Downer

Who went to a lot of trouble

ACKNOWLEDGMENTS

Writing this book required an enormous amount of help from friends. To them goes the credit. I'll take the money. Writing this book also required an enormous amount of help from enemies. Particularly, I'd like to thank Vice President Al Gore for being the perfect straw man on such subjects as the environment, ecology, and population. Sorry, Al, for repeatedly calling you a fascist twinkie and intellectual dolt. It's nothing personal. I just think you have repulsive totalitarian inclinations and the brains of a King Charles spaniel.

As always I owe a huge debt (and, pay advances considered, I mean that literally) to *Rolling Stone* magazine. Jann Wenner, friend and boss, has allowed me the latitude to rave and vociferate, although he disagrees with almost all my opinions. (I'll make a Republican of you yet, Jann. Just wait until you do your estate planning for the kids.)

Rolling Stone underwrote my trips to Somalia, the Amazon, Rio, ex-Yugoslavia, Haiti, and Vietnam. The "field work" in the chapters about famine, the environment, saving the earth, multiculturalism, plague, and poverty first appeared, in somewhat different forms, in *Rolling Stone*. Editor Eric Etheridge gave shape and sense to these stories, carefully applying large dabs of Gibberish Remover$_{TM}$ to my manuscripts. And Tobias Perse and Corey Seymour did the real work—phoning military juntas to see if they take the Visa card, making sure my war-zone hotel rooms had color TV and a heated pool, and scouring encyclopedias to find out if King Charles spaniels really do have lower IQs than U.S. vice presidents.

A number of other individuals and organizations deserve special thanks for their assistance and succor. Tina Mallon, Nick and Mary Eberstadt, Andy and Denise Ferguson, and Chris and Lucy Buckley listened to me prate about this book for two years and none of them surrendered to the temptation to stuff an oven mitt in my mouth or hit me over the head with a bottle. Instead they gave me ideas, encouragement, and help in my legwork. Nick Eberstadt used his expertise in population studies, economics, and statistics to aid me (and the reader) in making some sense of the numbers in this book (though I am sole author of all errors in same). And Nick explained to me the mysteries of the Georgetown University Library stacks and showed me where they keep the books with the good parts. (Fourth floor. Ovid. But you'd better be able to read Latin.)

The Cato Institute in Washington, D.C., made all its very considerable resources available to me and named me "H. L. Mencken Research Fellow," in case I needed a business card to upset liberals. Cato President Ed Crane also found the F. Scott Fitzgerald quote which prefaces this book. My thanks to him and to Cato Executive Vice President David Boaz and, especially, to Cato's Director of Natural Resource Studies Jerry Taylor. To Jerry I owe not only much of the information but most of the thinking and many of the jokes in my chapters about the environment and ecology. Jerry is to the idiot environmentalists what . . . well, what pollution is to the environment.

Wisdom, enlightenment, and inside poop were also provided by Grover Norquist of Americans for Tax Reform, John A. Baden of the Foundation for Research on Economics and the Environment,

Daniel S. Peters of Procter & Gamble and by the writers, scholars, and staff members at the *American Spectator,* the American Enterprise Institute, the Heritage Foundation, and Hillsdale College.

I'd like to thank Amy Kaplan Lamb for the extraordinary job she did fact-checking this book. Any facts found to be nonfactual are that way because of pigheaded author insistence, not because Amy didn't know better. And I'd like to thank Larry Gray for providing the author with Caribbean R&R after Christmases spent, successively, in Somalia and Haiti.

Thanks are also due to people for their written works: to the late Warren Brookes for his newspaper columns about bad public policy thinking; to the late Friedrich Hayek for his seminal condemnation of government planning, *The Road to Serfdom;* and to the unlate, fully extant, Peter W. Huber for *Galileo's Revenge,* his analysis of the evil effects of "junk science" on systems of law.

I have tried to make a list, as best I could, of people who helped me with individual chapters. Some names have been left out to save careers or protect reputations; other names are missing because of the amnesia of ingratitude. My apologies for any untoward exclusions (or inclusions, as the case may be).

Photojournalist John Giannini traveled with me to both Bangladesh and Vietnam. Not only was he a boon companion and a great picture taker but he also did extensive fact-finding about both countries and made all the labyrinthine tour arrangements with the Vietnamese government. Plus, in Bangkok, John took me to a bar full of the most amazingly beautiful half-naked . . . caring and sensitive individuals of the female gender, whom I respected as persons, honest.

In Somalia ABC Radio's John Lyons once again hired me as "Correspondent-Without-a-Clue." The broadcast professionals in Mogadishu were patient with my useless presence. Special thanks to Carlos Mavroleon, one of the few people (Somalis included) who know something about Somalia, and to Neil Patterson and Nasser Al Ibrahim, two of the original "combat accountants," who were always ready with a huge pile of dirty Somali banknotes when we needed them.

In the Amazon I had the great pleasure of traveling with Craig Nelson, Brenda Segel, Juan Tejada, and T. & B.S. (whose identities must remain secret because they are being pursued, very slowly, by sloths). Sean Macy provided me with heaps of material for the historical section of the Environment chapter.

Much of the research in the Ecology chapter was drawn from the labor of Ronald Bailey, whose book *Eco-Scam* was published by St. Martin's Press in 1993, and from the work of Ben Bolch and Harold Lyons, whose book *Apocalypse Not* was published by the Cato Institute the same year. A long talk with Bailey, Jerry Taylor, and Kent Jeffreys, director of Environmental Studies at the Competitive Enterprise Institute, gave me the outline for my ecological arguments.

My trip to the Czech Republic was organized by Therese Lyons at the National Forum Foundation, which organization is devoted to fostering democracy and individual rights in the former communist world. Therese also put together a giant package of background information about East bloc pollution. Forum Foundation's president, Jim Denton, met me in Prague and arranged to have Ivanna Husák and Martin Weiss show me around and translate. If I managed to explain anything of the political and economic complexities in the Czech Republic, it is as a result of the efforts of Ivanna, Martin, Jim, and Therese.

I was able to drive about in style and comfort behind the former Iron Curtain due to the good offices of my old friend David E. Davis, Jr., editor and publisher of *Automobile* magazine. David E. called Jürgen Hödel at the Mercedes-Benz press office and Jürgen persuaded Mercedes to loan me a splendid 300 diesel sedan. I would argue that the appearance of this marvelous crimson vehicle in Chabarovice, Libkovice, and Ústí nad Labem made more converts to capitalism in a week than Radio Free Europe did in four decades. My thanks also to Jürgen and Cindy Hödel for their kind hospitality when I returned to Germany.

In Rio de Janiero I fell in with Juan William Parke from Tulane University. Juan has a keen eye for the absurd and got an eyeful of it at the Earth Summit. I have borrowed liberally from his vision.

Rolling Stone's brother publication *Men's Journal,* under the fine editorship of John Rasmus, sent me back to my alma mater, where Miami University's Vice President for University Relations and Director of University Communication Richard D. Little arranged for me to pester everyone on campus. And Miami University President Paul Risser was a more than indulgent host. (Sorry about the food fight. That wasn't a real Renoir, was it?) I'd also like to thank David and Sue Frazier who, through their respective positions in the Miami English Department and Miami Student Aid Office in the 1960s, gave me the chance to get a college education in the first place. (Please know you're not responsible for what I've done with it.) And thanks, too, to Bill and Dee Dee Bartlett and Martha Williams, who've been my friends for more than a quarter of a century now. And we're still going out and having just as much fun as we ever did in the 1960s. Or let's say we are, anyway.

For assistance in my travels through former Yugoslavia (and for the loan of a flak jacket) I'd like to thank Bob Simpson of the BBC and his cameraman, Tuna. The ebullient and brave—as it turned out, too brave—Tuna would be killed in the fighting not long after I left Bosnia. And I'd like to thank Ed Gorman of the London *Times,* from whom I shamelessly stole the description of downtown Zagreb: "an old town of regulation charm, a hilltop cathedral inspiring the standard awe. . . ."

My doctor, William Hughes, prepared medical kits for all my journeys and made sure that I had the right shots, vaccinations, and, as it were, prophylactics. For the Plague chapter Dr. Hughes also delved into medical libraries in pursuit of technical literature about childhood diarrhea and explained to me what this technical literature meant. My thanks to him and to Dan Epstein at the Pan American Health Organization, Chris Isham at ABC News, Richard Morse and Ronald Derenoncourt in Haiti, and AP Caribbean News

Editor David Beard, author of the slogan "Diarrhea—It Can Be Contained."

And, finally, my trip to Vietnam was greatly aided by Senator John McCain, once a POW there, and by Garnett Bell, director of the U.S. Office for POW/MIA Affairs in Hanoi—sterling gentlemen both.

In closing I would like to express the greatest appreciation of—indeed, would fain write an encomium to—my editor and publisher, Morgan Entrekin; my publisher in Great Britain, Jacqui Graham; my lecture agent, Don Epstein; his chief of staff, Holly Berger, who arranged much of my travel; and my literary agent, Bob Dattila. My style of writing does not turn much toward praise or gratitude. Excuse me, each of you, if I am rusty in these forms of expression. Thanks.

—P. J. O'Rourke
March Hare Farm
Sharon, New Hampshire

"*I read somewhere that the sun's getting hotter every year,*" *said Tom genially.* "*It seems that pretty soon the earth's going to fall into the sun—or wait a minute—it's just the opposite—the sun's getting colder every year.*"

—F. Scott Fitzgerald, *The Great Gatsby*

CONTENTS

"MENCKEN'S LAW"
Whenever A annoys or injures B on the pretense of saving or improving X, A is a scoundrel.
—Newspaper Days, *1941*

ALL THE TROUBLE

IN THE WORLD

1 FASHIONABLE WORRIES

If Meat Is Murder, Are Eggs Rape?

❚

This is a moment of hope in history. Why doesn't anybody say so? We are no longer in grave danger of the atomic war which, for nearly fifty years, threatened to annihilate humanity and otherwise upset everyone's weekend plans. The nasty, powerful and belligerent empire that was the Soviet Union has fallen apart. It's nothing now but a space on the map full of quarreling nationalities with too many k's and z's in their names—armed Scrabble contestants. The other great malevolent regime of recent days, Red China, has decided upon conquest of the world's shower flip-flop market as its form of global domination. The bad political ideas that have menaced our century—fascism, communism, Ted Kennedy for President—are in retreat. Colonialism has disappeared, and hence the residents of nearly a quarter of the earth's surface are being spared visits from Princess Di. The last place on the planet where white supremacy held sway has elected a president of rich, dark hue. Apartheid-style racism is now relegated to a few pitiful and insignificant venues such as the U.S. Senate (and, if you think

Caucasians have any claim to genetic superiority, imagine majoring in U.S. Senate Studies).

Things are better now than things have been since men began keeping track of things. Things are better than they were only a few years ago. Things are better, in fact, than they were at 9:30 this morning, thanks to Tylenol and two Bloody Marys.

But that's personal and history is general. It's always possible to come down with the mumps on V-J Day or to have, right in the middle of the fall of the Berlin Wall, a piece of it fall on your foot. In general, life is better than it ever has been, and if you think that, in the past, there was some golden age of pleasure and plenty to which you would, if you were able, transport yourself, let me say one single word: "dentistry."

We know the truth of these matters from stories we've heard in our own homes. Existence has improved enormously within the lifetimes of our immediate family members. My Grandfather O'Rourke was born in 1877 and born into a pretty awful world, even if we don't credit all of his Irish embroidery upon the horrors. The average wage was little more than a dollar a day. That's if you had a job. O'Rourkes were not known to do so. The majority of people were farmers, and do you know what time cows get up in the morning? Working outside all day before sunblock or bikinis had been invented, agricultural laborers got very spotty tans. People had to make their own fun, and, as with most do-it-yourself projects, the results were . . . witness quilting bees. And the typical old-fashioned diet was so bad it almost resembled modern dieting.

Women couldn't vote, not even incredibly intelligent First Ladies who were their own people and had amazing inner strengths plus good luck playing the cattle futures market. (For all we know, Mrs. Rutherford B. Hayes had quite an eye for beef on the hoof.)

Without a voting First Lady, there was no health-care reform. Of course, there was also no health care. And not much health. Illness was ever-present, and the most trivial infection might prove fatal. The germ theory of disease as argued by Pasteur was just another wacky French idea with no more effect on the people of the 1870s than Deconstructionism has on us. Men customarily wed multiple wives, not by way of philandering but because of deaths in childbirth. The children died, too, sometimes before a suitable foot-long nineteenth-century name could be given them. A walk through an old graveyard shows our ancestors often had more dead children than we have live ones.

Pollution was unchecked and mostly unthought of. Sewage was considered treated if dumped in a river. Personal hygiene was practiced, when at all, on the face, neck, and hands up to the wrists. My mother's mother (from the indoor-plumbing side of the family) said that, when she was little, a hired girl had told her to always wear at least one piece of clothing when washing herself "because a lady never gets completely undressed."

Everything was worse for everybody. Blacks could no more vote than women could and were prevented from doing so by more violent means. About 10 percent of America's population had been born in slavery. "Coon," "kike," "harp" and "spic" were conversational terms. It was a world in which "nigger" was not a taboo name, but the second half of "Beavis and Butt-head" would have been.

Nowadays we can hardly count our blessings, one of which is surely that we don't have to do all that counting—computers do it for us. Information is easily had. Education is readily available. Opportunity knocks, it jiggles the doorknob, it will try the window if we don't have the alarm system on.

The highest standards of luxury and comfort, as known only to the ridiculously wealthy a few generations ago, would hardly do on a modern white-water rafting trip. Our clothing is more comfortable, our abodes are warmer, better-smelling, and vermin-free. Our food is fresher. Our lights are brighter. Travel is swift. And communication is sure.

Even the bad things are better than they used to be. Bad music, for instance, has gotten much briefer. Wagner's *Ring Cycle* takes four days to perform while "Mmm Mmm Mmm Mmm" by the Crash Test Dummies lasts little more than three minutes.

▌▌

Life is sweet. But you could spend a long time reading, going to the movies, and watching TV and not hear this mentioned. Especially, watching daytime TV. Of course, if you're watching a lot of daytime TV your life probably is dreadful. But, as I pointed out, that's your problem, not history's. History is on a roll, a toot, a bender. No doubt it will all come crashing down around our ears one day when a comet hits the earth or Sally Jessy Raphaël becomes Chief Justice of the Supreme Court. But, in the meantime, we should be enjoying ourselves, and we are not. Gloom enfolds the earth. Tales of woe reach us from every corner of the globe. Moans of "unfair," "unjust," and "poor me" are heard around the planet and are nowhere louder than in my own backyard.

Right now, at the end of the second millennium, is the best moment of all time, and right here, in the United States, is the best place to be at that moment. And do I hark to sounds of glee echoing midst purple mountains' majesty and rolling across the fruited plains? No. I hear America whining, crybaby to the world. I behold my country in a pet—beefing, carping, crabbing, bitching, sniveling, mewling, fretting, yawping, bellyaching, and being pickle-pussed. A colossus that stood astride the earth now lies on the floor pounding its fists and kicking its feet, transformed into a fussy-pants and a sputter-budget. The streets of the New World are paved with onions. Everybody's got a squawk. We have become a nation of calamity howlers, crêpe hangers, sour guts, and mopes—a land with the grumbles.

On the Fourth of July, 1993, the lead story on the front page of the *Boston Globe* read:

> The country that celebrates its 217th birthday today is free, at peace, relatively prosperous—but deeply anxious. . . . The American people are troubled, beset by doubts, full of anger.

And any peek into the media produces examples in plenty of the same sobs and groans, often from improbable Jeremiahs.

In the April 24, 1994, issue of the *New York Times Book Review*, Fran R. Schumer made reference to "the modern era, when anomie, caused by any number of factors—the decline of religion and community, the anonymity of modern life—gave rise to selfish, obsessive, 20th-century man." Ms. Schumer writes the Underground Gourmet column for *New York* magazine. All she was doing in the *NYTBR* was reviewing a book about food.

"In a world with the cosmic staggers, where the Four Horsemen . . . are on an outright rampage" began a profile of harmless comedian Jerry Seinfeld in the May 1994 *Vanity Fair*.

Licensed psychiatrist and tenured Harvard professor John E. Mack has written a book, *Abduction,* claiming that spacemen are kidnapping us. Why should the little green men bother? So they can, said Mack, tell earthlings that we're causing ecological ruin.

"Ecological ruin, shrinking white-collar job market and fear of intimacy confronting his generation" is how that journal of deep thinking, *People,* describes the subject matter of Douglas Coupland, latest young writer to complain his way to literary prominence.

Coupland's first novel, *Generation X,* was a detailed account of how wretched and spitty life is for middle-class white kids born after 1960. "Our Parents Had More" is the title of chapter 2. In case you missed the point (or fell asleep while the plot ossified) Coupland included several pages of depressing statistics at the back of *Generation X.* E.g., according to a *Time*/CNN telephone poll taken in June of 1990, 65 percent of eighteen- to twenty-nine-year-old Americans agree that "given the ways things are, it will be much harder for people in my generation to live as comfortably as previous generations."

Of course it's difficult for these youngsters to know if they're going to live as comfortably as their parents did because the kids are so immobilized by despair over ecological ruin, shrinking white-collar job market, and fear of intimacy that they're all still living at home.

But William T. Vollmann—the youthful author of *An Afghanistan Picture Show, Whores for Gloria, Butterfly Stories,* and numerous other books (who has been acclaimed a genius by the sort of people who acclaim those things)—knows it will take more than a split-level in the suburbs to redeem our ghastly existences. "I'd say the biggest hope that we have right now is the AIDS epidemic," Vollmann told Michael Coffey in the July 13, 1992, issue of *Publishers Weekly*. "Maybe the best thing that could happen would be if it were to wipe out half or two-thirds of the people in the world. Then the ones who survived would just be so busy getting things together that they'd have to help each other, and in time the world would recover ecologically, too."

Maybe we should also take dope. *Listening to Prozac* by Peter Kramer spent six months on the *New York Times* bestseller list. An article in the May 5, 1994, "Drugs in America" special issue of *Rolling Stone* said, "Given the psychic condition of the nation today [heroin] may be just what the doctor ordered. 'With heroin,' as a former user points out, 'your life can be falling apart around you and everything's still fine with you.'"

But no. It's worse than that. Being and creation are so horrible, even heroin can't make them better. Otherwise Nirvana lead caterwaul Kurt Cobain would still be with us. And what a tortured cry of existential despair that was when Kurt took a twenty-gauge shotgun and splattered his brains, or whatever it was he had in his skull, all over the Cobain guest house.

"That was his message, that life is futile," a twenty-six-year-old named Bob Hince told *Washington Post* reporter Jonathan Freedland. Freedland was writing a feature piece for the April 24, 1994, Sunday

Show section titled "Generation Hex." He found Mr. Hince drinking in one of the Seattle bars where Nirvana got its start. "We all feel the monotony, we all feel we cannot control our circumstances," said Mr. Hince, who is clearly a spokesperson not just for his generation but for all of America and maybe for space aliens.

Freedland reported that "[Hince] has completed six years of study in molecular biology but is now headed for Alaska to work as a salmon fisherman. His dyed red hair nearly covers his eyes, falling behind the lenses of his retro, Buddy Holly glasses. . . . 'It's just ambivalence,' he says. 'What am I supposed to be?' "

Personally, I think Bob Hince won't have to worry about what he'll be if the people who paid for his six years of studying molecular biology get their hands on him. But, as Nirvana would say, "Nevermind." The whole world is rotten. Everything stinks. Nobody loves me. Everybody hates me. My name is Legion. I'll be your server tonight. The special is worms.

Why are we so unhappy? Is it, as that Cassandra of food critics, Fran R. Schumer, would have it, "anomie" caused by "the decline of religion and community, the anonymity of modern life"? Sure. Going to church was always one of my favorite things to do. Zoning-board meetings are also a blast. And wasn't that great the way Mom knew exactly who was downstairs in the rec room with you? "Billy, Mary, Patrick, Susan—how come you kids have the lights off?" And what is it with this *anomie* stuff anyway? We all know perfectly well we've got no idea what the word means. We might just as well say we're suffering from yohimbine or rigadoon or Fibonacci sequence.

Are we depressed by lower expectations? Back in the sixties I expected Permanent Woodstock—a whole lifetime of sitting in the mud, smoking Oaxacan ditch weed, listening to amplifier feedback, and pawing a Long Island chiropodist's daughter who thought she'd been abducted by aliens from outer space. Show me somebody with lower expectations than mine.

Are we disheartened by the breakup of the family? Nobody who ever met my family is.

Or maybe what's got us down is that God created a world with evil in it. Saturday nights would be damned dull if He hadn't.

Yes, there is misery and suffering on earth. Thanks for adding to it, Killjoy. Life seems pointless. This isn't a reason to party? And the world's about to end. As if we were going to live forever otherwise. Will it matter in a hundred years if we went one by one or in a bunch? Besides, the world's been about to end for a long time, Hardly a mythology lacks its Götterdämmerung. The penultimate verse of the New Testament has Jesus saying, "Surely I come quickly." And he wasn't coming over for a swim. (Note to kids: Finish that math assignment. Somehow the world never manages to end before your homework is due.) Also, if the world's about to end, why aren't things more interesting? Why are people abandoning themselves to cares and gripes instead of to booze-ups and orgies? Why aren't I having an affair with Ava Gardner the way Gregory Peck was in *On the Beach?*

Fear and dread are not what make us upset, or alienation either. (If alienation is your problem, call John E. Mack and leave the rest of us alone.) We whine because it works. We used to be shunned for weeping in our beer. Now we go on *Oprah.* If our complaint is hideous enough, we get a TV movie made about our life. Congress passes legislation to give us money and special parking places. We get into college with two-digit SAT scores, and we can sue the school for discriminating against Sad Sacks if we flunk. The president feels our pain.

Grouching is a good excuse. We are, as even the pinko, querulous *Boston Globe* is willing to admit, "free, at peace, relatively prosperous." We have the opportunity and the means to do almost anything. How come we haven't done it? Here we've got all this material well-being, liberty, and good luck, and we're still our crummy old selves—flabby around the middle, limited out on our VISA cards. The job is a bore. The house is a mess. And *Melrose Place* is in reruns. It's not our fault, it's life's. The world is an awful place so we're not much good either.

We're all geniuses. We know that. But why haven't we had any genius ideas or done any genius deeds? Something terrible must be holding us back, repressed memories maybe. We forgot we were molested as children by someone we loved. It's coming back now. Milk and cookies weren't all Santa was chewing on after he came down the chimney.

Fretting makes us important. Say you're an adult male and you're skipping down the street whistling "Last Train to Clarksville." People will call you a fool. But lean over to the person next to you on a subway and say, "How can you smile while innocents are dying in Tibet?" You'll acquire a reputation for great seriousness and also more room to sit down.

Tragedy is better than comedy for self-dramatization, as every teenager knows. Think how little attention we pay to a teen who's bustling around the house with a big smile on his face, greeting parents and siblings with cheery salutations. . . . Actually, we'd pay a lot of attention and rush him to the drug detox center, post haste. But you know what I mean. Would you rather star in *Hamlet* or *Three's Company?*

Being gloomy is easier than being cheerful. Anybody can say "I've got cancer" and get a rise out of a crowd. But how many of us can do five minutes of good stand-up comedy?

And worrying is less work than doing something to fix the worry. This is especially true if we're careful to pick the biggest possible problems to worry about. Everybody wants to save the earth; nobody wants to help Mom do the dishes.

III

Thus, in fin de siècle civilization, we find ourselves with grave, momentous concerns galore.

The Clinton administration State Department has created a position of Worrywart-in-Charge, an "undersecretary of global affairs" who is to be responsible for "worldwide programs in human rights, the environment, population control and anti-narcotics efforts." Timothy E. Wirth, nominee for this dreary post, testified before the Senate Foreign Relations Committee. Fussed Wirth, "Growth that is all-too-capable of doubling—even tripling—today's global population in the next century is already a force contributing to violent disorder and mass dislocations in resource-poor societies. Some of the resulting refugees are our near neighbors." Oh those massively dislocated Nova Scotians, breeding like mink. "Others—refugees-in-waiting," said Wirth, "press hungrily against the fabric of social and political stability around the world." And that suit's going to have to go to the cleaner's.

Everywhere we see the imposition of grave concern into the most mundane and trivial aspects of life. Lightning Comics, a Detroit publisher of funny books, has created a super hero, Bloodfire, who is HIV positive. Which should cool Lois Lane.

A TV revival of *Bonanza* had, as its villain, a man who wanted to strip-mine the Ponderosa.

The Parliament of the World's Religions, meeting in Chicago in 1993, issued a statement called "Towards a Global Ethic" that opined, "We must move beyond the dominance of greed for power, prestige, money and consumption to make a just and peaceful world." A just and peaceful world full of powerless nobodies who are broke and have empty shopping malls.

On Earth Day, 1994, the National Council of Churches suggested that Protestants make a "confession of environmental sins": "We use more than our share of the Earth's resources. We are responsible for massive pollution of earth, water and sky. We thoughtlessly drop garbage around our homes, schools, churches, places of work, and places of play." (Which is why Episcopalian neighborhoods are always such dumps.) "We squander resources on technologies of destruction. Bombs come before bread." And Fran R. Schumer wonders at the decline of religion. I admit to sloth, gluttony, and coveting my neighbor's handmaiden, but I have not traded any Pepperidge Farm for nuclear devices.

Hanna-Barbera has a *Captain Planet and the Planeteers* animated cartoon about saving the you-know-what. Margot Kidder supplies the voice of "Gaia, the Spirit of the Earth." "I am worried about the planet for my daughter's future," announced Kidder in an interview with the *Chicago Tribune*. Kidder said her daughter had once told her, "Mom, when we grow up, the world may not be here."

The May 1994 issue of *Barbie* comics, featuring the adventures of the doll by that name, had a story about how deaf people are discriminated against. There was a page at the end where Barbie gave a lesson in sign language, showing us the signs for "push-up bra," "Let's go shopping," and "diamond tennis bracelet from middle-aged gentleman admirer." Just kidding. Barbie showed us the signs for "friend," "hello," "thanks," and that sort of thing.

The April 1994 issue of *Washingtonian* ran an article by my friend Andrew Ferguson about corporate "multicultural training." Andy quoted one of the trainers (or facilitators, as they like to be called), whose job it is to instill "sensitivity" about age, race, gender, disability, sexual orientation, and the kitchen sink into employees of Washington businesses:

> "It's a function of capitalism, isn't it?" says the facilitator. "Capitalism requires scarcity to function. It's built into the system—no scarcity, no profit.
>
> "That's the kind of power relationships capitalism creates. Sharing power is not something a male-dominated culture naturally gravitates towards, is it?"

The facilitator, a male, was being paid two thousand dollars a day.

And here is my favorite tale of pained solicitude, from an AP wire story that appeared in the *Arab News* in Saudi Arabia during the Gulf War, and which I have been saving ever since:

> Game wardens and wildlife biologists were among those gathered for nearly eight hours on a farm in northwestern Louisiana to save what they thought was a bear 50 to 60 feet up in a pine tree. A veterinarian fired tranquilizer darts at the critter in an effort to get it down. Deputies and wildlife agents strung a net to catch the bear when the tranquilizers took effect. . . . "People really wanted . . . to help and protect that bear and get him where he was supposed to be," Norman Gordan, the owner of the farm said. . . . It wasn't until the tree was chopped down . . . that they discovered they were rescuing a dart-riddled garbage bag.

Some of the folks propounding the above-listed anxieties, cavils, and peeves are amateurs: New Agers who will believe in anything but facts, environmentalist softies who think the white rats should be running the cancer labs, or bong-smoke theorists who would have the world be as stupid as they are. But many of the fretful—the "multicultural training facilitator" is an appalling example—are pros.

Professional worriers put our fears to use. Masters of Sanctimony have an agenda. The licensed and certified holier-than-thou work toward a political goal. And whether these agony merchants are leftists (as they usually are) or rightists (as they certainly can be) or whether they head off in some other and worse direction (the way religious fundamentalists do), the political goal is the same.

In fact, if we use the word *politics* in its broadest sense, there really is only one political goal in the world. Politics is the business of getting power and privilege without possessing merit. A politician is anyone who asks individuals to surrender part of their liberty—their power and privilege—to State, Masses, Mankind, Planet Earth, or whatever. This state, those masses, that mankind, and the planet will then be run by . . . politicians.

Politicians are always searching for some grave alarm which will cause individuals to abandon their separate concerns and prerogatives and act in concert so that politicians can wield the baton. Calls to mortal combat are forever being sounded (though only metaphorically—politicians don't like real wars, too much merit is involved). The idea is that people will drop everything for a WWIII. Remember the War on Poverty? And how Jimmy Carter asked Americans to respond to a mere rise in the price of crude oil with "the moral equivalent of war"? (What were we supposed to do, shame the gas station attendant to death?) Now we're "fighting pollution," "battling AIDS," "conquering racism," et cetera.

Ralph Nader is as much a politician as Senator Robert Packwood, even if Ralph isn't as smooth with the ladies. Such professional worriers as Al Gore, Paul Ehrlich, Jeremy Rifkin, Joycelyn Elders, Barry Commoner, Jesse Jackson, and Captain Planet want our freedom, on the grounds that they are better than us. (You may have noticed how politicians are wiser, kinder, and more honest than you are.) Because politicians worry so much about overpopulation, famine, ecological disaster, ethnic hatred, plague, and poverty, they must be superior people. And because they worry so much, they must be experts, too. (Said the Austrian political economist Friedrich Hayek, in his 1944 book *The Road to Serfdom,* "There could hardly be a more unbearable—and more irrational—world than one in which the most eminent specialists in each field were allowed to proceed unchecked with the realization of their ideals.")

The bullying of fellow citizens by means of dreads and frights has been going on since paleolithic times. Greenpeace fund-raisers on the subject of global warming are not much different than tribal wizards on the subject of lunar eclipses. "Oh, no, Night Wolf is eating the Moon Virgin. Give me silver and I will make him spit her out."

IV

Let us, for the space of this book, quit worrying and go take a look at what we are worrying about. And let us take a look not only at the worry but at the place where the worry is happening, the context within which the worry occurs, and the people who are doing the worrisome thing or having it done to them. And let us keep in mind about these people that, whatever their language, culture, or religion, whatever peculiar thing they are wearing through their nose, whatever caliber item they have pointed at our head, they are people, too. They are just as dumb, stinky, and ridiculous as we are.

Human problems are complex. If something isn't complex it doesn't qualify as problematic. Very simple bad things are not worth troubling ourselves about. Die and that's that. Survive, on the other hand, and we encounter all sorts of conundrums and puzzles. These are what the people in this book face. I admit to sight-seeing among their puzzlements. I get off the point. But so much of life seems to *be* off the point.

And worry itself is fairly pointless. Worrying is a futuristic matter. About that future, Sydney Smith said almost two centuries ago, "We know nothing of tomorrow; our business is to be good and happy today." To worry is an act of sublime ignorance. However, we can guess a few truths on the subject. One is that the usual solutions proffered for the usual worries are usually wrong.

Going around the poor parts of the world shoving birth-control pills down people's throats, hustling them into abortion clinics, and giving them cheap prizes for getting sterilized is to assume that those people don't want babies as much as we do, that they won't like those babies as well as we like ours, and that little brown and yellow babies are not as good as the adorable pink, rich kind. American children grow up to be valuable citizens. Bangladeshi children grow up to be part of the world population problem. They just aren't giving birth to any Marky Marks or Howard Sterns in Dhaka.

Modern famine is either the result of deliberate political policies (the Ukraine in the 1930s, Sudan right now) or of terrible economic ideas (Ireland in the 1840s, China in the late 1950s). To give food to the rulers of a famished country (as we did in Ethiopia) or to distribute food so that the rulers benefit from the distribution (as they did in Somalia) is simply to increase the power of the people who caused the famine. Then we are puzzled that our food donations don't stem world hunger.

Some kind of central planning seems to be the object of most environmental activists. But why is a politburo expected to work better for plants and animals than it did for Russians?

Giving certain races or ethnic groups special rights and privileges is no better (in fact, no different) than giving special rights and privileges to dukes and earls. Noblemen are a minority, too, after all.

Reacting to a plague by holding demonstrations, by loudly announcing how upset we are that disease exists is no more efficacious than sacrificing virgins (or, in the case of AIDS, than throwing drug-free, monogamous, heterosexual members of the middle class down a well).

And the poor of the world cannot be made rich by redistribution of wealth. Poverty can't be eliminated by punishing people who've escaped poverty, taking their money and giving it as a reward to people who have failed to escape. Economic leveling doesn't work. Whether we call it Marxism, Progressive Reform, or Clintonomics, the result is the same slide into the stygian pit. Communists worship Satan; socialists think perdition is a good system run by bad men; and liberals want us to go to hell because it's warm there in the winter.

The grave worries facing the world today mostly don't have solutions. That is, they don't have solutions outside ourselves. We can't vote our troubles away. Or mail them to Washington either. We can't give fifty dollars to the Sierra Club, read Douglas Coupland, and sing the *Captain Planet* theme song and set everything right. Instead we have to accept the undramatic and often extremely boring duties of working hard, exercising self-control, taking care of ourselves, our families, and our neighbors, being kind, and practicing as much private morality as we can stand without popping.

To the extent that our worries do have public, collective solutions, the solutions are quite simple. Though, like many simple things (faith, grace, love, soufflés), they are difficult to achieve. It was Thomas Robert Malthus himself, arguably the father of modern worrying, who set forth these solutions in the 1803 revision of his *Essay on the Principle of Population:*

> The first grand requisite to the growth of prudential habits is the perfect security of property; and the next perhaps is that respectability and importance which are given to the lower classes by equal laws, and the possession of some influence in the framing of them.
>
> We have been miserably deficient in the instruction of the poor, perhaps the only means of really raising their condition.

Property rights, rule of law, responsible government, and universal education: That's all we need. Though no society has achieved these perfectly. Our own nation is notably lacking on the fourth point. (And such things as huge federal regulatory agencies and the Menendez jury aren't helping items one through three.) Still, if we look around at the countries of the world that honor Malthus's societal virtues more or less, we see a minimum of the worries in this book. And when we do see worries in a free, lawful, democratic, and literate place, we see them being mitigated to the best of mortal man's ability to do so.

Let us seek out the worries but avoid the worriers. They are haters of liberty and loathers of individuals. They wish to politicize everything. Imagine Bill Clinton conducting your love life for you. And watch out, he may be trying to.

To quote Malthus again:

The most successful supporters of tyranny are without doubt those general declaimers who attribute the distresses of the poor, and almost all the evils to which society is subject, to human institutions and the iniquity of governments.

We should wipe the gnostic smirk of self-righteousness off the faces of the moral buttinskis. Anyone who thinks he has a better idea of what's good for people than people do is a swine. Let's give the professional worriers something to worry about. (And memo to Generation X: Pull your pants up, turn your hat around, and get a job.)

2 OVERPOPULATION

Just Enough of Me, Way Too Much of You

1

Bangladesh has some 118,000,000 people, nearly half the citizenry of the United States, all in a nation the size of Iowa. It's crowded. The population density of Bangladesh is 2,130 individuals per square mile. Of course, if the Bangladeshis would just spread out, that's enough space for each man, woman, and child to occupy a football field up to the eighteen-yard line. Plenty of room to fall back and punt. But this particular afternoon they were piling on.

I had gone to the Motijheel Commercial Area, in Central Dhaka, to buy a plane ticket. The offices of Biman, the state-owned airline, were—I consult a thesaurus—"congested," "thronged," "teeming," "packed in like sardines." Packed in like sardines will hardly do. A tin of sardines is a quiet thing and the fish are all lined up facing the same way in rows. These people were none of that and they were closer together besides. You can perform open-heart surgery with less intimate contact than is needed to get to a Biman ticket agent. Six or eight of these placid dignitaries were seated behind a counter doing nothing, and slowly too, while humanity in hollering gobs pressed upon them.

In the parts of the world where people are truly free, with personal liberties and democratic privileges, a crowd waiting for something automatically forms itself into a queue: a single file possessing militaristic discipline and aristocratic order of precedence. But in the parts of the world where people are mostly free to get shot by the military or starved by the aristocrats, any line for anything turns into an Irish wake. There's a lesson in that, but I didn't feel like pursuing it any more than I felt, at the moment, like pursuing the rest of the lessons in awfulness a long visit to Bangladesh was supposed to be teaching me.

Fortunately I had a guide and translator, whom I'll call Abdur, and Abdur was acting as my Virgil in this overbooked circle of Hades. (What *would* be the most populous section of a modern Dante's *Inferno?* These aspiring airline passengers couldn't *all* have been multicultural training facilitators in a previous life.) Abdur shouldered and elbowed—and kneed and hipped and footed—his way to the ticket counter while shouting the endless claims of special privilege that mark the underprivileged world. "This is a most important journalistic man! He is having a priority!"

In a trice (which, in Bangladesh, is two and a half hours) we were back in our hired cab, whereupon the Dhaka traffic, which normally doesn't move, quit doing even that. A bus driver had died. Not recently or anything, but a large number of his bus-driver comrades had driven their buses to a nearby corner in order to present (I guess) a bus bouquet as a memorial to the deceased. This blocked the street. As did a large protest march being led by what sounded like the Dhaka Municipal School for the Deaf marching band. Sixteen thousand railway workers were demonstrating against the firing of sixteen thousand railway workers by Bangladesh Railways. There was also a hunger strike in front of the National Press Club, which seemed an odd place to have a hunger strike (a cocktail fast, maybe). Although the Bangladeshis were savvy enough to know that if you're going to pester journalists, don't go to where they work: You'll never find them there.

So I was stuck in a taxi, a small, dirty, and extremely unair-conditioned taxi. First one beggar, then a hundred beggars noticed a foreigner stuck in a taxi. I rolled up the windows. They tapped on the glass. They waved ulcerated limbs. They waved deformed limbs. They waved no limbs at all because they only had stumps. "Baksheesh!" "Baksheesh!" Eyeless faces pressed against the windshield, and noseless faces and faces without any of the facial features left. The temperature rose above a hundred in the car. Abdur turned around in the front seat and began a disquisition on the theoretical difficulties entailed in transition from government central planning to a market-oriented economy. I caught such phrases as "great importantness of the infrastructural allocations" and "subsector of unemploymentship is woefully lingering" and "most positive inputs being of the social-fiduciary nature."

Abdur had a couple of drawbacks as a translator. For one thing it was hard to get a word in edgewise for him to translate. Also he sounded like Gunga Din imitating Ira Magaziner. I gather Abdur was arguing against privatization because it is too hard on the poor. They're losing their jobs, like the railway workers. A frighteningly skinny woman appeared at my window carrying two babies who appeared to be dead. "One taka, two taka, baksheesh," she chanted. A taka is worth two and a half cents. "No mother no father no brother no sister baksheesh," she droned in memorized English. She looked seventy, though I doubt she was out of her teens. I was startled. "Oh, she is come from the country," said Abdur. "She would rather go for begging."

"Could she *find* a job?" I asked.

"Why not?" said Abdur, who was charging me a hundred dollars a day to explain Bangladesh.

The bus-driver memorial broke up, the girl with the dead babies disappeared, our taxicab moved a couple of hundred yards, and then we got stuck in *really* bad traffic. We were surrounded by thousands of tricycle rickshaws crammed bike tire to bike tire for a mile in every direction. The rickshaws were so closely entangled that for half an hour Abdur and I couldn't even crawl out the window of our taxi and walk. A California freeway rush hour with three lanes closed by earthquake damage on the worst smog-alert day of the year is agoraphobic by comparison. And relaxed and quiet besides. Fans of "alternative transportation" should get a peek at a rickshaw jam. And a whiff.

Elsewhere in south Asia, in Vietnam for instance, tricycle rickshaws are compact little vehicles, something like wide-bodied wheelchairs, with the rickshaw "puller" perched above the third wheel behind you. The Bangladeshis have come up with a worse design, a sort of one-horse shay with an elongated bicycle frame protruding from the front. The result is clumsy and slow, and you spend your ride looking at the puller's sweaty butt. The canvas side curtains on the rickshaws are prettily decorated, however, with paintings of the wild animals which are now extinct in Bangladesh, and of the pastoral scenes the rickshaw pullers have just left to try their luck in the big city. Plus Rambo portraits. And I saw one rickshaw embellished, cargo cult–like, with a handsome rendering of a container ship.

"Here is our solution to the energy crisis," said Abdur with a fatuousness I thought you had to go through Yale Law School to acquire. A tricycle rickshaw is energy efficient like a Kuwaiti oil-well fire. The average food intake in Bangladesh is said by the Bangladeshi government to be 2,215 calories a day. One gallon of gasoline produces 125,000 Btus, which is equivalent to 31,250 calories. In other words, a gallon of gasoline is a box of sugar doughnuts, a half-dozen twelve-ounce steaks, three six-packs of beer, a pizza, an apple pie, a twenty-piece bucket of Kentucky Fried Chicken, one hundred chocolate chip cookies, a birthday cake, a quart of bourbon, and a Big Mac and fries—which is more than a rickshaw puller gets in two weeks, if ever. And a gallon of unleaded regular costs about seventy-five cents before taxes. Try feeding anybody for two weeks on seventy-five cents, even in Dhaka.

Abdur pointed out that the rickshaws also come in a flatbed

model suitable for carrying freight and suggested that these might be useful in New York City.

We managed to wiggle out of the cab at last, but when we tried to walk I discovered why nobody does that and why everyone is in a tricycle rickshaw instead. There are hardly any sidewalks, and what sidewalks exist merchants and beggars have appropriated for their trades. The beggars grab you by the hand if they are uncrippled enough to reach that high or by the ankle if they aren't. The merchants are nearly as insistent. The gutters are too filthy to step into and are punctuated with yard-wide abysmal pitfalls, which I suppose connect to a sewer system, though Dhaka shows no signs of having one. A man is not going to pad around in this terrain if he can help it. And a woman doesn't amble unescorted in a decent Muslim city. Besides, walking is a lowborn sort of thing. And a rickshaw ride costs only three taka, or twenty taka an hour if you're sitting in a rickshaw jam.

Abdur—who, having been paid to explain Bangladesh, would absolutely not stop explaining it—explained that there are one hundred thousand rickshaws in Dhaka and three hundred thousand men who pull them and that each of these men has an average of five dependents. A remarkable number of Dhaka's inhabitants make a living by giving each other rickshaw rides.

We squeezed between the pedals, spokes, and bodies until we reached the middle of an intersection. I climbed on a concrete plinth with a traffic policeman who had given up and was blowing his whistle in patternless blasts and waving his arms any old way. From there I watched a fire truck, lights flashing and siren ahowl, move fifty yards in twenty minutes.

We nudged and poked forward, south through the Old City, which was more jumbled than actually old. The architecture was all cement in soiled pastels, and the streets were so narrow and confused that it was sometimes hard to tell if we were indoors or out—standing in the road or in someone's front parlor. At the end of this we emerged on the Bund, the wharf road along the Burhi Ganga, one of Bangladesh's myriad waterways and a part of the great Brahmaputra river system, I think, though it's hard to tell from consulting maps, where Brahmaputra, Ganges, Jamuna, Padma, and Meghna constantly shift names and courses while their tributaries, branches, creeks, and estuaries wave like all the arms on one of those Hindu goddesses if she happens to be spastic.

Here on the Bund was the Sadarghat, the principal Dhaka boat landing. Vast presses of people were moving in every direction, the men in shabby *lungi* wraps and dirty shirts, the women in cheap saris or *shalwar kameez* pajama suits and drab *dupatta* shawls, the children in not much at all and everybody very skinny. Stacked on the mud quays were piles of firewood three and four stories high, cut illegally in the mangrove swamps at the coast. The mangrove swamps form little islands, *chars,* of fertile new farmland. Without the mangroves the soil of Bangladesh washes away into the Bay of Bengal. The Brahmaputra alone carries nearly a billion tons of silt a year. Filth and ordure were everywhere along the Sadarghat. How can a country not have enough to eat and still smell so much of crap?

But it was just sunset, and dust and wood smoke gave an argent glow to the air above the filthy riverbank. And there were pinpricks of beauty in this mess. A Hindu bride, maybe thirteen, ascended from a water taxi with an entourage of in-laws. She was returning, after the wedding, for the ceremonial visit to the house of her father. Gilt threads twinkled in the scarf draped over her head and shoulders, a few bangles flashed at her wrists and a little gold stud winked above one nostril—all the wealth she'd probably ever have. A beautiful girl and, hey ho, there goes the birthrate.

I looked out across the river at the junks and rafts and fishing boats with big square barn-red sails and at the scissors-rowing taximen in their crafts no bigger than canoes, at a thousand boats of every kind—coasters, punts, skiffs, and the thatch-topped dories that are home to the Badhi, the river gypsies. Kids splashed in the putrid water at my feet. Ship bells rang and ship horns blew and nautical shouts resounded. Huge ferries plied the current, so overcrowded that they'd capsize if everybody on board looked in the same direction. It was the yacht club on the River Styx.

II

That the world is overpopulated and overpopulation is a terrible thing seems to go without saying. Not that this keeps people from saying it over and over again. "Famine, low living standards, unemployment, political instability and ecological destruction. Society . . . must seek ways to curb population growth," says *Scientific American.*

"Either nations with burgeoning populations will take steps to limit their numbers, or Malthusian misery—starvation and epidemic will accomplish the same goal," says *Newsweek.*

"Malthus," says Vice President Al Gore in *Earth in the Balance,* "was right in predicting that the population would grow geometrically." Al, as the father of four children, should know. With an air of twerpy concern as thick as his literary style, the vice president announces, "No goal is more crucial to healing the global environment than stabilizing human population."

Such talk isn't new. In the third century B.C., bossy Chinese philosopher Han Fei-tzu said, "People at present think that five sons are not too many and each son has five sons also, and before the death of the grandfather there are already twenty-five descendents. Therefore people are more and wealth is less." And that was in the days before anyone even bothered to count women.

Plato, in his *Laws,* maintained that the ideal number of households in a city state was 5,040 and thought that this number could be maintained if fathers married off their daughters to people from out of town, then picked one son as an heir and gave up any leftovers for adoption. If there was too much procreation or—given Plato's sexual proclivities—too little, the government was supposed to step in and regulate family planning "by the proper distribution of honors and marks of ignominy." Something like the programs to build self-esteem and the Norplant implants presently being tried in our inner cities.

But the number of people in the world did not become something with which to frighten vice presidents and journalists until the 1798 publication of *An Essay on the Principle of Population* by the afore-cited Thomas Robert Malthus. Malthus used the mathematical buzz-words of the Enlightenment, terms that had the same slightly incomprehensible but very important sound to his readers that "ozone depletion" and "biodiversity" have to us. "Population, when un-checked . . . increases in a *geometrical ratio,*" said Malthus (my italics), and "means of subsistence . . . could not possibly be made to increase faster than in an *arithmetical ratio.*" In other words there's no end to the number of babies that can be made, but you can only plant so much wheat before you run the plow into the side of the house.

It was a brilliantly self-evident idea and left a number of cut-ting-edge thinkers—John Stuart Mill, David Ricardo, Charles Darwin, Thomas Macaulay—whacking themselves on the forehead for not seeing it first. However, like many brilliantly self-evident ideas (free love, leveraged junk-bond buyouts, New Coke), it wasn't so brilliant.

Malthus said that population tends to increase faster than wherewithal, that there is a "constant tendency in all animated life to increase beyond the nourishment provided for it." He was wrong.

The Organization for Economic Cooperation and Develop-ment is an international research agency formed by some two dozen of the world's wealthiest nations in order to promote the kind of eco-nomic policies that are supposed to make nations wealthy. The OECD collected economic statistics from everyplace where respectable statis-tics have been kept this century—thirty-two countries ranging in pros-perity from Bangladesh and China to the United States and Japan. When the OECD got done nerd-wrestling this lump of numbers it was determined that, for each person in these countries, gross domestic product—measured in constant 1980 U.S. dollars—grew from $841 a year in 1900 to $3,678 in 1987. In the very period marked by the most astonishing population growth in mankind's million-year history, mankind got real rich.

Life expectancy in industrialized nations is now 74.6, much longer than it ever has been anywhere before. And, according to combined World Bank and UN Department of Economic and Social Development figures, life expectancy in developing nations has increased from 44.2 years to 62.4 years just since 1960.

The World Bank publication "Social Indicators of Development 1990" states that worldwide infant mortality, a reasonable yardstick of diet and health care, decreased from ninety-six to fifty-three deaths per thousand live births between 1965 and 1988.

And the UN Food and Agricultural Organization says that, from 1968 to 1990, per capita global food production rose by over 10 percent and chronic malnutrition declined by more than 16 percent. Meanwhile 2.8 billion people had been added to the world's population.

There happens to be no empirical evidence to support the Malthus theory.

However, if mere disproof were enough to rid us of ideas, think of the things we'd be free from: the social sciences, group therapy, raising taxes to decrease government spending.

And so, in 1968, 170 years after the publication of *An Essay on the Principle of Population,* came Paul R. Ehrlich with *The Population Bomb,* one of the most exasperatingly influential books of the last quarter century. Once again big-time intellectuals were giving themselves epiphany-induced thumps on the noggin. Dr. Ehrlich, an insect biologist, had about the same qualifications as a demographer as Reverend Malthus, an Anglican minister. It is to be noted, however, that Malthus was not a Malthusian. He never predicted that everybody would die in famines or plagues or wars. Malthus said only that all societies provide checks upon their populations because, if they didn't, nature would do it for them in a less kindly way. Ehrlich felt himself under no such constraints of logic or observation. *The Population Bomb* announced on its cover, WHILE YOU ARE READING THESE WORDS FOUR PEOPLE WILL HAVE DIED FROM STARVATION. MOST OF THEM CHILDREN. (Thus—assuming things have gotten no better, and the likes of Paul Ehrlich will tell you they haven't—750 people have died from starvation so far in this chapter, most of them children. You could have gone out and fed them, but you were too busy reading a book.)

The first words of Ehrlich's prologue are "The battle to feed all of humanity is over. In the 1970s the world will undergo famines— hundreds of millions of people are going to starve to death in spite of any crash programs embarked upon now. At this late date nothing can prevent a substantial increase in the world death rate. . . ."

Dr. Ehrlich gives us several predictions. In his *best case* scenario, America, in 1974, stops food aid to "India, Egypt, and some other countries which it considers beyond hope." There's "mild" food rationing in the United States. The pope approves birth control and abortion. Famines and food riots "sweep Asia." Ditto Africa, Latin America, and the Arab world, plus plagues and warfare. Russia has a lot of internal problems. "Die-backs" continue until 1985. What's left of the world sets a global population goal of 2 billion for the year 2025 and 1.5 billion for 2100.

He was right about Russia.

In Ehrlich's worst-case scenario, famine, plague, war, and all that kind of thing have repeatedly visited Asia, Africa, and Latin America by the late seventies. Thermonuclear holocaust ensues and everybody dies.

Has this nonsense discredited Dr. Paul Ehrlich? By no means. He is still regularly trotted out as a expert on matters populationish. And the bibliography of *Earth in the Balance* cites Ehrlich's new book, which is titled, with dogged persistence in metaphor, *The Population Explosion*.

But, if *An Essay on the Principle of Population* and *The Population Bomb* and all that ilk are wrong, what do we call this Malthusian detonation of humans in Bangladesh? Well, a man may be an idiot in his worries—scared that he's going to be hit by a car when he's drowning—but this doesn't make automobile accidents less dangerous or the idiot's lungs less full of water. Besides, there may be a Kennedy driving in the neighborhood. The population of Bangladesh *is* enormous and impoverished. The crowding is real. And the reality is overwhelming to an American fan of elbow room.

But that American—which is to say me—has to quit panicking about Bangladesh and begin some actual investigation of the place. It's easy to make first-glance assumptions, but what proves them right? Crowded as the country is, is overcrowding even its main problem? Hong Kong and Singapore both have greater population densities (14,315 and 12,347 per square mile, respectively) than Bangladesh, and they're called success stories. The same goes for Monaco. In fact, the whole Riviera is packed in August, and neither Malthus nor Ehrlich have complained about the topless beaches of St. Tropez.

III

Downtown Dhaka in full afternoon dither was an assault on the senses, but that was the only kind of assault it was. No one tried to hurt, rob, intimidate, or insult me because America, with only 4.7 percent of the earth's population, uses 20.6 percent of the earth's energy resources. A visit to the poor part of any big U.S. city is, in point of danger and unpleasant behavior by the locals, a worse experience. Even Dhaka's importuning beggars never raised their voices and when chased away stayed chased.

Bangladeshis are unfailingly, even exhaustingly, polite. Trying to find Mr. Atiqul Alam, the Reuters bureau chief whose office is in the Dhaka Sheraton, I was accidentally sent to Mr. Shafiul Alam, the Sheraton's rooms division manager. Shafiul Alam had served me two cups of tea and entertained me with half an hour of pleasantries before he was able to bring himself to tell me I was in the wrong place. The telephone receptionist at the Dhaka Chamber of Commerce tried for

a full two minutes (a long time on the telephone) to correctly pro-
nounce my last name. "I will break my teeth," he said at last.

Outside the big cities—and there are only two of these, Dhaka
and Chittagong—Bangladesh is a flat, green place with lots of open, if
not unpeopled, space. It's all pleasant enough, though rather tame.
Everything is being farmed and there's not much to see. Villages of
close-set mud-wall and thatch-roof houses perch on the little rumps of
land that rise above the rice paddies. By the side of the road there's an
occasional tomb of a *pir,* a Muslim saint, or a crumbling Buddhist stupa
or—looking more venerable than either of these—a battered red brick
Victorian building from the raj civil service. And once in a great while
there's a little group of yellow-leafed sāl trees. They used to be an
important hardwood export, and rhinos once lived in the sāl forests,
but now it's hard to find a wooded patch big enough that the rhino's
horn wouldn't stick out one end and its heinie out the other. Abdur
had traveled a bit in the United States, and while we drove though the
Bangladesh countryside he held forth on the scenic grandeur of the
Lake Erie area. "So beautiful a place," said Abdur. "Trees on *both* sides
of the road!"

You don't see many trees in Bangladesh, but you don't
see many disasters either—even though Bangladesh is nothing but another word for disaster in most of our minds. I half expected to turn
on the television in my hotel room and find the local Dhaka weath-
erman standing up to his waist in flood water, with debris and dead
cows floating by, saying, "slightly lessening terrible death in the
southeast this evening and an increased chance of horrifying mortality
tomorrow."

"We are not as bad as it is projected outside," said Chowdhury
Kamal Ibne Yusuf, Bangladesh's minister of health and family welfare.
He told me that when he had visited the United States people had
asked him, "How are you so healthy?" and expressed surprise that he
could speak English. One lady told him she didn't want to come to
Bangladesh because she couldn't swim. On a visit to China in 1979, the

minister said a U.S. senator had mistaken him for the Bangladeshi delegation's chauffeur and had taken him aside to ask, with great kindness, if there was anything the minister needed, was he hungry?

Mahbubur Rahman, president of the Dhaka Chamber of Commerce, said that Bangladesh's former president, Hussain Moham-mad Ershad, had once been asked whether his country had an airport and if there were roads. "This," said Rahman, with great merriment, "by the president of *Zimbabwe!*"

My hotel in Dhaka was quiet, clean, and comfortable in the ordinary characterless way of international hotels, except it had an acre of garden next to it where someone would bring you a chair and you could sit in the afternoon shade and sip pink gins. Which, every afternoon, I did. Flocks of pesky house-crows hopped about in the mango trees. A fellow from the hotel staff wearing a neat white mess jacket would come out on the lawn and shoot them with an air rifle. There was a tennis court at the bottom of the garden where tennis was played as it should be, with the pace and fervor of badminton. One day the local girls' swim team held a meet at the hotel's pool. Being from good families, the girls wore their *shalwar kameez* instead of bathing suits. Thus fully dressed, with the lineaments of big, serious Sears catalogue–type underwear visible beneath the wet clothing, it took most of the young women ten minutes to do a lap.

After sundown I would retire to the hotel bar where everyone who owned a necktie in Dhaka also seemed to be. There was no Muslim rigamarole about drinking, as there is in Pakistan, no showing your foreign passport or swearing that you're Christian. And no dread-ful local brands either. (A bellhop in Peshawar, and a well-bribed one, too, once brought me a bottle of "Old Collie.")

Some cocktails later I'd head off in search of dinner, always an indifferent one. The town has a number of perfectly dreadful Chinese restaurants, and at the hotel buffets there's English cooking as bad as you can find this side of England.

The three principal native dishes are *biriyani,* rice with chicken, beef, or mutton (as if you could tell which was which); *pullao,* rice without chicken, beef, or mutton; and *baht,* rice without flavor. There are also maybe-chicken-maybe-beef-maybe-mutton kebabs and a lot of meatball things of the type that are more ball than meat.

The meatlessness was probably just as well. I'd visited the Dhaka cattle market, a big open space near a rail head. The market had neither fences nor stalls. The herdsmen seemed to keep their animals in place by force of will. Here I'd noticed that you could get an entire old water buffalo weighing close to half a ton for 3,000 taka—seven or eight cents a pound—whereas eating beef was going for $1.75 a kilo. So the reason the chicken can't be told from the beef from the mutton is because of the strong water buffalo flavor it all has. Also, hygiene wasn't excellent at the cattle market, and only local thrift kept it from getting worse. I saw a little girl about eight or nine balancing a basket on her head, the basket heaped high with neatly arranged cow flops.

The cattle market was a large enterprise for a country I had so often heard was on the verge of starving. And $1.75 a kilo (80¢ a pound) is a bargain price for beef. I got Abdur to ask about this and about why so many of the cows were the white Brahmin kind, though I hadn't seen any of these in the countryside. They are, it turns out, sacred cows from India. The Indians worship cows, but deity can get under foot. And the Indians aren't the first people to make money shopping God around.

So Indian gutter-scrap browsing was another reason Dhaka dinner entrées weren't much good. Nonetheless I kept looking for someplace decent to eat. Driving was easy enough to do at night. Dhaka is empty after dark. I don't know where everybody goes or where there could be room for them either, but even most of the beggars are off duty. And, except for a few university students shooting each other over political matters, it is completely safe.

One of my sometimes dinner companions, a British civil engineer who'd lived in Bangladesh, on and off, for the past decade, had a group of about twenty children who would meet him outside my hotel gate every night after the cocktail hour. They came not really to beg but just to see him, though he'd pass out sweets or a bit of pocket change or maybe buy a shell necklace that one of the older kids had made. On weekends the engineer would pack this score of urchins into rickshaws and take them to the zoo or a soccer game. He'd more or less adopted the bunch. "Not that they don't have families," said the engineer. "But their folks aren't in a way to give them any treats."

"People here do love their children," said the engineer. "The way some aid workers talk, you'd think Bangladeshis didn't have children for the same reasons the rest of us do. But you'll seldom ever see a kid mistreated." And indeed I didn't. Even the woman with the dead-looking babies was holding them carefully.

Dhaka has not only restaurants, hotels, and a meat market but plush suburbs. The modern stucco houses are mostly set in guarded compounds the way they are in the worse parts of the world, the way they're coming to be in the United States. Dhaka even has a golf course. An American photojournalist friend of mine, John Giannini, went to play eighteen holes and said it was very much what you'd expect in a country so crowded that three average-sized local farms could fit into the fairway of a par 4 hole. John's foursome had four caddies, four assistant caddies, and a number of assistants to the assistants to hold umbrellas and go get drinks. Practically every divot had its own greenskeeper, and next to the flag on each green was someone standing by to remove it. Plus there were dozens of boys waiting in the rough to find your ball and, for a modest fee, find it in a pretty good lie. "I swear to God," said John, "if I hadn't brought my own tees, there would have been someone to get down on all fours and use his thumb." John said it was "the most in-your-face golf course in the world."

(Although John was not literally right about that. A couple of days later I was in Cox's Bazaar, where there is another golf course.

Here the tees have to be fenced off to keep the goats away. I watched a Japanese man take a mighty swing with a three wood. The ball went into the top rail of the fence and came straight back at the guy's head.)

IV

It's not the right question to ask what's wrong with Bangladesh. Everything's wrong. The question is how does the place manage to exist at all. When it became independent from Pakistan in late 1971, Bangladesh had only two international distinctions—being the world's largest poor country and the world's poorest large one. Bangladesh's per capita income was one-third of Red China's. The total economic production of the country equaled less than seventy-seven cents a day for each person, and that tiny amount had been shrinking for most of the century. Furthermore, as many as a million people had died during the civil war. Armed guerrillas were still wandering in the countryside. And eight to ten million refugees were returning penniless and everything else–less from India.

The situation was so bad, even rock stars thought they could help. But—despite critically acclaimed benefit performances by George Harrison, Bob Dylan, Ringo Starr, Leon Russell, and a number of other talented musicians back when they were still talented—the Concert for Bangla Desh couldn't put things right. (In later years talented musicians would discover that they couldn't feed Africa, save the family farm, or cure AIDS either.)

Bangladesh—East Pakistan, as it was then called—had already suffered a social injury in 1947. The country was deprived of its hated, grasping, but semicompetent ruling class when the raj was partitioned. Not only did the British colonial administrators leave, but so did the Hindus who had prospered under British protection. In Bangladesh before partition, Hindus controlled business, finance, and the professions, held more than three-quarters of the civil-service jobs, and owned 80 percent of large agricultural holdings and urban real estate.

It would be as though our nation suddenly lost all its college graduates and Rotary members. What a relief, in a way. On the other hand, who's going to put braces on the kids' teeth and do our taxes? West Pakistanis and Biharis—Muslims from northern India—came carpet-bagging to fill the vacuum. At independence in 1971 these people, too, were thrown out. So Bangladesh lost three educated middle classes in one generation.

The first government of Bangladesh called itself a "People's Republic" and nationalized 90 percent of the nation's industry—with the same happy results that have attended such schemes in Cuba, Bulgaria, and North Korea. Economic life, and the rest of life besides, became politicized. The Federal Research Division of the U.S. Library of Congress publishes a series of "Area Handbooks" about foreign countries. These are fairly politicized items themselves, but even so, the *Area Handbook on Bangladesh* scolds: "Party affiliation, political contacts, and documented revolutionary service became the main prerequisites for admission to the rapidly growing new elite of political and industrial functionaries." Nor were the peasants left unbothered. "In the countryside, new elites with links to the villages bought property to establish their socio-political control." Knowledge, ability, and good breeding suddenly went for nothing. Poverty became worse than ever. And the ordinary Bangladeshi found himself in a position as absurd as ours would be if our well-being depended upon whether we had, say, gone to school with the wife of the governor of Arkansas.

Bangladesh was meanwhile being blown halfway to the Himalayas by the usual cyclones and washed clear out to sea by the normal floods. (Even on the relatively high ground around Dhaka, there are phone poles with water stains eight feet in the air.) And the Bangladeshi population was growing by two-thirds—from about 70 million at independence to the present 118 million plus.

But Bangladesh didn't turn into a Somalia or a Cambodia or even an East L.A. The nation endured. In fact, it actually made a little progress, at least in the cities and towns. A military coup in 1975 got rid of the extreme leftist government, and, since then, there's been an average annual per capita economic growth rate of 2.1 percent adjusted for inflation, which would have been enough to have kept George Bush in office.

After Bangladesh became a country of its own, life expectancy lengthened from 44.9 years (a chilling 1.6 less than my own years as I write this) to an improved if not Methuselahean 52.8. The infant mortality rate dropped from 140 per 1,000 live births to 108. (That still leaves an awful number of dead babies, though in the United States the rate of abortions per 1,000 live births is 404, if dead babies happen to be what you worry about.) And, despite Bangladesh's 23 percent increase in kids who didn't die right after they were born, the annual rate of population growth diminished from 2.68 percent a year at independence to 2.39 percent now.★

★Note About Exact Numbers in Chapter Two and Everywhere Else in This Book:

You may wonder how the government of Bangladesh—not renowned for its competence in other fields—is able to give us the country's annual rate of population growth to the hundredth of a percentage point. It can't. For that matter the Organization for Economic Co-Operation and Development, cited a few pages back, cannot measure GDP growth since 1900 within a dollar. Nor can the UN and the World Bank know how many tenths of a year average global lifespan has increased. We have here the first law of the social sciences: "The more precise the figure, the more general the lie."

These exact—and hence absurd—numbers exist because the UN, the World Bank, the OECD, and the government of Bangladesh need them to get funding and foreign aid. Spending money on commercial transactions is a rational matter. We want something. We've got cash. We buy it. But spending money on geopolitical transactions is not so rational. We can't call the UN and say, "Send me a pound of world peace." And we can't go to Bangladesh and ask, "How much for a gallon of landless peasant economic opportunities?" Attempts to obtain these goods require acts of faith, otherwise known as irrational decisions. Whenever we're making irrational decisions, we like to do a lot of reasoning about them. Nothing sounds more reasonable than a number, and nothing makes a number look more carefully ratiocinated than a couple of decimal places.

Thus the UN, the World Bank, the government of Bangladesh, etc., give us ridiculous statistical exactitude. And I use the statistics in this book. I do so with a more or less clear conscience for two reasons:

The number of people per doctor in the country has been reduced from 8,810 in 1980 to 4,755 in 1990 without benefit of Hillary Clinton. Maternal mortality, in a society not famous for care of its women, went from 7 per 1,000 childbirths to 4 in the same period. From 1982 to 1989 average daily calorie intake increased by a chocolate éclair or so from 1,925 to 2,215, and protein intake per day increased from 56 to 64 grams although meat and fish consumption declined somewhat.

Bangladesh is not a wild success of a nation, but it's not a "basket case" or a helpless sponge for endless aid sops. A cyclone struck Bangladesh in November 1970 and killed approximately 225,000 people. (And it sometimes seems, when writing about Bangladesh, that I could put any number in that last sentence and people would believe me. I could say a million people died in a Bangladeshi train wreck, and readers would scrunch their brows and shake their heads in little mimes of concern, then wonder if Ortho-Novum can't be sprayed from planes.) Anyway, another tremendous cyclone hit Bangladesh in the fall of 1988 and this time "only" 2,200 people died. Evacuations had been planned, cyclone shelters had been built, weather predictions— and means of telling people what those predictions were—had been improved. One and a half million tons of food had been stockpiled along with adequate medical supplies; 3,000 civilian and military medical teams were on call.

Of course in 1991 along came one more cyclone and killed

---

1. The statistics come from the most reliable sources I can find. I believe that the people generating the statistics are trying to be accurate even if the degree of accuracy to which they lay claim is a laugh.

2. I think the statistics have some comparative use. That is, the errors which went into the calculation of "Blah blah blah 1940" are the same errors that went into the calculation of "Blah blah blah 1990." While both numbers might be wrong, there may still be value in contrasting them. It is true that, in the groves of academia, the orchards of the statisticians produce fake fruit. But I have tried to compare wax oranges only with wax oranges and plastic bananas with same.

140,000 people. So it's strictly one day at a time in the big Bangladesh twelve-step recovery program.

I say that Bangladesh isn't a wild success of a nation, but actually, in some sense, I must be wrong. Otherwise what are 118 million people doing there? One hundred eighteen million people don't live in Kenya. Kenya is where human beings evolved, so it's been populated, really, forever. It is four times the size of Bangladesh and has famously good climate and soil. Yet Kenya has a population of only twenty-six million.

One hundred eighteen million people do not wind up in a place just to make charity donors feel important or give OxFam volunteers something to do on weekends. And all those people didn't breed like gerbils because they were starving and without hope. So how did Bangladesh get to be such a brilliant sensation? And has it been, as with many another brilliant sensation, a bit too much of a good thing?

What first attracted humans to this place and made them, in Neolithic terms, well-to-do when they got there was the astounding fertility of the land. Bangladesh was formed by the confluence of three of the largest rivers on the Indian subcontinent—the Ganges, the Brahmaputra, and the Meghna. These meander, bifurcate, twine, and join in some seven hundred distinct watercourses, forming what is traditionally called "the Mouths of the Ganges." From the air Bangladesh looks like blood capillaries or nerve ganglia or some other C^- lab report thing that had to be viewed through a biology-class microscope. Runty hills rise in the east and northeast but nine-tenths of Bangladesh is no higher above the ocean than a fourth-floor beachfront condominium. This is the largest estuarine delta in the world, an enormous alluvial plain, a great big mudflat. At the turn of the last century, before modern agricultural improvements had even been applied in Bengal, some areas were known to support as many as nine hundred people per square mile by farming alone. Each person was obtaining his livelihood from the cultivation of a plot 175 feet square, smaller than many suburban house lots. And this assumes they all slept standing up, leaning against the tomato stakes.

As real estate, it has its downside. One of the oldest stone inscriptions found in Bengal urged people to store food in preparation for future floods, and a fourteenth-century Moroccan traveler, Ibn-Batāuta, said the Bengalis themselves called the place "a hell crammed with blessings." But the soil is so perfectly dark and rich that you think it must have come from the plant store in little bags. The ground is moist and friable and possessed of the dark, mellow, sweet-and-sour bumper-crop smell I remember from a childhood of getting my face shoved in Ohio loam while playing football. It is the stuff compost heaps are supposed to turn into, instead of the stinky slime they do. Plant a foot on the dirt of Bangladesh and you'll grow more toes.

In the 1911 edition of the *Encyclopaedia Britannica,* Bengal is described as

> one of the most fertile and densely populated tracts of country in the world. It teems with every product of nature. Tea, indigo, tumeric, lac, waving white fields of the opium poppy, wheat and innumerable grains and pulses, pepper, ginger, betelnut, quinine and many costly spices and drugs, oil-seeds of sorts, cotton, the silk mulberry, inexhaustible crops of jute and other fibers; timber, from the feathery bamboo and coroneted palm to the iron-hearted *sāl* tree—in short, every vegetable product which feeds and clothes a people, and enables it to trade with foreign nations, abounds.

And the article goes on to say that "since the advent of British administration the history of Bengal has substantially been a record of prosperity."

Per capita income in the area was actually about the same then as it is now, so note that our standards of prosperity have changed (and so, unfortunately, have our standards of encyclopedia writing). Note also that "densely populated" was not, in 1911, a term of disapprobation.

There were other reasons for Bengal's relative wealth. The

Hooghly river, some sixty miles west of the present border of Ban-gladesh, was the place where the British originally barged in on India in 1650. No one likes having a lot of Brits around, but the British East India Company did found the city of Calcutta there in 1690. Thus the produce of Bengal was provided with an enormous market and with roads and, eventually, railways by which to move that produce, and with soldiers and policemen to protect those roads and rails.

Islam was also a benefit. In the twelfth century, Bengal had been ruled by the Sena dynasty, militant Hindus who were obnoxious in their enthusiasm for the caste system. When the Muslim Mughal Empire conquered Bengal in 1202, low-caste Hindus converted to Islam with dispatch. Being Muslim gave the Bengalis some measure of equality before the law and a set of laws worth being equal in front of. Mughal rule also introduced Bengal to the technical innovations, intel-lectual vigor, and business sophistication of the medieval Arab world.

However, what truly made Bengal rich was jute. Jute is a fish pole of a plant, five to ten feet high, nearly branchless and only as thick as a finger. Mention its name anywhere but Bangladesh and you will be greeted with a "huh?" But a century ago jute was big agriculture. It was grown for its fibers, which are similar to hemp (though without, as far as I know, any of hemp's smokable spin-off benefits). Only cotton and flax were more important to the weaving and textile industries. Not that jute was very good stuff. It was weaker than flax and coarser than cotton and less durable than either. But it was cheaper by a third or a half. Jute is what's used to make burlap, and thus, before the advent of synthetics, most sacks and packaging were jute. All the sandbags of both world wars were made of jute. And jute was used to make string, rope, cord, bargain-priced carpets and floor mats, tarpaulins, cheap yard goods, and inferior-grade paintbrushes. In 1906 the world con-sumed three and a half billion pounds of jute. It was the polyester of its day.

Jute is native to Bengal, and Bengal is the only place where jute grows well. Jute, the "golden fiber" as it was called, brought cash and consequence, industry and export earnings to the place that would become Bangladesh. Jute was the key to Bangladesh's success.

V

Unfortunately, jute is still the key to Bangladesh's success. Jute is Bangladesh's largest hard-currency earner. Jute and jute products constitute one-third of Bangladesh's exports. Jute is the only significant cash crop in a country where 82 percent of the population depends upon agriculture for its livelihood. And no one wants jute anymore.

The government of Bangladesh actually has a Ministry of Jute. And the whole while I was in Bangladesh I got phone calls at my hotel from the jute minister's office. "Yes I am speaking to Mr. Oh-Dork-Ee, please? The government ministry is most anxious to inform you of the official willingness to grant personally an interview with the minister of jute." Unsolicited phone calls. I had absolutely nothing to ask the jute minister except how he kept a straight face when he had to tell somebody his title.

But jute's the thing in Bangladesh. And a journalist was in town, so jute must be discussed. When I went to the Dhaka Chamber of Commerce to talk to Mahbubur Rahman (the man who'd told me about the president of Zimbabwe asking if Bangladesh had roads), Rahman, too, wanted to chat about jute.

The chamber of commerce was in the Motijheel Commercial Area, right around the corner—and therefore thirty or forty minutes away—from the Biman Airline office. I went up a couple of flights of dusty stairs in a rapidly aging modern concrete building and into a big, humid room full of male secretaries scratching in enormous ledger books and clattering and dinging on the kind of manual typewriters only seen in the U.S. in little theatre productions of *The Front Page*. Rahman was steely-haired and well turned-out, one of those men middle age is made for, its dignity topping off his charm. He made as good a pitch for jute as anyone could. Why, there is no end of its uses.

Carpet backing, just for instance. A kind of particleboard, also. Did I know that jute had been used to make not only the sandbags in World War I and World War II but the sandbags in the Korean War as well? Rahman had tea and biscuits brought in on a tray. Jute is a *natural* fiber. Natural fibers are very fashionable just now. True, jute has minor shortcomings as a textile, but jute can be blended with other materials to make, well, a blend of other materials and jute. And now there is a way to manufacture paper from jute. "My business card is made of jute paper," said Rahman, handing me a business card neatly printed on wrinkled, lumpy, brown, discolored cardboard. "And jute is very good for making rugs. You can make rugs that look just like wool, and quite durable. The rug in this office is jute." I peeked at the rug. It didn't look a thing like wool and was coming to bits.

The price of jute has been falling since plastics were invented. And in the 1980s, when the petrochemicals from which plastics are made became cheaper than they ever had been, jute prices collapsed. The government of Bangladesh had the same reaction to the advent of plastics as the Dustin Hoffman character had to mention of that word in *The Graduate*. Actually, worse. What the government of Bangladesh did was more expensive than just looking smug and staying unemployed. The price of jute fell below the cost of growing jute. So the government, one of the least rich governments in the world, decided to subsidize jute growers and jute product manufacturers. "Ironically," says the *Area Handbook,* "Bangladesh's indispensable foreign exchange earner was thus itself a drain on the economy." Lively prose style is not, I suppose, a mandate given to the writers at the Federal Research Division of the Library of Congress but, even so, "ironically" is a tepid adverb.

"Insanely" is the word the Library of Congress was looking for. Nor is jute the only observable insane thing in the Bangladesh political economy. In the 1990–91 fiscal year, government-owned companies were given three and a quarter billion taka free of charge and even then couldn't make a profit. In fact they went on to lose some twenty billion more taka, for a total equal to U.S. $612 million down the drain.

Here are just a few of the companies that the Bangladesh government owns:

> Osmania Glass Sheet Factory
> Dhaka Match Factory
> Bangladesh Diesel Plant
> National Tubes Ltd.
> Dhaka Vegetable Oil Industries
> Kohinoor Battery Manufacturing Co.
> Bangladesh Cycle Industries
> Khulna Hard Board Mills
> Bangladesh Blade Factory
> Eagle Box Cartoon [sic] Manufacturing Co.
> Bangladesh Steel Engineering Corporation Can Making and
>   Tin Printing Plant
> Bangladesh Insulator and Sanitary Ware Factory

These are from a list of enterprises the government is trying to sell off, and I'd like to shake the hand of—well, meet, anyway—the man who buys Bangladesh Insulator and Sanitary Ware.

Paging through the Dhaka Chamber of Commerce's monthly magazine, one comes across such items as: "Cloths worth about [U.S. $14 million] were lying unsold in the domestic mills during 1990–91," and in the very next paragraph a Mr. Mannan, who holds the absurd portfolio of "Minister of State for Textiles," is quoted as telling the national legislature that "the country was likely to be self reliant in cloths by 1993" but that, as yet, "the cloths production in the country was not capable of meeting the requirements."

Or consider this for a nation whose only resources are human, whose only hope is an educated workforce and whose present rural literacy rate is 17 percent: "Minister for Forest, Fisheries, Livestock and Environment Abdullah Al-Noman said . . . the government had decided to stop import of foreign books excepting those required for research and reference." How the minister for forest, fisheries, livestock and environment got to be in charge of book-banning was a subject too depressing for inquiries. Anyhow, Mr. Al-Noman went on to say, "The government decision to stop import of books which are not in conformity with our culture and heritage, will help flourish our own literature and culture."

Let me suggest to the minister that among books exempt from his proscription should be books of the phone type. The only useful source of phone numbers in Bangladesh is a xeroxed sheet passed out by the chamber of commerce and the chamber has its own number wrong on the list.

Not that this matters. No two dialings of a phone number on a Bangladeshi telephone result in being connected with the same person twice (unless, apparently, you're calling from the jute minister's office). A better communications system could be put together with carrier pigeons, indeed with carrier mice. Nor is the high-tech revolution which would solve this problem likely to arrive in Bangladesh soon, at least not to judge by what my friend John Giannini had to go through to bring his laptop computer into the country. You would have thought John had arrived at customs carrying 118 million copies of Salman Rushdie novels and no permission slip from the forest and fisheries department.

Giannini didn't quite know what to do. There's a fine line in the Third World between half a dozen customs officials waiting for you to offer them a bribe and half a dozen customs officials waiting for you to offer them a bribe so they can throw you in jail. But it didn't turn out to be a baksheesh problem. There were just papers to be filled out, reams and sheaves and quires of papers, all in quadruplicate at least and all to the effect that John was not going to sell this computer in Bangladesh "and," said John to a customs officer, "wreck the incredibly important Bangladeshi computer-manufacturing industry by dumping cheap imports on the local market." Fortunately the customs officer had been flourishing his own literature and culture, and his English wasn't up to detecting sarcasm.

LEARN COMPUTER BUILD YOUR CAREEAR read a billboard on the way into town from the airport. And next to this was an ad for the annual TEXTILE, LEATHER AND JUTE FAIR, the rides, sideshows, and midway attractions of which I leave to your imagination.

Every encounter with officialdom in Bangladesh, every visa application, hotel registration, or currency exchange set off the same typhoon of paper. Paying with an American Express card at a government store selling village handicrafts took nearly two hours. And heartbreaking handicrafts they were: embroidered bedspreads with a million hand stitches for about a hundred dollars each. Beautiful, but contemplate what that works out to as an hourly wage. While I examined these at very great leisure indeed, the clerk—who had already copied out all the information on my credit card, passport, New Hampshire driver's license, and *Rolling Stone* press card—was calling the central bank on a phone that didn't work and the central bank was wiring American Express on a telex that didn't function and American Express was faxing approval to a facsimile machine that didn't exist.

Government orders and regulations as intricate as any millionstitch bedspread cover every aspect of Bangladeshi economic life and make microscopic hand embroidery seem, by comparison, a wildly productive use of time. There are over forty government ministries including the Ministry of Food, the Ministry of Land, the Ministry of Youth and Sports, the Ministry of Works (which is separate from the Ministry of Labour and Manpower), and the Ministry of Cabinet Division, which is to say, the Ministry of Appointing Ministers.

In Abdur's endless elucidative chitter-chat, every sign of material progress was greeted with the comment, "Oh, the government has just released funds for this now." A block of middle-class garden apartments on the outskirts of Dhaka, a spate of freshly mudded huts in a rural district, an industrial park: "Oh, the government has just released funds for this now." As though funds were a genie and only government could rub the lamp.

And it seemed the rest of the country agreed with Abdur that government was the source of all good things, since every vertical surface in Bangladesh was decorated with political graffiti. Well, not with graffiti, exactly, because most people can't write or read, but with symbols of the political parties such as a sheaf of rice for the ruling Bangladesh National Party, a boat for the opposition Awami League, a plow for ex-President Mohammed Ershad's Jatiyo Party, a pair of scales for the Jamaat-E-Islami fundamentalists, and an umbrella, a chair, a pineapple, a car, a bus, and so forth for the hundred-odd minor parties. (When are the world's political parties going to get appropriate symbols: snake, louse, jackal, outhouse, trash can, clown face, dildo, dollar bill with wings on it?)

The Bangladesh Supreme Court, a great faux-Mughal pile of a building, is three times the size of the U.S. Supreme Court and by sheer bulk gives the impression of deciding every rickshaw-fare dispute and goat-rustling case in the nation. The Jatiyo Sangsad, Bangladesh's parliament, is a huge, horribly modern raw concrete complex designed by cranky architect Louis I. Kahn, who once said, "To make a thing deliberately beautiful is a dastardly act," and meant it.

Not all of the government's buildings are so prepossessing, but, if it's big and it isn't a hotel for foreign-aid honchos, it probably belongs to the government. There are dumpy breeze-block structures from the first modest days of postcolonialism and retarded-looking prefabricated cement constructs from the early seventies era of Soviet influence and contemporary concrete rectangles not worth describing.

Chowdhury Kamal Ibne Yusuf, the minister of health and family welfare who'd been mistaken for a chauffeur, was in a breeze-block edifice, a drab one painted blue like the swimming pool in an abandoned motel. The ministry's outer office had, in its one window, a broken air conditioner racketing away and making the room ten degrees warmer than the outside air. A dozen petitioners sat waiting, and the minister's secretary, a young man in jeans and a tank top, was shuffling papers. It's a cliché, but this fellow was actually doing it— flipping and dealing the documents as if they were foolscap-size cards in a solitaire deck. A single unanswered dial-face phone sat ringing incessantly on a desk.

The minister's office proper was decorated in fake wood paneling and a jute carpet in a dog-mistake shade of beige. The carpet was very damp. It's a wet country and jute is remarkably absorbent, able to blot up nearly a quarter of its weight in moisture—nature's bath mat. The minister had half a dozen junior ministers gathered about him. They were debating some detail of family-planning policy and invited me to join the discussion. With as much international assistance as Bangladesh receives, they're used to having perfect strangers butt in on their business.

The minister was a compact man of academic demeanor unaccountably dressed in a leisure suit. He didn't look a thing like a chauffeur, although he might have passed for one of Ravi Shankar's backup sitar players. When we'd decided upon the average number of male children jute weavers should father by age forty, or whatever, I asked Minister Yusuf to tell me about foreign aid. Annual charity from overseas—U.S. $1.5 billion of it—makes up 10 percent of Bangladesh's gross domestic product and provides 85 percent of the country's development capital. But does it work? Foreign aid is a huge industry in Bangladesh, and there's some evidence that the government of Bangladesh is no better at running it than it is at running the Eagle Box Cartoon Manufacturing Company or the Bangladesh Insulator and Sanitary Ware Factory. By the late 1980s "undisbursed project assistance"—that is, foreign aid money the Bangladeshis had but couldn't figure out how to spend—exceeded U.S. $5 billion.

Minister Yusuf was not, of course, about to quit standing at the international street corner with his WILL QUIT OVERPOPULATING FOR MONEY sign. But he did admit that many of the big aid projects of the past—steel mills, cement plants, et cetera—had ended up losing cash for his government instead of providing benefits for his countrymen. And these big projects often resulted in expensive consulting fees, which went right back to the countries that had donated the money.

"The type of aid that works," said Yusuf, "is more transfer of technology." (Although this is what Giannini had been expressly forbidden to do with his laptop computer.) "And more foreign investment." (Although if 85 percent of a development budget isn't an investment, what could it be?) "However," said Yusuf, "what would be more important would be for the United States and the European Community and others to lower their trade barriers, their textile quotas, for example, and allow us to sell our products in their markets."

That is, it's more comfortable to give somebody a handout than it is to let him have a crack at taking your job. What are the aid donors really donating? The steel mills were obviously a bad idea. Bangladesh has no iron ore or coal with which to smelt it. Cement-making is a simple technology. Surely free enterprise, even such as it is in Bangladesh, could have been left to figure out cement. Bangladesh gets money not only from the United States, Britain, Germany, and Japan, but from Canada, Sweden, Finland, the Netherlands, Switzerland, and Australia. Are national experts being sent out to instruct the Bangladeshis in hockey, nudism, reindeer taming, tulip appreciation, yodeling, and drinking until they heave?

In fact, the aid has concentrated on agriculture. The World Bank has financed immense irrigation and flood control programs and built a factory to produce five hundred thousand tons of fertilizer a year. Half the Asian Development Bank's financing has gone to projects involving farming and farm products, as has two-thirds of U.S. aid. And while all that agricultural aid was being parceled out, rural poverty worsened in Bangladesh. At independence 25 percent of agricultural laborers were landless, now 40 percent of them are. An estimated 47 percent of the population in the countryside is presently below the poverty line—a line which, in Bangladesh, is drawn not very high above the grave.

There has been a great encouragement of agriculture in a country that desperately needs to escape from its grip. Well over 40 percent of the laborers in Manhattan are landless, if you don't count condominiums. But the trees in Washington Square have not been cut for firewood, nor is the median strip in Park Avenue overgrazed by goats.

I went to visit the Dhaka office of the World Bank, a snappy new red brick building whose occupants were, it seemed, faring better, in a healthier environment, than the minister of health and family welfare. The World Bank is an agency of the UN. What it does is tap rich countries for money. Then it uses this money to make loans to poor countries, the kind of loans that will be paid back when the pope sits shiva. The World Bank mooches U.S. tax dollars, so some of this money they're loaning out is mine. I wanted to ask the World Bankers if they were doing the kind of things with my money that I'd be doing with my money if it were still my money, if the World Bank hadn't run off with it.

This is the only real test of any aid or assistance, be it of the national, international, or bum-on-a-steam-grate kind. Is this the way you'd help someone yourself? If it isn't, why are you having the UN do it for you? If you loan someone money to pursue a bad idea—a chain of soda fountains featuring meat-flavored ice cream, for in-stance—you're not only wasting your own money but you're harming the borrower as well (not to mention nauseating his customers). The same is true with a charitable contribution. It's good to give money to the poor, but not for drugs or—in the case of Bangladesh—jute.

I also wanted to ask the World Bankers if I could get a World Bank MasterCard so I could charge hydroelectric dams and stuff. But everybody at the World Bank was out to lunch.

I went to the Grameen Bank, instead. The Grameen Bank was started by somebody who actually did make loans from his own per-sonal funds, Muhammad Yunus, head of the economics department at Chittagong University. Professor Yunus was so appalled by the eco-nomic situation in Bangladesh in the 1970s that he decided to quit just professing economics and start getting involved in the economy. He loaned a total of $30 to forty-two impoverished village artisans so they could buy the materials for their crafts. Now the Grameen Bank has 910 branches with more than a million borrowers. The average loan size is $75, and the maximum loan is $180, unless you want to build a house, in which case you can get $300.

Grameen, though it loans money only to the poorest Bangladeshis, is a going concern. It charges 16 percent interest and has a default rate of only 8 percent. Grameen borrowers are formed into five member groups to mutually guarantee the loans. Only two members of each group can have loans outstanding at the same time. Several groups form a "centre," and each centre is visited by a Grameen representative once a week. Ninety-two percent of the borrowers are women because the Grameen people believe an increase in women's income directly benefits households. Professor Yunus said, "A man has a different set of priorities, which do not give the family top position," by which I think he means cigarettes and floozies.

Grameen urges the women not only to be economically self-supporting but to follow a set of tenets called the "Sixteen Decisions." These include such resolutions as "We want to change our life," "We want to grow trees," and "We shall not take any dowry when we're getting our sons married and we shall not give any dowry when we are marrying off our daughters." The Grameen Bank also does such things as sell vegetable seedlings to its customers to improve their diets. Although vegetables are easy to grow in Bangladesh (as everything is), people aren't accustomed to eating them and vitamin-deficiency diseases are rife.

The Grameen Bank has run into opposition. Leftists claim it teaches capitalism to the Bangladeshi poor. The village mullahs hold that it is sacrilege for women to fool with money. And local traditionalists are shocked at brides without dowries and probably at vegetables. Grameen is a little piece of a society trying to reconstruct itself. In the office of Khandaker Mozammel, the bank's number two man, I noticed the bookshelf contained Rousseau's *Social Contract,* Milton and Rose Friedman's *Free to Choose, Selected Works of Chairman Mao,* and

Beyond Love. No stone, however dense or mossy, is being left unturned in the process of this reconstruction. (Don't tell the minister of forest, fisheries, livestock and environment.)

The Grameen Bank is obviously a better sort of thing for Bangladesh than massive airdrops of soft money from the World Bank or having the Peace Corps send flocks of idealistic comparative lit majors to teach people who have been farming for three thousand years how to farm. But it is tempting to expect too much from a Grameen Bank. Grameen only has thirty-six million dollars in assets. And the product of Grameen-financed enterprise is, when all's been said, that million-stitch bedspread it took me two hours to buy. Better that than no product, but bedspreads are not what Germany and Japan based their postwar economic miracles upon.

VI

Before I left Bangladesh I visited the worst slum in Dhaka. Just judging the choice was difficult. But I think I managed. It was a neighborhood of twenty-five thousand people in a space that wouldn't park the cars at a minor-league ballpark, a neighborhood of tin-roofed rattan huts seven feet wide by ten feet long without windows or chimneys or even smoke holes. Each hut was built smack up against its neighbors at the back and sides and opened on a dirt lane that was four feet wide. At the end of these lanes were a few water spigots sticking a foot or so out of the mud and some latrine holes in cement-block sheds. I tried to ask how many people lived in each hut. "More than possibly can," was, I believe, the answer.

I can't tell you much more about this place because every time I stopped to take notes I was enveloped in a swarm of giggling, hopping, begging, grabbing, pawing children, hundreds of them. During a moment when I'd broken free from the kids I looked through a low doorway and saw a woman squatting on the floor preparing a dinner of wiggly salamanders. I'm no expert on the Koran, but I'm almost certain salamanders aren't allowable food for a Muslim. Or for this Christian either.

These neighborhoods often burn. This particular one has burned down half a dozen times in the past twenty years. There's no way to know how many people die in the fires, nobody tries to find out. And there's no way for the residents to move, because they're not really here in the first place, they're squatters. They can't get three-hundred-dollar Grameen Bank house loans. They have no legal place to put a house. And they can't get a legal place to put a house because they're not citizens, they're Biharis.

Biharis, the Indian Muslims who came to East Pakistan when the raj was split in 1947, chose the wrong side in the Bangladesh war for independence. They had considered themselves superior to the Bengal natives, whom they thought too Hindu-acting. They had refused to learn Bengali and had been treated with preference by the West Pakistan–dominated government. Abdur said the Biharis had even formed special brigades to fight alongside the West Pakistan army against Bangladeshi guerrillas. Abdur had been imprisoned during that war and tortured—pins stuck under his nails.

When Bangladesh won its freedom in 1971, West Pakistani soldiers were given safe passage home. West Pakistan natives were repatriated, and wealthy Biharis were able to go to Pakistan, too. But, as Abdur put it, "the wretched ones stayed back." And here they remain, some 600,000 of them, spread through refugee camps and squatter slums. There's nothing for them in Bihar State. Most weren't even born when India was partitioned, and Hindus own all the property in Bihar now. Pakistan doesn't want them. And they're hated in Bangladesh.

A Bangladesh banker I met at my hotel bar, a man who said he'd been doing volunteer work in refugee camps since World War II, said he thought the Biharis were simply lazy. But this wasn't true. There were rows of little lean-to shops all around the edges of the slum. The shops were full of young boys sewing the elaborate gold-embroidered wedding trousseaus that are a Bihari specialty. Just the scarf for one of these wedding gowns, the scarf the little Hindu bride was wearing on the Sadarghat, will sell for 780 taka. The boys make about 200 taka a week. In other shops Biharis were repairing dreadful old jute carpets, splitting illegal mangrove firewood, and otherwise doing the nation's scut work.

Abdur claimed that until recently he hadn't known these Bihari slums existed. No one else seemed to know yet. We had to ask directions five or six times to find this one. Abdur said he used to despise the Biharis, but now he felt pity for them. So he came with me, even though he couldn't translate here, and Abdur and I spent an afternoon walking around in a haze of buzzing urchins, looking at what seemed to be poverty but was actually politics, at what seemed to be a country with too many people, but which was actually people without a country.

VII

What could change Bangladesh? How different could the place be with other economic practices, other political institutions, other social structures?

Fremont, California, has the same population density as Bangladesh. It might seem absurd to compare an American city of 177,500 with an Asian country of 118,000,000. But I'm not sure if I know why. Fremont is not a self-sufficient nation. Neither is Bangladesh. Fremont is part of a larger political entity. Bangladesh used to be and was even worse-off then. Fremont has sparcely inhabited spaces nearby. The northern border of Bangladesh is only a hundred miles from Tibet. And Fremont is much smaller than Bangladesh. But Taiwan is much smaller than Red China, and Beijing seems to have learned a lot from its tiny neighbor.

If over-population is something to worry about and Bangladesh's degree of crowding constitutes overpopulation, then Fremont should be a worry, too. In fact, with 2,250 people per square mile compared to Bangladesh's 2,130, Fremont is slightly more worrisome.

Fremont is on the east side of lower San Francisco Bay, across the Dumbarton Bridge from Stanford University and the kind of people who agonize about overpopulation, and twenty-five miles south of the Oakland slums and the kind of people who don't. There is absolutely nothing remarkable about Fremont. The city is laid out on a piece of flat land between the bay marshes and the foothills of the Diablo Range. It was incorporated in 1956 and everything is new aside from a few nineteenth-century farmhouses, 1920s storefronts, 1950s gas stations, and an overrestored 1797 Spanish mission.

Fremont has a lot of malls, and office parks for companies such as Kaiser Permanente and First Interstate Bank, and it has industry. The GM/Toyota joint venture, New United Motor Manufacturing Inc. (NUMMI), is here, as are such impressively modern concerns as Logitech, LSI Logic, GRID Systems, Syquest Technology, Seagate Magnetics, and LAM Research Corporation. The industry is neatly zoned, contained in buff-colored hygienic buildings set midst lawns and shrubs. Fremont's factories have more landscaping than its malls do. And Fremont is ecology conscious. The big local news story when I visited in 1993 was a forty-five-million-dollar expansion at the NUMMI plant being held up because a single burrowing owl had been discovered on the proposed building site, burrowing. The burrowing owl isn't even an endangered species. "But its population and habitat are dwindling," said California Department of Fish and Game wildlife biologist Joanne Karlton (who is not, incidentally, empowered to ban books).

The Fremont natives do care about their birds. Twenty thousand acres adjacent to the town were ceded to the San Francisco Bay National Wildlife Refuge to form the largest urban duck marsh in the world. Fremont has some thirty other parks and playgrounds including, in the very middle of the city, a lake that's large enough for windsurfing. And I saw more ducks waddling around this lake than I saw in the wildlife refuge.

Bangladeshi thickness of settlement may make for crowded Third World farmland but, in Californian suburbia, yawning space is the result. Fremont's boundaries encompass 10,000 acres of biologically significant ooze and goo used as evaporation ponds by the Leslie Salt Company. A 205-acre historic farm is maintained on the north side of town, as is a reconstructed Ohlone Indian village. The original transcontinental railroad ran through what is now Fremont. The whistlestop burg of Niles has been preserved in a reasonable amount of its entirety. Niles was used as a "Wild West" set for silent pictures starring Bronco Billy, Ben Turpin, Wallace Beery, and Charlie Chaplin. Movies featuring the Little Tramp were filmed in Fremont forty years before Fremont existed.

Fremont has a hang-glider launch pad on Mission Peak, lots of little horse pastures and hobby ranches and even some for-profit cattle grazing in the Mission Hills. And, still within the city limits, is the entire Weibel Champagne Vineyards, America's fifth-largest producer of not very good sparkling wine.

Few of Fremont's buildings are over five stories high and most are only one. You could spend weeks in Fremont without climbing a flight of stairs. So spread-out are homes and businesses that any attempt to be a pedestrian turns into an expedition trek. Not that anyone does attempt it. This is California, so among the many open spaces surrounding you in Fremont are spaces of the parking sort, probably two or three for everyone who lives there. No parking meters either.

Fremont is quartered by ample freeways, all its major streets are six or eight lanes wide, the traffic lights are timed and the traffic, even at rush hours, rushes.

The city has, as of last count in 1990, 39,212 single homes, 3,784 semidetached houses, 18,531 apartments, and 618 trailers. And there is yard enough at these for practically everybody to have a gas grill, basketball hoop, flowerbed, above-ground pool, pet dog, and parked RV.

There are no bad parts of town. Although the chamber of commerce, in a brochure for prospective residents, goes so far as to admit, "Fremont does have neighborhoods that are generally well maintained but spotty in quality. Some lawns have been let go . . ."

No litter is evident, nor much graffiti. In one of the deep cement culverts that run from the hills to the bay, I saw THRASH METAL RULES spray-painted. Actually it was TRASH METAL RULES, but someone had corrected the spelling, inserting a defining H. A nearby sign forbade use of skateboards or bicycles in these tempting half-pipes. I suppose the vandalism was fair recompense.

I saw only three beggars, and one of them wasn't very professional. She was a plump woman who had an eight- or ten-year-old girl with her. It was six in the evening and the woman was holding a placard saying she'd work for food. But she was standing beside an off-ramp, where it was almost impossible for a car to stop, and she was standing there at an hour of the day when people are hurrying home and unlikely to have either food or work in the car with them. Fifty yards behind the beggar woman was a McDonald's with a NOW HIRING sign in the window. A middle-aged man came out of the McDonald's parking lot and gave the woman and girl Big Macs.

Fremont is middle-class, though it doesn't quite deserve that slur. Eighty-two percent of Fremont's children live with both parents. Fremont kids test in the top third among California's public school students. About two murders a year take place in the town. And the crime rate is 30 percent below the national average. So Fremont still has some nice, solid, lower-class values intact.

The population is integrated: about 19½ percent Asian, 4 percent black, and 13 percent Hispanic. Cultural mix seems complete. The supermarket produce departments have vegetables so alien-looking that if one of them came up in my garden, I'd take a ball bat to it. And I saw a Volvo low rider.

Fremont started out, after World War II, as a blue-collar bedroom community. And the chamber of commerce's survey of local salaries still shows nothing in three figures and not much in the high twos. Housing is, however, expensive. The real estate section of the *Fremont, Newark and Union City Argus* showed no single family Fremont homes for sale under two hundred thousand dollars. And people don't get overmuch for their money. The houses are blandly comfy, indistinguishable from each other, built in a "ranch style" that would puzzle California's original *rancheros*. The most prominent architectural feature is usually the attached two-car garage.

Fremont is itself blandly comfy. And indistinguishable, in a very nice way, from much of the rest of America. The chamber of commerce brochure confesses "few classy restaurants." California has been having a recession for several years. There are some empty shops in the Fremont malls. People are having trouble paying the bills. But no one I talked to was calling for international aid. There were no angry demonstrations in the street.

Fremonters are nearly as friendly as Bangladeshis. I was out jogging one morning and slogged by a beer truck making a delivery. "Too bad you're running this stuff off," shouted the driver, "I was about to offer you a case." I accidentally left my change on the counter of a 7-Eleven. "No tips to the proprietor under ten dollars," said the man behind the counter. When I asked a park ranger if he had any trail maps for the wildlife refuge, he said, "got thousands of 'em—this is a government project." And, at the chamber of commerce, when I told the lady behind the front desk I was doing a comparison between Fremont and Bangladesh, she gave me a pile of literature and a warm and encouraging smile. I was obviously crazy but how nice for me that I had something to occupy my time. (The Fremont Chamber of Commerce, by the way, has a *nylon* rug and *regular paper* business cards.)

Fremont is just an ordinary place. Not the stuff of dreams, perhaps, but all the substance of a decent life is there. Or maybe Fremont *is* the stuff of dreams. I bought a painting outside the Bihari squatter camp in Dhaka. It showed a boxy, featureless one-story house with a prominent garage. There was a lawn and plenty of flowers. A TV antenna perched on the rooftop and a little car was parked outside. It was a Bangladeshi vision of paradise on earth, and it looked exactly like Fremont, California.

The two places have more in common than humans per square

mile. They are about the same height above sea level. Both are extraordinarily fertile. Fremont's climate is drier but with plenty of water for irrigation and warm enough for multiple crops. Until the 1950s Fremont's economy, like Bangladesh's, was entirely agricultural. No place has disasters like Bangladesh, but Fremont gets earthquakes, flash floods, and brushfires. And Fremont has undergone an amazing population increase—from 22,443 in 1956 to the present 177,500—a growth rate that makes Bangladesh look like an onanistic nation of Planned Parenthood activists, with every male permanently sheathed in a full body prophylactic.

VIII

Is there any basic, scientific reason why Bangladesh can't be like Fremont, California? Of course, a whole world as populous as Bangladesh (or Fremont, California) would contain some 112 billion people and be a very busy and doubtless tiresome place. But no reasonable person, not even any reasonable alarmist, believes that's going to happen.

The present population of the world is about 5.3 billion. Charles C. Mann, in a very big and serious article about population in the February 1993 *Atlantic Monthly* magazine, points out that world fertility rates peaked a while ago. Quite a while ago, in developed countries. But, even in very poor countries with the greatest amount of baby-having, fertility rates dropped 30 percent between the late sixties and the early eighties. If this trend continues, world population growth could reach replacement level by 2005, when the UN estimates there will be 6.7 billion people. (Actually, the population would keep growing for a while after that because of something called "demographic lag." But, on the other hand, the rate of fertility-rate decrease could increase, too—if you're following this, you're doing better than I am—so, what the hell, let's use 6.7 billion as our most optimistic number.)

The *1993 Information Please Almanac*—that august source of

research info for all eighth-graders who have a science report due on Monday morning and didn't begin it until nine-thirty Sunday night—takes a grimmer view. *Information Please* claims population will be 8.2 billion by 2020. That's my approximate checkout date if my liver holds.

Vice President Gore, who is even more pessimistic than a plagiarizing eighth-grader, says, in *Earth in the Balance,* that the number of living humans may reach 14 billion someday.

Of course we have to be careful when playing with arithmetic. Numbers can prevaricate with a straight face that words never assume. And mathematical projections are especially suspect. A 1970 *Look* magazine article about all-time champion population doomsayer Paul Ehrlich stated that Ehrlich's Zero Population Growth organization "now has a membership of over 8,000 and is doubling every two months." You'll remember how there were 17.6 quadrillion ZPG members by 1977.

And how many people are there in the world, really? You go try to count heads in Azerbaijan or even in your own house when your teenagers are having a party. I'll bet you've missed at least three who were in the utility closet toking down. The 1992 revision of the "UN World Population Prospects" says 5,295,300,000. The Comparative International Statistics section of the 1991 *Statistical Abstract of the United States* says 5,318,013,000. And *Information Please* says 5,321,000,000. A whole country's worth of people—25.7 million—is missing in the differences. In effect we can't find Canada. Like we care.

Nonetheless, arguments about population lend themselves to fun with numbers. Let us take 5.3 billion as a fair estimate of the number of us breathing at the moment. How crowded does this make the world? If we exclude Antarctica—assuming this will continue to be an unpopular place for home towns—a figure of 5.3 billion gives the earth's land surface a population density of 101 people per square mile, a bit less than that of Tennessee, which has 118 people per square mile. Of course a lot of the earth's land surface is not very habitable, but neither is a lot of Tennessee. If a 6.7 billion population peak comes true, we'll have 128 people per square mile. If *Information Please* is right, by the time I die there will be 156 people per square mile. If Al Gore has accurately frightened himself, we should eventually wind up with 267 people per square mile.

New Hampshire has 124 people per square mile, Indiana has 154, Pennsylvania 265. We are thus moving from a world as congested as Tennessee toward a world at least as thronged as New Hampshire, possibly as teeming as Indiana, and maybe even as packed as that seething mass of pitiful humanity, the state of Pennsylvania (nearly two billion acres of state forest and nine million acres of farms, producing thirty-eight billion dollars a year in food and agricultural products).

At the present, if the world wants to live in Fremont, California–type suburban sprawl—and a lot of the world seems to—then every one of us on the globe can have a single family home in Europe, with most of Russia west of the Urals left over for landfill. If we'd prefer a more cosmopolitan environment—such as San Francisco, with its density of 15,502 per square mile—then all 5.3 billion of us can fit into Texas and Oklahoma, with a few million left over to keep the planet's bird-feeders full and rake and weed the rain forests. If we want a more get-down, def and slammin' zip code, then—at the Manhattan population density of 52,415 per square mile—everybody on earth can live in former Yugoslavia. And, if we're going to act like New Yorkers, Yugoslavia is what we deserve.

This leaves us with the question of what people mean when they say the earth is overpopulated. What these concerned citizens usually mean is that they've seen a whole bunch of the earth's very ordinary people up real close, and the concerned citizens didn't like what they saw one bit.

Paul Ehrlich starts the first chapter of *The Population Bomb* with a description of "one stinking hot night in Delhi" when he and his wife and daughter took a taxi ride (a taxi ride that sounds, if I may say so, like a stroll in the Tivoli gardens compared to my Dhaka cab sojourn):

"We entered a crowded slum area. The temperature was well over 100. . . . The streets seemed alive with people. People eating, people washing, people sleeping." Ehrlich goes on to combine "people" with eight other verbs that describe typical human activities and winds up with this memorable sentence: "People, people, people, people." Says Ehrlich, "All three of us were, frankly, frightened."

Charles C. Mann concludes his otherwise numbingly well-balanced *Atlantic* article with a little horrified shudder at our too-populous future world: "My guess is that it will be something like living in New York today." Which, as I have pointed out, it will be if we all move to Yugoslavia.

And in Malthus, too, there is a strong aesthetic element underlying what seem to be coolly rational arguments. Although Malthus, at least, had the good grace to be concerned with the sufferings of others rather than himself. He describes "the wretched inhabitants of Tierra del Fuego": "We cannot be at a loss to conceive the checks to population among a race of savages, who, shivering with cold and covered with filth and vermin, live in one of the most inhospitable climates in the world, without having sagacity enough to provide themselves with such conveniences as might mitigate its severities, and render life in some measure more comfortable."

In other words, people are—present company always excepted—just awful. And "People, people, people, people" are that much more so. Especially if these people happen to be not-quite white. Notice that Paul Ehrlich is not panicked by being caught in the tremendous squash and jostle of rich folks around the bar in the Churchill Downs clubhouse on Kentucky Derby Day. Nor is Charles C. Mann worried about the opening-night crush at New York's Metropolitan Opera. And Malthus, when talking about a race of unwashed brutes who live in a miserable spot and don't have enough sense to come in out of the rain, is not discussing Highland lairds.

Fretting about overpopulation is a perfectly guilt-free—indeed, sanctimonious—way for "progressives" to be racists. *Time* magazine, in a 1990 article titled "Beyond the Melting Pot" and published to coincide with those vaguely worrying census forms we all got in the mail that year, began paragraph one with "Someday soon . . . white Americans will become a minority group." And paragraph two said, "If current trends in immigration and birth rates persist, the Hispanic population will have further increased an estimated 21%, the Asian presence about 22%, blacks almost 12% and whites a little more than 2% when the 20th century ends." *Time* then indulged itself in a few column inches of pious noise about cultural and racial sensitivities and the ever-changing complexion of the American body politic before getting back to scaring the Lean Cuisine out of its ofay readers. "History suggests that sustaining a truly multiracial society is difficult, or at least unusual," claimed *Time*. The Babylonian Empire? The Persian Empire? The Indian Empire? The various empires resulting from the conquests of Alexander the Great? (He *insisted* that his officers marry foreign women.) The Roman Empire? The Mughal Empire? The British Empire? America? Canada? Australia? Brazil? "A truly multiracial society will undoubtedly prove much harder to govern," said *Time*. As opposed to monoracial societies such as Somalia.

The idea that too many people exist leads to unfortunate and even lethal plans for those people. One of Thomas Malthus's motives for writing *An Essay on the Principle of Population* was to argue against the Poor Law of his time, which gave aid to pauper families in accordance with the number of their children. This, thought Malthus, bred more paupers. Malthus was also writing in support of Britain's Corn Laws, which imposed large tariffs on imported grain. During the potato famine of the 1840s, these laws would contribute to the deaths of more than a million Irish. Malthus didn't mean any harm, of course. He was a clergyman. "I would never wish to push general principles too far," he said, "though I think they always ought to be kept in view." So we shouldn't actually *shove* paupers and Irishmen into the grave, but we shouldn't lose sight of the option either.

And Paul Ehrlich, in *The Population Bomb,* states flat out that

India—where he'd had such an unfortunate experience in a taxi—was one of "those countries that are so far behind in the population food game that there is no hope that our food aid will see them through to self-sufficiency."★ Ehrlich thought America should stop all help to India and just let the dusky heathen croak.

There *are* too many people. Anyone who's spent a week in the library with Thomas Malthus, Paul Ehrlich, Albert Gore, and the writers of *Time* and *Newsweek* can tell you—even one of these people is too many.

★Twenty-five years and a lot of population increase later, India no longer needs to import food and the Indians aren't starving—although they are blowing each other up quite a bit.

3 FAMINE

All Guns, No Butter

I

We do not, in the modern world, have famine, plague, and war caused by a population crisis; we just have famine, plague, and war. Of these, war is the easiest to condemn, plague is the most frightening, but it's famine that makes us squirm.

Famine is too close to dieting. We snap at our spouses, jiggle on the scale, and finish other people's cheesecake. If we're turned into angry, lying thieves by a mere forgoing of dessert, what must real hunger be like? Imagine a weight-loss program at the end of which, instead of better health, good looks, and hot romantic prospects, you die. Somalia had become just this kind of spa. I went there in December 1992, shortly after U.S. troops had landed in Mogadishu.

I was hoping famine would prove to be a simpler issue than overpopulation. Population alarmists have forgotten that each numeral in a census represents an individual human with as much interest in living and as much right to do so as a population alarmist. Hunger alarmists are professional worriers, too, but they don't wish the rest of humanity dead. Quite the contrary. And in Somalia the good intentions that professional worriers forever profess were being combined with—how rare this mixture is—good deeds. Food was being shipped to the country and international peacekeepers were being sent to deliver the food.

"Feed the hungry" is one of the first principles of morality. Here it was in operation. So where *were* the starving children of Mogadishu? Where were the pitiable little fellows with the gone-away expressions, faces already turned to some less painful world, limbs as thin as the lines of type in a newspaper obit column and bellies gravid with death? A glance at these tykes racks the soul. They are the emblem of Third World misery, the inevitable cover of news magazines, the constant subject of videotape on *Eyewitness News*. I half-expected to be met by a delegation of them at the Mogadishu airport.

What I met with instead were guns. Arrayed around the landing strip were U.S. guns, UN guns, guns from around the world. Trucks full of Somalis with guns came to get the luggage. These were my guns, hired to protect me from the other Somalis with guns, and they all had them. And I thought I might get a gun of my own besides, since none of these gunmen—local, foreign, or supranational—looked like they'd mind shooting me.

Everything that guns can accomplish had been achieved in Mogadishu. For two years the residents had been joining, dividing, subdividing, and rejoining in a pixilation of clan feuds and alliances. Previously Somalia had been held together by the loathsome but stable twenty-two-year reign of dictator Siad Barre. But Barre gained loathsomeness and lost stability, and when he took a walkout powder in January 1991, all and sundry began fighting each other with rifles, machine guns, mortars, cannons, and—to judge by the look of the town—wads of filth.

No building was untouched, and plenty were demolished. It was a rare wall that wasn't stippled with bullet holes and a peculiar acre that lacked shell damage. Hardly a pane of glass was left in the city.

There was no potable water and no electricity. At night the only illumination was from tracer bullets. Mogadishu's modern downtown was gone, the steel and concrete architecture bombarded into collapse. The old city was deserted rubble, a no-man's-land between two envenomed clan factions. Rubbish was dumped atop wreckage everywhere and goats grazed on the offal. Mounds of sand had blown through the streets. Sewage welled up through what pavement was left.

The destruction had squeezed people into the roads, where they built market stalls from pieces of scrap wood and flattened olive-oil cans—market stalls which seemed to sell mostly pieces of scrap wood and flattened olive-oil cans. Young men waving AK-47 assault rifles pushed among the crowds. Rusted, dent-covered, windshieldless pickup trucks with gun mounts welded into their beds sputtered down what remained of the right-of-way, outnumbered by donkey carts and overtopped by pack camels.

It was a scene of Paleolithic ruin except for the modern weapons. The Somalis used to paint the outside walls of their shops with crude pictures of canned goods, television sets, photocopiers, and the like. Cartoon murals on abandoned storefronts were the only evidence that the twentieth century had produced anything pleasant.

Compared to Mogadishu, starving children would be cute. In fact, somewhere in the psychic basement of the sob-sister sorority house, in the darkest recesses of the bleeding heart, starving children *are* cute. Note the big Muppet Baby eyes, the etiolated features as unthreatening as Michael Jackson's were before the molestation charges, the elfin incorporeity of the bodies. Steven Spielberg's E.T. owes a lot to the Biafran-Bangladeshi-Ethiopian model of adorable suffering.

It's easier to advertise our compassion for innocents in misery than it is to face up to what happened in a place like Somalia. What happened was not just famine but the complete breakdown of everything decent and worthwhile. I spent two weeks in Somalia and never saw a starving child, not because they didn't exist but because they were off somewhere dying, pushed into marginal spaces and territories by people with guns. Going to Somalia was like visiting the scene of a crime and finding that the murderer was still there but the body had fled.

II

The world has enough food. In 1990 the World Hunger Program at Brown University published a book, *Hunger in History,* edited by Lucile F. Newman. World Hunger is the kind of program (and Brown, the kind of university) that would, I think, be eager to tell us if the world didn't have enough food. But they don't tell us this. In the book's final article, "On Ending Hunger: The Lessons of History," Robert W. Kates and Sara Millman say that "global food sufficiency" was reached in the 1960s and that, as of the mid-1980s, the world was "nearing diet sufficiency," by which they mean the earth has enough protein, carbohydrates, vitamins, minerals, and whatever else is currently supposed to be good for us to go around.

Hunger in History's penultimate article, "Organization, Information, and Entitlement in the Emerging Global Food System," was written by six experts in the hunger field. They conclude, "If food were distributed equitably, current supplies would be more than adequate to provide an ample diet to all." Though these experts cannot resist a dig at us gluttonous bourgeoisie who've climbed way up on the food chain where we don't belong. The *Hunger in History* idea of equitable distribution would require a cuisine "in which animal products are considerably less abundant than they are in the diets of the developed countries." If I don't eat this steak, the cow will come back to life, vomit its corn and silage, and these can be fed to people in Chad.

But never mind, the world has enough food—enough food, according to Kates and Millman, to provide 120 percent of global needs on a "near vegetarian" regimen and more than half of what's necessary for everyone to eat like an American and get fat.

Plus there's more food where that came from. Only 2.7 percent of the U.S. labor force is employed in agriculture, versus 60 percent in China and 43 percent in Russia. Yet the United States exports forty thousand metric tons of wheat a year, enough to supply China and Russia with all the wheat those two countries need to import despite their hordes of farmworkers. Nor is this just a matter of America being a big, lush country. Cramped, industrialized Japan produces as much rice as Burma, which is twice Japan's size and utterly rural. And dumpy little France grows more wheat than Argentina and Australia combined.

In most of the world, food production has well outpaced the growth of population. In the 1930s American wheat growers had an average yield of thirteen bushels per acre. By 1970 the yield was thirty-one bushels. In the same period the corn yield went from twenty-six bushels per acre to seventy-seven. And the distribution of food has also improved. According to the UN Food and Agriculture Organization, almost a quarter of the people on earth went hungry in 1950 while only 10 percent do now.

The modern era has witnessed an enormous increase in food, an enormous increase in people being fed—and an enormous increase in famine. This would seem to defy physical law. William A. Dando, in his 1980 book *The Geography of Famine,* estimates that, worldwide, about two million people died of starvation in the seventeenth century, ten million in the eighteenth, and twenty-five million in the nineteenth. Then comes the twentieth century. Between 1958 and 1961 as many as thirty million people starved in just one famine in China. At least five million more starved in the Ukraine during the 1930s. Three million starved in another Chinese famine in 1928–29, three million in Bengal in 1943, a million in Cambodia in the late 1970s, and uncounted millions more in Biafra in 1967–68, Ethiopia in 1973, Bangladesh in 1974, and sub-Saharan Africa in 1983–84.

When a thing defies physical law, there's usually politics involved. Drought, floods, crop failures, and insect pests played a part in some of the disasters listed above, but not one of these famines was *caused* by nature. The Chinese famine of 1958–61, the worst famine in history, had nothing to do with weather or "acts of God." In fact, it could be said to have resulted, literally, from an act of Godlessness—the imposition of Marxist theory on traditional peasant agriculture. The same thing caused the Ukrainian famine of 1932–34 and the Cambodian famine of 1975–79.

Some famines were deliberately created. The Nigerian government used starvation as a weapon of war against the Biafrans. The Ethiopians did the same thing to the Eritreans, and the Muslim Sudanese are doing it now to their Christian and animist countrymen.

Some famines came not from political organization but from lack thereof. A government can't very well provide famine relief when there is no government, as there was none in China in the late 1920s.

And some famines have political causes of maddening complexity. The British in Bengal in 1943 had no weird ideas or evil designs. But they wanted to keep rice supplies out of the hands of possible Japanese invaders, and they wanted to feed the masses in Calcutta and keep the vital industries there running. So the British confiscated rice that was stored in rural Bengal. This set off a price panic, and mass starvation followed, even though there was no great scarcity of food.

Indeed, famine can occur when and where there's a food surplus. Sylvia Nasar, in an article on the political causes of famine in the January 17, 1993, *New York Times,* says, "one of the worst recent famines—Bangladesh's in 1974—took place in a year of unusually high rice production." Unfounded rumors of a rice shortage caused prices to double. Then the government of the "People's Republic of Bangladesh," led by self-styled socialist Mujibur Rahman, set about making things worse. The army was sent to arrest hoarders, "convincing people," says Ms. Nasar, "that [Mujibur] had lost control and fueling the price surge." The price surge led to a huge black market. Black marketeering exacerbated the already-wonderful corruption of the

Mujibur regime. And people starved for no reason. Ms. Nasar adds, "The United States contributed by announcing that it would withhold food aid to punish Bangladesh for, of all things, selling jute to Cuba." And there's that damn jute again.

Plenty is no guarantee against famine, but neither does scarcity guarantee that famine will happen. Indian economist Amartya Sen was one of the first scholars to argue against regarding famine as a natural disaster. His 1981 book *Poverty and Famines* was, in academic circles, whatever the academic-circle equivalent is of a new animated Disney feature. Using the 1943 Bengal famine as his principal example, Sen proved (as well as anything can be said to be proved in the social sciences) the political nature of food distribution in modern society.

Later Professor Sen studied the 1983–84 drought in sub-Saharan Africa. He found that Sudan and Ethiopia had experienced, respectively, 11 percent and 12½ percent declines in food production. Those countries suffered severe famines. But Botswana had a 17 percent decline in food production, and Zimbabwe had a 37½ percent decline, and there wasn't any famine in either place. The reason was that Sudan and Ethiopia didn't mind if certain troublesome portions of their populations starved to death while Botswana and Zimbabwe did mind.

If famines are now political, how long has this been true? How far back in history can we go and find human privation caused by human folly?

The Great Hunger in Ireland, 1846–51, was started by potato blight, which can't be blamed on the British (though don't try telling that to certain members of my family). But England's Corn Laws made other sources of food in Ireland expensive, so expensive, in fact, that Ireland was still exporting grain during the worst of the famine years. And the British-imposed system of absentee landlords let the gentry keep a comfortably distant perspective on the suffering of their tenants.

David Arnold, author of the 1988 book *Famine: Social Crisis and Historical Change,* argues that the persistent famines of nineteenth-century China were the result of a corrupt and listless Manchu Dynasty's failure to maintain the infrastructure of peasant agriculture. He cites evidence that, for over a thousand years, more vigorous Chinese governments had practiced various famine-control measures including relief provisions of food and money, subsidized grain sales, encouragement of imports into stricken areas, tax abatements, refugee resettlement, water conservation, pest eradication, land reclamation, and employment of the impoverished on public works such as roads and canals. During the famine of 1493, Ming Dynasty officials gave aid to more than two million people.

Dando, in *The Geography of Famine,* claims to have studied the entire long and gruesome history of Russian hunger and says, "All of the famines which have occurred in Russia from 971–1970 can be predominately attributed to human factors."

University of Chicago economist Robert Fogel examined five hundred years of food records from Britain and France and concluded that, although there have been a number of famines in those countries since 1500, not one of those famines coincided with empty national granaries.

Decent governments and worthwhile citizenries have known, for a long time, how to deal with famine. Peter Garnsey, in his book *Famine and Food Supply in the Graeco-Roman World,* avers that in the classical age "while food crises were frequent, famine was rare." He notes that the three best-attested famines in ancient Athens were siege-induced and gives examples of famine relief such as the Emperor Augustus dispensing aid to two hundred thousand people in A.D. 6.

Garnsey also quotes the Roman physician Galen's second-century treatise *On the Properties of Foodstuffs,* where Galen describes the resourcefulness of the Roman peasantry: "Often when forced by hunger people eat pyethrum, sia, alexander, fennel, wild chervil, chicory, gum soccory, gingidium, wild carrot, and the tender shoots of a great many shrubs and trees." Thus the more elaborate kinds of modern salad owe their existence to ancient famines.

No disagreement seems to exist among experts about the political—or, at least, social—nature of famine. Amartya Sen says famine "is the characteristic of some people not *having* enough to eat. It is not the characteristic of there *being* not enough to eat." William A. Dando says, "Natural factors cause crop failures, but humans cause famines." And Andrew B. Appleby, in an article, "Epidemics and Famine in the Little Ice Age" in the *Journal of Interdisciplinary History,* says, "The crucial variable in the elimination of famine was not the weather but the ability to adapt to the weather."

Some would even go so far as to argue that before mankind became politically organized people didn't starve to death, or at least not in heaps and piles. Mark Nathan Cohen, in his article "Prehistoric Patterns of Hunger" in the Brown University *Hunger in History* book, says, "Early human groups were relatively well nourished and well buffered against starvation."

Mr. Cohen maintains that archeological evidence "suggests that qualitative nutrition was relatively good in the earliest hunter-gatherer populations in any region, more commonly declining than improving with agriculture. The effects of civilization appear to be mixed and patchy."

Too true. Nonetheless, for someone who has been to Somalia, Mr. Cohen's views sail precariously close to Romantic primitivism. Mogadishu is no place to argue in favor of Rousseau's ideas about "natural man." Attribute superior virtues to simple natives, if you will, but the Somalis are about as untainted by civilization as they could be, and no one who's met the Somalis is calling them noble savages.

III

In order to go to Somalia, I took a job as a radio reporter for ABC news. It wasn't someplace I could go by myself. News organizations had to create fortresses for themselves in Mogadishu and man those forts with armies.

ABC sent in its most experienced fixers, men known in the

news business (and not without respect) as "combat accountants." The accountants hired forty gunmen and found a large walled house that used to belong to an Arab ambassador. The house was almost intact and close to the ruins of the American embassy, which—the accountants hoped—would soon be occupied by U.S. Marines.

Satellite dishes, telephone uplinks, editing equipment, half a dozen generators, fuel, food, water, beer, toilet paper, soap, sheets, towels, and mattresses all had to be flown in on charter planes from Nairobi. For some reason we wound up with five hundred boxes of a Kenyan chocolate chip cookie that tasted like bunion pads. Cooks, cleaning people, and laundry men were employed, as well as translators—dazed-looking academic types from the long-destroyed Somali National University.

Some thirty of us—journalists, camera crews, editors, producers, money men, and technicians—were housed in this compound, bedded down in shifts on the floor of the old audience hall while our mercenaries camped in the courtyard.

It was impossible to go outside our walls without "security" ("security" being what the Somali gunmen—gunboys, really—liked to be called). Even with the gunmen along, there were always people mobbing up to importune or gape. Hands tugging at wallet pockets. Fingers nipping at wristwatch bands. No foreigner could make a move without setting off a bee's nest of attention—demanding, grasping, pushing crowds of cursing, whining, sneering people with more and worse Somalis skulking on the fringes of the pack.

One of the first things I saw, besides guns, when I arrived in Mogadishu was a pack of thieves creeping through the wreckage of the airport, sizing up our charter cargo. And the last thing I saw as I left was the self-appointed Somali "ground crew" running beside our taxiing plane, jamming their hands through the window hatch, trying to grab money from the pilot.

A trip from our compound to Mogadishu's main market required two kids with AK-47s plus a driver and a translator who were usually armed as well. The market was walking distance but you wanted a car or truck to show your status. That there was a market at all in Mogadishu was testimony to something in the human spirit, though not necessarily something nice, since what was for sale was mostly food that had been donated to Somalia's famine victims. CON-TRIBUÉ PAR LES ENFANTS DE FRANCE said the stenciled letters on all the rice sacks. (Every French school child had been urged to bring to class a kilo of rice for Somalia.)

Meat was also available, though not immediately recognizable as such. A side of beef looked like fifty pounds of flies on a hook. And milk, being carried around in wooden jugs in the hundred-degree heat, had a smell that was worse than the look of the meat. But all of life's staples, in some more or less awful form, were there in the market. If you had the money to get them. That is, if you had a gun to get the money. And a whole section of the market was devoted to retailing guns.

I wanted to buy a basket or something, just to see how the ordinary aspects of life worked in Somalia in the midst of total anarchy and also, frankly, to see if having my own gunmen was any help in price haggling. I was thinking I could get used to a pair of guys with AKs, one clearing a path for me and one covering my back. I'd be less worried about crime in the States, not to mention asking for a raise. And, if I happened to decide to go to a shrink, I'll bet it would be remarkable how fast my emotions would mature, how quickly my insights would grow, how soon I'd be declared absolutely cured with two glowering Somali teens and their automatic weapons beside me on the couch.

They were, however, useless at bargaining for baskets. Nobody gets the best of a Somali market woman. Not only did the basket weaver soak me, but fifteen minutes after the deal had been concluded she chased me halfway across the marketplace screaming that she'd changed her mind. My bodyguards cringed and I gave up another three dollars—a sort of Third World adjustable basket mortgage.

She was a frightening lady. Ugly, too, though this was an exception. Somali women are mainly beautiful: tall, fine-featured, and thin even in fatter times than these. They are not overbothered with Muslim prudery. Their bright-colored scarves are used only for shade and not to cover elaborate cornrows and amazing smiles. Loud cotton print sarongs are worn with one shoulder bare and wrapped with purposeful imperfection of concealment. There is an Iman doppel-gänger carrying every milk jug. You could do terrific business with modeling agencies hiring these girls by the pound in Somalia and renting them by the yard in New York.

The men, perhaps because I am one, are another matter. They're cleaver-faced and jumpy and given to mirthless grins deco-rated with the dribble from endless chewing of qat leaves. Some wear the traditional *tobe* kilt. Others dress in Mork and Mindy–era American leisure wear. The old clothes that you give to charity are sold in bulk to dealers and wind up mostly in Africa. If you want to do something for the dignity of the people in sub-Saharan countries, you can quit donating bell-bottom pants to Goodwill.

When we emerged from the market our driver was standing next to the car with a look on his face like you or I might have if we'd gotten a parking ticket just seconds before we made it to the meter with the dime. Shards of glass were all over the front seat. The driver had been sitting behind the wheel when a spent bullet had come out of somewhere and shattered the window beside his head.

Mogadishu is almost on the equator. The sun sets at six, prompt. After that, unless we wanted to mount a reconnaissance in force, we were stuck inside our walls. We ate well. We had our canned goods from Kenya, and the Somalis baked us fresh bread (made from famine-relief flour, no doubt) and served us a hot meal every night—fresh vegetables, stuffed peppers, pasta, lobsters caught in the Moga-dishu harbor and local beef. I tried not to think about the beef. Only a few of us got sick. We had a little bit of whiskey, lots of cigarettes, and the pain pills from the medical kits. We sat out on the flat tile roof of the big stucco house and listened to the intermittent artillery and small-arms fire.

Down in the courtyard our gunmen and drivers were chewing qat. The plant looks like watercress and tastes like a handful of something pulled at random from the flower garden. You have to chew a lot of it, a bundle the size of a whisk broom, and you have to chew it for a long time. It made my mouth numb and gave me a little bit of a stomachache, that's all. Maybe qat is very subtle. I remember thinking cocaine was subtle, too, until I noticed I'd been awake for three weeks and didn't know any of the naked people passed out around me. The Somalis seemed to get off. They start chewing before lunch but the high didn't kick in until about three in the afternoon. Suddenly our drivers would start to drive straight into potholes at full speed. Straight into pedestrians and livestock, too. We called it "the qat hour." The gunmen would all begin talking at once, and the chatter would increase in speed, volume, and intensity until, by dusk, frantic arguments and violent gesticulations had broken out all over the compound. That was when one of the combat accountants would have to go outside and give everybody his daily pay in big stacks of dirty Somali shilling notes worth four thousand to the dollar. Then the yelling really started.

Qat is grown in Kenya. "The Somalis can chew twenty planes a day!" said a woman who worked in the Nairobi airport. According to the Kenyan charter pilots some twenty loads of qat are indeed flown into Mogadishu each morning. Payloads are normally about a ton per flight. Qat is sold by the bunch, called a *maduf,* which retails for $3.75 and weighs about half a pound. Thus $300,000 worth of qat arrives in Somalia every day. But it takes U.S. Marines to deliver a sack of wheat.

IV

I went to the Marine Corps encampment at Mogadishu Port on the day before Christmas. The docks and quays and warehouses had been so heaped with wreckage and muck that the first pieces of military equipment the marines landed were bulldozers. The marines plowed away the debris and sprayed the wharves with firefighting equipment from the U.S. Navy ships. It took three scrappings and hosings before Mogadishu was only as dirty as an ordinary seaport. Then the marines built a twenty-foot wall of cargo containers around the space they'd cleared, not so much for military reasons but to make a sort of citadel of hygiene.

Only one of the port's warehouses had enough corrugated tin left on top to provide shelter, and this was pinked with galaxies of bullet holes. Somalis must have stood inside and fired through the roof for the sheer noise of it. Seven or eight hundred marines were sleeping here, their mosquito net–draped cots in rows as close as auditorium chairs. It was 100, 110, 115 degrees every day in Mogadishu, with air so humid that the wind felt like shaving lather. Even in our thick-walled, shaded house the only way I could sleep was to lie naked on the mattress with an electric fan pointed at me. There were no fans in the warehouse and not even much of that hot, sopping breeze.

A branch of some reasonably firlike plant had been set up by the warehouse doors, its needles decorated with miniature Tabasco bottles, Chiclets, and other of the less-esteemed items from the MRE ("Meal Ready to Eat") ration packs. In place of a star was a plastic envelope of beef stew. The navy claimed it would try, the next day, to get some turkey in from the ships' galleys. And satiric carols had been composed:

> *On the first day of Christmas,*
> *The Marine Corps gave to me*
> *Forty injections for tropical disease . . .*

The troops were crabbier than they'd been in the Gulf War. They were sticky and dirty and bored. They had no showers, no hot meals, and, even with female military personnel all over, no private place to take a crap. But all these conditions had existed in Saudi Arabia and for months on end. The problem in Somalia was more abstract. This was the first large-scale military operation in history to be launched for purely altruistic reasons. Nobody knew how to go about such a thing. In a war against hunger, what do you do? Shoot lunch?

I went out on patrol with a squad of marines. I borrowed one of the flak vests that make jogging around in the Mogadishu weather truly miserable. I skipped the Kevlar helmet, which feels like a hollowed-out bowling ball. Neither the jacket nor the helmet will stop an AK-47 round, just slow it down, and I didn't want any slow bullets in my head.

The patrols were being run because the marines, when they weren't unloading boats or guarding aid convoys, couldn't think what else to do. We went in open Humvee trucks to the most battle-frayed parts of town. The idea was, I guess, to look for snipers and goons, and people too blatantly displaying arms and to see if anyone wanted to shoot marines and to shoot them first. Hard to say what the average Somali—the man-in-the-gutter, if you will—thought about this. There was a large group hanging out at the entrance to the port, begging. Sometimes they tired of begging and threw stones until a few marines rushed out and beat them with truncheons, then they'd beg again. But when we stopped our trucks in the ravaged downtown a solitary old man said, in a carefully enunciated shout, "Shoot everybody who makes trouble! We like peace! Long life to America!" This was in front of the city's only Christian church. Someone had tried to brick up the doors and windows. Someone else had pillaged the place.

Schools had long ago disappeared in Mogadishu, and the streets were filled with kids, not starving but good and dirty. The kids would put things out in the road when they saw us coming—bricks, stones, pieces of pipe. Then, when we drove closer, they'd run out and snatch this stuff back. They were playing "roadblock." They liked to try out their English. Earlier that day, when I was driving to the port, a little boy had leaned in my window, flashed an enormous winning smile, and said, "I will kill you." The kids seemed to like the marines, however. Sometimes a marine would open an MRE packet and scatter its contents. In return the kids would point to certain buildings and yell to the effect that snipers were inside.

The marines said the kids were sometimes right. We gave a Humvee-ride reward to one ten-year-old who, a couple days before, had shown the marines where a machine-gun-equipped Toyota pickup—a "technical," as it's called—was hidden. The marines had shot its occupants.

The kids would run in packs behind the speeding Humvees, their sandals flapping like applause. If there's ever a ten-kilometer-in-shower-flipflops Olympic event, it will be won by a prepubescent Somali.

The kids also act as mine canaries. Suddenly they *aren't* running behind the Humvees, suddenly they all disappear, then the marines know they're in a conclusively dangerous place. For instance, the "Green Line," so called after the famous boundary in Beirut, though Mogadishu's Green Line isn't a line but a whole area so fought over that there's nothing left to fight over. Then there's the "Bridge of Death" (actually a culvert) and "Bermuda," for the triangle of the same name, because if you go in there you'll never come out.

Like many people with a mean streak the Somalis have a way with nicknames. A thoroughgoing bad hat may be called *Mattukaday*—"man who's never been seen in a mosque." There is a warlord yclept "Fuji" for inscrutability and a doctor who goes by "Cholera." A particularly hasty defeat of one subclan is remembered as "Kuwait." The most congested intersection in the city is named "Kamakazi Corner" not from the driving but because of suicidal quarrels that break out among the gunmen there. Siad Barre was known as "Big Mouth" due to his speeches, and his cronies were called "Four Pockets" in honor of their ability to line same.

We got out of the Humvees and began to patrol on foot. Mogadishu has a sort of Capitol Hill from when there used to be a government. The way the marines said the kids sometimes vanished, the kids vanished that way here. The marines went down the street in a hollow rectangle, the men on one side checking the walls and windows above the men across the way. One man was walking backward in the rear. One man was darting ahead, his M-16 preceding him around corners.

A minibus full of young Somali men nosed into an intersection in front of us. There was a big grinding of gears and the Somalis sped backwards at cartoon speed.

We went into a ruined government office. Two marines flopped in the doorway behind us and sealed the entrance. Two men went up the steps, scanned the hallways, and pressed back against the walls. Two more men shouted, "Coming up!" and went on to the next floor, the patrol leap-frogging thus until we were on the roof.

The whole mess of Mogadishu spread below us. The place probably never did amount to much, though it's more than a thousand years old. In the distance the blue and yellow stripes of desert meeting surf were pretty enough, albeit the land was covered with thornbushes and the ocean infested with sharks. Wide strips of dirt with tree stumps were visible where handsome avenues might once have been. Maybe the narrow Omani stone houses near the port used to evoke the charm of *Arabian Nights,* if you didn't mind that they were built by slave-trading elephant murderers. They were slums now. And the rest of Mogadishu, what was left of it, was a joke. The taller buildings, nearly all of them abandoned, were built in that ever-present Third World *wog moderne* style, cement puns on Le Corbusier. Siad Barre had constructed an immense reviewing stand for himself, but its grandeur was foiled by its perfect resemblance to a parking garage. The Italians, who were the colonial power in southern Somalia from the 1880s until 1960, had put up a fake Middle Eastern castle on a bluff above the harbor, giving the old part of town a "Seven Package Tours of Sinbad" look. Here and there were bogus classical monuments from when Mussolini was in charge, notably a vaulted gateway to nowhere with dumpy proportions and lots of fasces on it. The postimperialist Somalis had done as well as they could to better this item, and in the center of a roundabout near the airport stood a huge, ill-crafted, out-of-plumb, Taco Bell–façade concrete thing with peeling white paint and big blue letters reading ARCH OF POPULAR TRIUMPH. Somalia is a civilization in ruins but not grand ones.

The marines came down from the roof of the government building, retracting their pickets like a coiling snake. You don't realize how much paper there is in a government until you see it all busted out of its filing cabinets and spread in drifts down floors and through courtyards. Then it seems as though government must be nothing but paper, and I suspect the Somali government wasn't much more than that. Paper and, of course, guns—the guns are still in working order.

Our patrol went on up the hill to the parliament building. This had been subjected to something more like evisceration than looting. The very marble of the floors had been pulled up, and the electrical fixtures had been yanked with such vehemence that the wires were pulled right out through the plaster, leaving vertical trenches in the walls. The National Assembly chamber had been stripped of carpet and décor. Its floor was covered with human excrement. All the chairs and desks had been torn from their mountings. Somalia's seat of government had been wholly, soundly trashed. How many people in how many countries have wanted to do this? Somalis gave in to the temptation.

V

Where did this strange nation come from? The Somalis have a joke: God was bored. So He created the universe. But that was boring, too. So God created Adam and Eve. But He was still bored. So God created the rest of the human race. And even then He was bored. So God created the Somalis. He hasn't stopped laughing since.

As with all nomads, Somalis come basically from nowhere. Roving, quarreling, pillaging bands of Somalis show up in the Horn of

Africa—the biblical land of Punt—about the same time that roving, quarreling, pillaging bands of Normans show up for the Battle of Hastings. The Somalis are, and seemingly always have been, divided into clan families. There are six of these: Dir, Isaaq, Hawiye, Darod, Digil, and Rahanweyn. They hate each other. Not that those are their only hatreds. The two worst Somali warlords extant at the time of my visit, Mohammed Farah Aidid and Ali Mahdi Muhammad, were both Hawiye. Each clan family is divided into numerous subclans. They hate each other, too. And each subclan is likewise split and irked. The first Europeans, visiting Mogadishu in the sixteenth century, found the then-tiny city already riven into warring clan sectors.

Back when one culture could say what it thought of another without risking a massive Donna Shalala explosion, the 1911 edition of the *Encyclopaedia Britannica* (the only reference work I really trust) opined, "The Somali are a fighting race and all go armed. . . . They are great talkers, keenly sensitive to ridicule, and quick tempered . . . love display . . . are inordinately vain and avaricious. . . ." And, said *Britannica,* "The Somali have very little political or social cohesion." In fact, the basic unit of Somali society is something called the "diya-paying group," *diya* being the Arabic word for blood money.

Besides the members of the six clan families, there are other nonclan Somalis known as *sab,* or "low." These are hunters, barbers, leather-workers, metalsmiths, and other productive citizens much looked down upon by nomads. Noble camel thieves think *sab* vocations are degrading. The six clans themselves are divided in prestige according to degree of idleness. The Dir, Isaaq, Hawiye, and Darod call themselves "Samale," from whence comes the name of the country. The Samale clans consider themselves to be strictly nomads—fighters and herdsmen. They call the Digil and the Rahanweyn "Sab clans," and *Rahanweyn,* in Somali, means merely "large crowd." The Sab are farmers, and nomads regard farms with the same violent distaste I have for law offices.

The gunmen who are currently destroying Somalia, who are

wrecking the livelihoods of innocent Somalis and robbing them of their sustenance, are largely Samale. And many of the people who are starving are Sab. It is one of Somalia's plentiful supply of grim ironies that the victims of its famine are the people who grow its food.

Of course the nomad clansmen doing the wrecking and robbing aren't traditional nomads any more than a Toyota pickup truck with a machine gun mounted in its bed is a traditional element of a caravan. But the Samale don't need to go on any Robert Bly wildman weekends to get in touch with their inner warrior. Somali became a written language only in 1972. Just a few miles from the main towns you see itinerant families of Darod and Dir who could pass for Mary and Joseph on their flight into Egypt. Here all the men are dressed in *tobe* kilts, with sword-length daggers in the waistbands, and the women are wrapped in homespun instead of Kenyan chintz. The camel bridles, donkey blankets, pannier baskets, and milk jugs have been made by hand. The nomad life is possessed of almost as much honest, natural, rough-hewn folksiness as a New England crafts fair. Only the occasional flash of a bright yellow plastic wash bucket tells you what millennium you're in.

I have a friend, Carlos Mavroleon, who works as a freelance TV reporter for ABC and who has spent a lot of time among nomads in the Muslim world. Carlos found a very good translator and went off with a minimum of security and baggage to the far parts of the Somali desert to talk to the real Samale. They were shy of strangers—given current events in Somalia, they'd be crazy if they weren't—and it took Carlos several days of lolling around making gifts of tea and tobacco before the nomads would chat. Finally they invited him into their camp, and, when a suitable length of pleasantries had been exchanged, Carlos asked the nomads, "How has this war affected you?"

"Oh, the war is terrible!" they replied. And they told Carlos that just last week some goats had been stolen and a month before a valuable camel was lost. It was a very horrible war indeed. More goats might be lost at any time and only a couple of years ago a wife had been carried away.

Carlos said he didn't realize for a while that the war the nomads were talking about was the war they had been conducting, time out of mind, with the next subclan down the wadi. "No, no, no," said Carlos, "I mean the big war in Mogadishu."

"Oh, *that* war," said the nomads, and there were shrugs all around.

Carlos liked the Somalis. "Men in skirts killing each other over matters of clan," he said. "People call it barbaric savagery. Add bagpipes and a golf course, and they call it Scotland."

And, like good Scots Presbyterians, the Somalis can be religious fanatics when they feel like it. Sayyid Muhammad 'Abdille Hassan, known as the "Mad Mullah," fought the British Empire to a standstill in northern Somalia in the Dervish Wars of 1900 to 1920. The British were forced to withdraw to coastal garrisons, causing famine among the Somali clans who were not allied with the Mullah. An estimated one-third of the population of British Somaliland died during the Dervish Wars, a period that Somalis call "The Time of Eating Filth."

The British never intended to rule Somalia but found themselves continually forced to intervene in Somali affairs to ensure the supply line to their strategic outpost at Aden. In the words of I. M. Lewis in his *A History of Modern Somalia,* "The problem of the future status of these areas was complicated; no one friendly or fully acceptable . . . seemed to want them." And they still don't. Various internationalist schemes were attempted, which is where Italian Somaliland came from. The Mad Mullah was unimpressed. During World War I he wrote a letter to the British Commissioner at Berbera:

> You . . . have joined with all the peoples of the world,
> with wastrels, and with slaves, because you are so weak.
> But if you were strong you would have stood by yourself
> as we do, independent and free. It is a sign of your
> weakness, this alliance of yours with Somali, menials,
> and Arabs, and Sudanese, and Kaffirs, and Perverts, and
> Yemenis, and Nubians, and Indians, and Russians, and

Americans, and Italians, and Serbians, and Portuguese, and Japanese, and Greeks, and cannibals, and Sikhs, and Banyans, and Moors, and Afgans, and Egyptians . . . it is because of your weakness that you have to solicit as does a prostitute.

Seventy-five years before the fact, Sayyid Muhammad was able to accurately predict the composition, effectiveness, and moral stature of today's UN.

The Mullah is still revered in Somalia. And the day I arrived in Mogadishu a flyer was being distributed in the local mosques showing a servile Somali rolling out a carpet for a pair of armed men mounted tandem on a horse. One man was marked with a cross and the other with a Star of David. Two fighting men on one horse was the seal of the Knights Templars, a Christian military order formed in the twelfth century to fight Muslims in the crusades. Sense may be short in these parts, but memories are long.

VI

So here we were on another crusade, this time one of compassion (though Richard the Lionhearted thought his cause was compassionate too). Enormous stores of food aid were arriving in Mogadishu, food donated by international governments and by private charities. Armed convoys were being formed to deliver that food. It takes a lot of weapons to do good works (as Richard the Lionhearted could have told us). And this is not just a Somali problem. We have poverty and deprivation in our own country. Try standing unarmed on a street corner in Compton handing out twenty-dollar bills and see how long you last.

I went with an ABC camera crew on the first convoy to Jalaaqsi, 120 miles north of Mogadishu up the Shebeli river. For the sake of making America's allies look less worthless, the Italian army was given the escort job. A company of Italians in Fiat jeeps and troop carriers led a dozen aid-agency food trucks. Two U.S. Army platoons in Humvees brought up the rear.

The convoy was not a work of logistical genius. It left town a day late because (my American military sources swear this is true) the Italians lingered too long over lunch. Then the Italians, who in their own country are homicidally fast drivers, insisted on a twenty-mile-per-hour convoy speed. They also took three meal breaks. Then one of the Italian drivers fell asleep at the wheel and ran into practically the only tree in the Somali desert. After the sun went down, the convoy got off course somehow. I'm not exactly sure what happened, but I believe the lead driver saw what he thought were the lights at the Jalaaqsi airstrip and headed toward them, but those were actually the lights of the last vehicles in the convoy. Anyway, we wound up with an enormous merry-go-round of trucks, jeeps, and Humvees circling in the desert.

The trip took fourteen hours. Then, with thousands of square miles of parched sand in every direction, the Italians found a mudflat for us to camp in.

The Somalis had been busy, too. Before we even left Moga-dishu, the Italian colonel in charge of the convoy had caught one of the Somali drivers draining the radiator of his own truck. That way he'd have a "breakdown" en route and his cargo would be "stolen." A number of other such sabotages were detected. The Somalis were also quarreling with each other, and their qat-addled driving was bad even by Italian standards. Then, during meal break three, the Somalis decided they couldn't eat Italian rations and they couldn't eat American MREs. They would have to leave the convoy, go to a local village, and get Somali food.

"This is a famine, goddamnit," said an American sergeant. "There *isn't* any Somali food. If there *was* any Somali food, we wouldn't have to fucking *be* here."

The Italian colonel said he wanted to shoot all the Somali drivers.

An American lieutenant commented, "I'm quitting the army.

I'm going on welfare. I'll sell the cars to my folks, sell the house to my sister, and get benefits. This thing sucks—helping people who don't give a shit.''

ABC's Somali employees had also claimed they needed special food. The Kenyan canned goods we were going to pack for them might have pork inside. They wanted a million shillings. Which they got. But they didn't buy any food with it. And, when we weren't looking, they ate all of ours. We had to get the ABC satellite phone out, set it up in the mudflat, and trade soldiers long-distance calls to Mom for MREs.

We didn't have any camping gear either, and when we got ready to go sleep in our trucks, we found our gunmen already stretched out on all the seats, roofs, and hoods. I took three Halcion tablets and lay down in the mud, and I understand the entire U.S. military presence in Jalaaqsi was kept awake all night by my snoring.

When the sun came up, we could see a refugee squatter camp stretching for a mile along the Shebeli river. These people were not starving; that is, they weren't starving *to death*. Their misery had not quite reached the photogenic stage. But they were living in huts no bigger than the houses children make by putting a blanket over a card table. These homes weren't even hovels, just little humps in the landscape formed with sticks bent in half-circle hoops and covered with grain sacks and pieces of scrap cloth.

The refugees had none of the proud shyness that Carlos had found among the nomads. You could approach these people at random, and they were only too glad to talk. They had nothing to do but talk.

I talked to a woman named Habiba Osman. She had fled from the fighting in someplace called "Burrui," which I cannot find on a map. She was a Hawiye, a member of the Hawadli subclan, and had been chased away from her home by other Hawiye, members of the Abgaal subclan. She had nine children, she said, holding up four fingers, and she was forty-five. Her husband, Muhammad, stood in the background. They were getting one portion of coarse cornmeal a day. It was hard to eat. They made it into porridge.

I counted her possessions: a wooden bowl, a long pestle for cracking grain, an empty two-gallon olive-oil can, an aluminum pot, a few aluminum dishes. The goats and camels had been stolen.

I went to watch one of our convoy trucks unload food for the Save the Children charity in Jalaaqsi. The town itself hardly existed anymore, though it hadn't been ruined by the war or abandoned by its population. It was just—like the rest of the Somali nation, citizenship, and culture—a neglected, entropic, crumbling mess. The Save the Children headquarters was a tumbledown school sitting in a small yard inside the high walls with which everything needs to be surrounded in Somalia. The food we'd brought to them was something called Unimix, a sort of Purina Famine Chow made of 50 percent corn, 30 percent beans, 10 percent sugar, and 10 percent oil, all ground together. It makes a nourishing gruel when stirred into water, if you can find clean water. A great number of Somalis had to be hired to unload the food: some to carry the fifty-pound sacks, more to stand around yelling commands, and even more, armed with long switches, to argue with the others and take swipes at townspeople who gathered in a nosy cluster around the truck.

Save the Children had managed to keep some food coming into Jalaaqsi. In the midst of the worst chaos they had eight kitchens operating to feed kids. They were able to do this, they said, because they worked closely with clan elders. More importantly, there isn't much of a thieves' market for Unimix. Save the Children was losing only 10 percent of its food shipments. But, even so, as many as ten children a day were dying in the refugee camp where I talked to Habiba Osman.

Several reporters were interviewing a Save the Children aid worker. One of the reporters must have flunked journalism school because he asked a question that went straight to the point. "Who cares?" he said, looking around at the wretchedness, squalor, muddle, and despair. "Back in the United States, in the rest of the world, who really cares about these people?" The man from Save the Children started to laugh. He was possessed of Christian charity—or Muslim or Jewish or whatever. The idea that someone could look at this suffering and *not* care was absurd to the aid worker, utterly ridiculous. So he laughed, the only laugh of kindness I've ever heard.

Much uglier jokes were available. About food, for instance. It was all over the place. In fourteen hours of travel the previous day, we'd never been out of sight of the stuff. The American sergeant yelling at the Somalis for trying to grocery-shop in a famine was wrong. Just as I'd been wrong about parched sands when I'd seen our bivouac area. The Shebeli river valley is wet and fecund and contains the richest farmland in Somalia. The road from Mogadishu traversed miles of corn and sorghum, the fields marked out with animal skulls set on stakes. (Scarecrows, maybe, or scarepeoples. I saw a human skeleton beside the pavement.) Even in the drier areas, away from the river, there were herds of cows and goats. We'd been carrying thousands of pounds of food relief through thousands of acres of food.

It was not a supply-side problem they had in Somalia, as our drivers and gunmen pointed out to us that afternoon when they refused to take us back to Mogadishu. They said they'd be robbed and shot. "But," we said, "you knew we were coming to Jalaaqsi, and you knew we'd have to go home. We talked about this before we left. We asked for volunteers. You weren't afraid then," we said. They said they'd changed their minds.

So we left the little army that our corporation had hired with the larger army that our tax dollars pay for and hitched a ride to Mogadishu on a relief agency plane.

Somalia is amazingly roofless. Almost every building we flew over had its ceiling off. How much of this was from neglect and artillery and how much from looting of corrugated tin sheets I don't know, but you could look right down into the rooms and hallways, and it made the entire country seem like a gigantic game board of Clue. Probable correct answer: Everybody. In the toilet. With an AK-47.

Beautiful beaches, however. As we came into Mogadishu we
could see miles of tawny sand with not a hotel or time-share condominium in sight. At this very minute some real estate developer is
probably saying, "We got your two baby-boom major obsessions here:
oceanfront property and weight loss. Bingo, it's the new Hilton
Head."

VII

On New Year's Eve I went with another convoy west a hundred miles
to Baidoa, this time with U.S. Marines in the lead. We made the trip
in three hours despite long sections of road that weren't there anymore.
Marines drive like qat-influenced Somalis except they don't litter.
American troops in Somalia were scrupulous about not tossing empty
water bottles out Humvee windows or scattering MRE trash on patrol.
They policed their areas and always left the campground cleaner than
they found it. We tried to explain to the marines that the locals *wanted*
those water bottles and MRE scraps. Somalia is so bad that making a
mess improves the place.

    The land was less fertile here than in Jalaaqsi. Western Somalia
is one great thorn scrub savannah gradually rising toward the mountains
of Ethiopia and utterly featureless except for two gigantic limestone
rocks, Bur Acaba and Bur Eibi, which jut out of the surrounding plain
as big and steep and out of place as ski resorts. But, although this was
desert, it had wells and irrigated fields, and between the fields was
grazing land dotted with cows, goats, and camels. Again, we were
never out of the sight of food. And never out of the sight of hunger
either.

    Children were begging frantically by the roadside, pointing to
their bellies and making terrible faces. Older boys twirled rags to attract
attention. That they had enough energy for theatrics meant they were
among the better-off. We weren't going to stop for them anyway. The
road was famous for bandits.

    On New Year's Day we would come back down this highway

without marines. The beggars were gone, and in their place were a dozen freelance roadblocks. These were lengths of iron pipe, each balanced on an oil drum and counterweighted with a chunk of concrete. Half a dozen armed creeps lurked in the thornbush shade while one harmless-looking fellow squatted by the drum, ready to raise the pipe and obsequiously wave you through—unless you looked as harmless as he did, in which case you'd be robbed and shot. We'd found some doughtier gunmen than the Jalaaqsi bunch, and we had a dozen of them with us in three trucks. We drove fast right at the blockades with much scowling and bristling of gun barrels, and we were unmolested.

We went on the trip to Baidoa to see George Bush, who was making the kind of high-speed kiss-and-promise tour of Somalia that seemed, I thought, indistinguishable from presidential campaigning—as though the man had suffered complete memory loss, forgot he was beaten the previous November, and forgot he was in the wrong country besides.

Baidoa had been completely destroyed: "Somollified," as we'd taken to calling it. And it stank with the same smell poverty has around the world—stale smoke and fresh shit. The only buildings left intact were the fortified charity offices. The charities also had the only vehicles left running, all filled with gunmen and sporting the flags and logos of various relief agencies. A total innocent, set down in these environs, would say by the look of things that Baidoa had been conquered and pillaged by the Red Cross, OxFam, and CARE.

We found lodgings of a sort in Baidoa at the Bikiin Hotel, named not after the bathing suit but, very approximately and very unaccountably, after the capital of China. The Bikiin was a disintegrating thatch-and-cement establishment that served dirty plates of spaghetti and warm Kenyan beer. But it had the one thing you want most in Somalia—a high wall. It also had an antiaircraft gun and a howitzer outside the front gate.

No rooms were to be had, not that we wanted one of the dank

little cubicles. And there were no bathrooms that we would go into more than once voluntarily. We commandeered an empty hut at the back of the compound, made pallets on the floor, and draped mosquito nets around as best we could. We got our gunmen squared away, fed on the spaghetti and staked out around our trucks. Then we found a table and some chairs and set these out under a palm tree.

There were four of us ABC employees: a reporter from New York, a South African soundman, a cameraman from Cairo, and me. We'd requisitioned two bottles of scotch from the ABC emergency larder. Huge red clouds rolled through at sunset like blood pouring into water. The sky turned ruby then maroon then mahogany then black. A breeze came up. The temperature went down to only ninety degrees. The clouds blew away again and there was a moonless equatorial sky undimmed by the lights of civilization or anything resembling it. The sky was so clear that the starlight cast shadows, and so many sparkles and glitters and glints appeared above us that it looked like something really expensive had been dropped and shattered in heaven—God's Steuben ashtray, maybe.

We began to drink and think big thoughts. What the hell were we doing here? We thought that, for instance. And we thought, well, at least some little bit of good is being done in Somalia. The director of the Baidoa orphanage had told us only one child died in December. Before the marines came, the children were dying like . . . "Dying like flies" is not a simile you'd use in Somalia. The flies wax prosperous and lead full lives. Before the marines came, the children were dying like children. Would this last? No, we thought. Everything will slip back into chaos as soon as the marines are gone. But to do some good briefly is better than doing no good ever. Or is it always? Somalia was being flooded with food aid. The only way to overcome the problem of theft was to make food too cheap to be worth stealing. Rice was selling for ten cents a pound in Somalia, the cheapest rice in the world. But what, we thought, did that mean to the people with the fields of corn and sorghum and the herds of goats and cattle? Are those now worth nothing, too? Had we come to a Somalia where some people some-times starved only to leave a Somalia where everybody always would?

We had some more to drink and smoked as many cigars and cigarettes as we could to keep the mosquitoes away—mosquitoes which carry yellow fever, dengue, lymphatic filariasis, and four kinds of malaria, one of which is almost instantly fatal. Was this the worst place we'd ever covered? We thought it was. We had, among the four of us, nearly forty years' experience of journalism in wretched spots. But Somalia . . . tiresome discomfort, irritating danger, amazing dirt, prolific disease, humdrum scenery (not counting this night sky), ugly food (especially the MREs we were chewing), rum weather, bum natives, and, everywhere you looked, suffering innocents and thriving swine. True, the women were beautiful, but all their fathers, brothers, uncles, husbands, and, for that matter, male children over twelve were armed.

Still, we thought, this wasn't the worst New Year's Eve we'd ever spent. We had a couple more drinks. We certainly weren't wor-ried about ecological ruin, shrinking white-collar job market, or fear of intimacy. All that "modern era anomie" disappears with a dose of Somalia. Fear cures anxiety. The genuinely alien banishes alienation. It's hard for existential despair to flourish where actual existence is being snuffed out at every turn. Real *Schmerz* trumps *Weltschmerz*. If you have enough to drink.

But what do you do about Somalia? We had even more to drink and reasoned as hard as we could.

Professor Amartya Sen says, "There has never been a famine in any country that's been a democracy with a relatively free press. I know of no exception. It applies to very poor countries with democratic systems as well as to rich ones."

And in the *New York Times* article featuring that quote from Professor Sen, Sylvia Nasar says, "Modern transportation has made it easy to move relief supplies. But far more important are the incentives governments have to save their own people. It's no accident that the familiar horror stories . . . occurred in one–party states, dictatorships or colonies: China, British India, Stalin's Russia." She notes that India has had no famine since independence even though the country suffered severe food shortages in 1967, 1973, 1979, and 1987.

Says Professor Sen, "My point really is that if famine is about to develop, democracy can guarantee that it won't." And he goes on to say that when there is no free press "it's amazing how ignorant and immune from pressure the government can be."

Well, for the moment at least, Somalia certainly had a free press. The four of us were so free nobody even knew where we were. But how do you get Somalia one of those democratic systems Amartya Sen is so fond of? How, indeed, do you get it any system at all? Provisional government by clan elders? Permanent international occupation? UN Trusteeship? Neo-colonialism? Sell the place to Microsoft? Or . . . Or . . . Or . . .

We were deep into the second bottle of scotch now, and boozy frustration was rising in our gorges along with the MRE entrées. It's all well and good to talk about what can be done to end famine in general. But what can be done about famine specifically? About this famine in particular? About a place as screwed-up as Somalia? What the fucking goddamn hell do you do?

There's one ugly thought that has occurred to almost everyone who's been to Somalia. I heard a marine private in the Baidoa convoy put it succinctly. He said, "Somalis—give them better arms and training and seal the borders."

4 ENVIRONMENT

The Outdoors and How It Got There

∎

Hunger, overcrowding, dying a horrible death—these are understandable worries. Of course we love our food, our health, and having enough room on our side of the bed. But why are we so worried about nature's welfare? How did we get to be enamored of the outdoors? Just go out there for a minute, and no fair taking the indoors with you. Doff the little Donna Karan frock, that rumpus room for your torso. Shed those lacy Christian Dior knickers, gazebo for your butt. Eschew your Joan and David pumps, small personal floors for feet. Enter nature as you, indeed, entered nature. Then get arrested. Police, we mustn't forget, are part of nature, too.

But let's say you're on your own land and properly secluded, and the kids are at camp, and the cleaning lady has gone home, and today isn't the day the boy comes to mow the lawn, and your husband's too busy watching ESPN to notice. Go outdoors and cavort. Scamper through the foundation plantings. Roll in the gladiolus. Vault the lawn furniture. Romp 'neath clothesline and bird-feeder. You'll learn about yourself. And what you'll learn is that *you itch*.

Ticks, lice, fleas, mites, poison ivy, poison oak, mosquitoes, black flies, deerflies, horseflies, sunburn, prickly heat, allergies, rashes, and fungal infections . . . One thing that's certain about going outdoors: When you come back inside, you'll be scratching.

With me it was chiggers.

I was in an Orejón Indian village on the Sucusari River in the Peruvian Amazon. A few slapdash thatch-topped shacks were set around a weedy common. The jungle stood behind with its excess of greens: celadons, olive drabs, chartreuses, envies, gullibilities, golf courses, and Saint Patrick's Day parades. The locals lolled in their hammocks. Midday hush obtained. The sky was a fine, light, equatorial blue with just a few tubby cumulus clouds as pretty as foam on a beer.

It was Eden, a scruffy Eden, Eden after the apple had been eaten but before anybody realized they'd have to go to work. Anyway, there was a one-room schoolhouse in the village and a beautiful schoolteacher barely out of her teens and very shy. I was thinking, if I were a younger man, maybe I'd get into this ecology stuff. With altruistic enthusiasm born of undying love, the two of us could save a rain forest and a half. And rescue mountain ranges. And give the Heimlich maneuver to an occasional small continent. While I was thus woolgathering, one of the beautiful schoolteacher's tiny charges booted a soccer ball into my knee.

It was ninety-five degrees. I'm as old as the president of the United States. I have a body like a sack of Gummy Bears. And it's been thirty years since I was a third-string forward on my high school's JV soccer team. But such is male vanity that for the next half hour I was America's one-man World Cup team battling a half-dozen midget Pelés. Running through the verdure, I got chiggers. Who got the schoolteacher, I can't say. She wandered away unimpressed.

∎

I'd flown to Peru from Florida. There's a corner of Miami International Airport devoted to off-brand Latin American airlines: Chacha Air,

Trans Mato Grosso, Malvinas National, Aero Tierra del Fuego, and so forth. American "eco-tourists," seeking solitude in untrammeled wilderness and lonely communion with the natural world, jammed the ticket counters. There's a look about these sightseers. They haven't been out in the weather enough to get skin-cancerous, and they haven't been in an office or shop for fourteen hours a day either. Theirs is the healthy glow of people without enough to do. They are in their thirties or forties but sit on the airport floor cross-legged as though they were fifteen. They touch each other a lot and make prolonged eye contact, and their conversations are filled with little noises of affirmation. The men are not actually unshaven but look as though they are nerving themselves not to shave. The women wear their hair plain and their faces scrubbed and go undecorated except for large pieces of "native" jewelry—that is, jewelry from cultures where women spend as much time dolling themselves up as they can spare from baby-having and yam-field-tilling.

Why do the eco-tourists have neon-blue hiking shorts? And fluorescent-purple windbreakers? Caution-signal-yellow sweat socks? Crap table–toned fanny packs? Hojo-tinted luggage? T-shirts the hue of sex dolls? What is the connection between love of nature and colors not found in ditto?

Ahead of me in line was an all-female tour group, Amazon-bound, as it were. They talked about being an all-female tour group. This, they told each other, was meaningful. Also meaningful were herbal medicines, spiritual healings, astral projections, auras, and other things not subject to empirical observation or experimental proof. Natural creatures showing appreciation of nature by holding natural science in contempt—nature *is* mysterious.

"Party of ten women?" said the Peruvian airline ticket agent.

"Party of ten *loud* women!" said one of the women, loudly.

I'd signed up for my own Amazon trip more or less at random. I had a pile of tour-company brochures, each saying the rain forest was a marvel and all promising "experiences you'll never forget." I guess the people who write the brochures—or the people who read them—

haven't had many such experiences or the tour companies would tout "experiences you'll wish you could remember more of," those being the fun kind. The brochures also pointed out that I wouldn't be exploring for oil or cutting down tropical hardwoods. In fact, I'd be doing the rain forest a kind of favor by going there and thanking it for sharing. And every brochure had a large picture of a poison frog. I don't know why this was a selling point.

I hoped, of course, to be thrown in with, well, ten loud women, for instance. But I had no luck. News of coup attempts and Shining Path excesses had given Peruvian adventure travel too adventurous a name just then. I wound up with just four other people on a tour designed for thirty.

We landed in Iquitos, an old rubber boom city far back behind the Andes and reachable only by river or air. It was late at night and violently hot. The air was wet and immobile. We stood around in a cement-floored hall decorated with murals of Machu Picchu, which we were nowhere near, and ads for "Inca Cola." The baggage handlers threw our luggage in all directions. A clutter of begging musicians played the Simon and Garfunkel Andes theme, leaving me with that "I'd-rather-be-a-hankie-than-a-snot" tune stuck in my head the whole week.

The ten loud women were assembled by their tour guide and led loudly away. The guide for my tour, Julio, came to get us in a bus made of wood, like one of those arts-and-crafts-store toys that people without children give to kids. "The lush rain forest of the Amazon wilderness supports the most prolific and diverse array of flora and fauna found anywhere in the world," began Julio.

"Where can we get a beer?" said Tom, an ex-rodeo rider. Tom turned out to be a Republican. His wife, Susan, may have been one, too. (Ever since the Republican party got overexcited about fetus empowerment at the 1992 convention, it's been hard to get women to admit this.) If so, we were the first eco-tourist group with a Republican majority since Teddy Roosevelt explored the Amazon in 1913.

The fourth member of our party, Michael, was the executive editor of a publishing house in New York and had just commissioned a book from an old college friend of mine. "I know what *you're* doing," Michael said to me. "You're writing an article viciously satirizing large plants. Don't anybody do anything plantlike. He's taking notes." Michael was traveling with the marketing director of his company, Shelley, who'd come to the Amazon because of a lifelong fascination with three-toed sloths.

"Their top speed is .16 miles per hour," said Shelley. "They sometimes spend their entire existence in one tree. They only come down to shit. And they only have to do that once a week. They lead a wonderful life."

Julio looked confused. "The Amazon rain forest occupies over 2.5 million square miles and includes major portions of nine South American countries," he said. "There are eleven hundred tributaries to the Amazon river system, which contains sixty-six percent of all the earth's river water. It has been calculated that the Amazon contributes twenty percent of the oxygen . . ."

It took us two days to make Julio stop this. We knew that we'd gotten through to him when he quit saying "Amazon rain forest" and started saying "jungle."

"We *really* need some beer," said Susan.

"Or some of that Peruvian coca-leaf tea," I said.

"And we need to know how to get the little bags up our nose," said Michael.

We had a few hours' sleep in an Iquitos hotel that was trying hard to be clean and air-conditioned. Then we went to find coffee on Iquitos's modest esplanade. We watched the sun advance in a giant sky over an immensity of water and herbage. It was a noble vista, grand and calm and reaching off past the two-mile-wide river into a vast distance. A blush of haze obscured the horizon, giving an impression of true endlessness, as though the earth really were flat and you could see all of it from Iquitos. It was like a vision of, to be honest, Illinois. It was especially like a vision of Illinois in the flooded summer of 1993. But if you stand on the Missouri bluffs anytime when the Mississippi is high, you'll see that the Amazon is nature's Midwest—a featureless, prone spot with too much river in it. Speaking as a native midwesterner, that's reason enough to leave the Amazon alone.

Iquitos is not as majestic or as dull as its surroundings. It's a mildly pleasant city of 250,000, fairly tidy and not completely impoverished. The architecture is low and pastel, arranged in an orderly grid with the houses blank and flush against the sidewalk, Latin style. Monument-filled plazas appear at regular intervals, although I don't think anything monumental has ever happened in Iquitos. There's one novel feature, a floating slum named Belén full of tenement rafts and pushcart boats and beer cellars on stilts. Belén is sometimes called the Venice of the Amazon, but not very often.

Iquitos has a feel, a very Estados Unidos feel, of being a place with no reason to be in that place, like Springfield, Illinois. Iquitos was founded in the mid-1700s by Jesuits in order to pester local Indians with religion. The Indians, of course, have long ago all been pestered, many to death. Modern Iquitos dates from the rubber boom of the late nineteenth century. The famous rubber baron Fitzcarraldo made a fortune here, or lived here, or passed through. Local history is obscure on the point. Anyway, *Fitzcarraldo,* the movie, was shot in Iquitos. "Signs of the great opulence of those rubber boom days may still be seen in mansions and edifices," said my guidebook. By which was meant, I think, that there's an old hotel with balconies and that some of the narrow, squat, fin de siècle stucco town houses have doorways decorated with Portuguese tiles.

Iquitos is the nethermost deep-water port on the Amazon, twenty-three hundred miles upstream. But not many oceangoing freighters call anymore. It's a seventeen-day trip from the Atlantic, and there's no pressing reason to make it. Rubber comes from factories now. Iquitos exports some Brazil nuts, some plywood, some tobacco, some mahogany, and photos of poison frogs. Most of the locals seem to make their living in the open-air market, selling each other the same enormous catfish—a shovel-nosed thing the size of a bunk-bed mattress and marked with the dun-colored camouflage that was used in the quite-different environment of Desert Storm. There is oil being looked for in the region, however. And some has been found already. Another boom approaches, perhaps. More decorative tiles and hotels with balconies are on their way. In fact a skyscraper was even started in Iquitos. But the contractors were building it between two of the eleven hundred tributaries that contain 66 percent of the earth's river water, which means 66 percent of the earth's river mud, and the thing began to sink. The empty shell stands eight or ten stories high, moldy and just slightly out of plumb.

Julio collected us in the clapboard bus and took us to the tour-company dock. Here we got on board a very long and narrow boat with an absurd palm-frond roof. The boat had a large outboard motor dropped in a well near the stern and a little steering wheel at the bow connected to the engine by thirty-foot strands of scraping, twanging coat-hanger wire.

We went fifty miles down the Amazon in three and a half hours, traveling not quite fast enough to water-ski but fast enough to dangle a hand over the side and not get it eaten by piranhas. The big sun and big clouds made dapples of Impressionism light on the water, and the breeze was as good as that moment in a noontime parking lot when the car AC finally kicks in. The fashionably earth-toned river complemented the green jungle verge. It was a scene of inordinate charm that stretched along the Amazon's banks . . . and stretched and stretched and stretched—uniform, unvarying, same and identical for fifty miles. Fortunately, the boat driver sold beer from a cooler.

And the boat had an interesting bathroom. It was a little outhouse on the very end of the ship, hanging over the water aft of the outboard motor. To get there you had to climb across the top of that outboard, its propeller churning horribly below. Then, when you pulled up the toilet-seat lid, you realized you were right over the engine's rooster-tail wake—death douche.

Our tour company's lodge was tucked up a creek in the jungle.

Tree-trunk pilings supported a ramble of thatch and board buildings all roofed in the same manner as the boat, though more appropriately. One tennis court–sized screened area enclosed a dining room and a bar. Guitars leaning in a corner threatened folk music. The rooms themselves were just partitioned nooks, open beneath the roof. Mosquito nets covered the beds. There was no electricity or plumbing, and the showers were fed from gravity tanks full of river water more or less warmed by the sun.

Michael called the style of the lodge "primitive *primitif.*" Although this tour company is owned by an urban corporation, the people who run it and who built its facilities are either Indians or *ribereños,* the poor people who live along the river banks and are a mixture of Indian, Spaniard, rubber planter, river boatman, and whatever. It would be interesting to know what people who live in humble circumstances think of creating humble circumstances for people who live in luxury to come visit. But they were too polite to say.

Whatever the employees' opinion of their task, they accomplished it with grace. The lodge had ice for drinks, plenty of hammocks, fresh fruit, fried plantains, wonderful little Peruvian potatoes, and excellent (very large) catfish fillets. And, except for a biology professor from Lima and his assistant, we were the only guests. There was twice as much staff as us. A perfect wilderness adventure, or it would have been except Julio inveigled us into a nature hike.

Some people would think it odd to go all the way to the Amazon and never get out and take a close-up look at . . . Yow! Did you see the size of that bug?! Personally, I believe a rocking hammock, a good cigar, and a tall gin-and-tonic is the way to save the planet. From a recumbent, and slightly buzzed, perspective, Mother Earth is a fine specimen of womanhood, a cutie. And the environment is something for which everyone should give his all, if somebody will go get my wallet. Pour me a couple more G&Ts, and I'll be making solemn eye contact, passing out hugs, and saying things like "We are only guests upon this planet, so let's make our renewable-resource beds and not leave a mess in the ozone kitchen."

I have accumulated a three-foot stack of books and articles about the rain forest. (Just think of the dead trees. And, by the way, do you send a decorative arrangement of cement to a plant funeral?) From this reading material, I gather that, if the rain forest disappears, we'll have to get our air in little bottles from the Evian company, and biodiversity will vanish, and pretty soon we'll only have about one kind of animal, and with my luck that will be the Lhasa apso. The indigenous peoples will all become exdigenous and move to L.A.; and this will be tough on them because it's hard to use a car phone when you've got a big wooden disk in your lower lip. Furthermore, we'll never discover all the marvelous properties of the various herbal treasures that are found in the rain forest, such as Ben & Jerry's Rainforest Crunch. Also, rain forests are disappearing so fast that by the time you read this you're dead anyway.

In my reading about the rain forest, however, I have found very little description of what it is like to actually *be* in a rain forest. There's a good reason for this, the same reason that little girls' baby dolls don't actually smell like babies. Not that the rain forest smells. You'd think something so wet, hot, and biological would stink like boiled Times Square, but it doesn't. Jungle has a nice fresh scent, the reason being that there's so much life in the jungle that anything which dies or is excreted or even gets drowsy is immediately a picnic for something else.

A tree keels over and it's termite Thanksgiving. A termite slows up and it's lizard hors d'oeuvres. The lizard takes a nap—kinkajou lunch. And so on up the food chain—and back down it. There's a spider in the jungle so big it eats birds. The ravenousness of rain-forest appetites is such that the floor of the jungle is nearly bare. If you don't count ants. And you can't. There are ants in numbers large enough to confuse the people who calculate national debt. There are ants all over every leaf and stem (not to mention every shoe and sock), ants all over the ground and around all the tree trunks, and ants climbing in droves up the jungle vines. Which is something they don't tell you in the Tarzan books: He went ahhEEEahhEEEahhEEEahhEEEahh as he swung through the jungle because he had ants in his loincloth.

There are ants as big as AA batteries and ants as small as, well, ants. Leafcutter ants regularly go forth in columns of ten thousand to pick up dime-sized bits of foliage and carry these back to their nests for the purpose, I believe, of making public-television nature movies. My guidebook asked me to imagine that the half-inch leafcutter ants were six feet long. I have my own fantasy life, thank you. Anyway, my guidebook insisted, each of these six-foot creatures would be capable of carrying 750 pounds and moving at fifteen miles an hour. Which makes the leafcutter ant nature's lawn tractor.

The intense, even NBA-like competition among living things in the rain forest means that almost every plant and animal has some kind of stinger, barb, thorn, prickle, spur, spine, poison, or angry advocacy group back in the United States boycotting your place of business. There's a fierce competition for the nutrients in the ground, which is why rain-forest soil is notoriously poor and easily damaged by horticulture. The tremendous hardwood trees of the jungle, rising 120 feet with prodigious rocket-ship tail-fin buttresses and trunks as big around as tract houses, are rooted in earth where you couldn't grow petunias. It's hard to imagine something so enormous and complex based upon virtually nothing. Unless you've had experience with large American corporations.

But what it is like to actually *be* in the rain forest is hot and sticky. When you get out of your hammock and go nature hiking, you're immediately covered in sweat. Your underwear clings, your shirt clings, your pants cling, and things that EEK! aren't part of your clothing at all cling to you. You're also immediately covered in bugs. And the rain forest is, as its name would imply, rainy. Hence, WHOOPS! slippery. You're immediately covered in mud, too.

While we were trying to remove the sweat, bugs, and mud with handkerchiefs, moist towelettes, and Deep Woods Off (in the environmentally friendly pump containers), Julio was showing us insects that look like sticks and frogs that look like leaves and moths that look like birds and lizards that look like anything they sit on. There seem to be problems with identity in the jungle. Among the various things the rain forest needs is, probably, psychiatric help.

The rain forest is not, however, scary, not even in the dark. Though the rain forest is dense, tangled, and filled with remarkably icky things, the conifer woods of Maine are spookier. Not to mention the bushes of Central Park. Maybe this is because anacondas aren't really inclined to attack people (probably because we taste like towelettes and Deep Woods Off) and the *ribereños* have eaten most of the crocodiles. Or maybe it's because the largest land mammal anywhere nearby is the capybara, a sort of giant guinea pig. But I think it's the sound. The jungle sounds exactly like the jungle sounds in every jungle movie. There are even distant drums, though these turn out to be from popular songs being played on the lodge staff's boom box. Even in the middle of the night, when you have no idea where you are, it's impossible to believe there isn't someone selling popcorn and Milk Duds right around the corner.

Actually, right around the corner was someone collecting bats. The biology professor was stringing fine mesh nets across the jungle paths. These are invisible to bat radar. The bats get as tangled up as jungle hikers who have come around a corner and walked into a fine mesh net full of angry bats.

The professor extracted the bats—and us—and held the bats with wings outspread so we could examine them in the light of Tom and Susan's video camera.

Why do people spend so little time contemplating the ugliness of nature? How many ordinary humans can get all the way through even the most fabulous sunset without getting up for a beer or going inside to check the evening news? But you can watch an enraged Jamaican fruit bat trying to bite a professor from Lima for hours. A Jamaican fruit bat looks like a colonel in the rat air force. And it's got a set of teeth on it that you could use to perform an appendectomy. If

I were Jamaican, I'd keep the fruit out in the garage or maybe rent a mini–storage space. There was another bat, I didn't catch the name, which ate pollen or pollinated plants or did something in the pollen line. Anyway, it had a tongue that was a surprise. If bats wore blue jeans, this fellow would be able to get change out of his hip pocket with his tongue. It must make bat date night interesting. Then there was a leaf-nosed bat that was honestly uglier than Ross Perot.

All these bats were furious, swiveling their necks and snapping their heads from side to side, trying to get at the professor's fingers, taking thumb-sized chunks out of the air with their jaws. And all these bats were male; and, in the throes of their fury, they had erections— tiny, pink bat penises sticking out of their fur. Some feminist theory of something-or-other was being validated here, maybe. Susan and Shelley declined to comment.

For those of us who were not enraged male bats, however, the jungle wasn't very sexy. That cannot, of course, be literally true, given the reproductive riot and galloping fecundity around us. But, for average *norteamericanos,* the prospect of romance was something like moving our beds into a sauna, dumping bug spray on the hot rocks, and making love under down quilts.

The gummy swelter of the rain forest only gets worse after dark. When the sun goes down, the air is becalmed, and a humid, gagging smother settles upon the body. Sundown makes the heat get worse, and so, for that matter, does everything else. When the rain comes, the air gets so dense you could serve it as flan. When the wind blows, the atmosphere is as horrid as ever; there's just more of it. And, when the sun comes up again, it brings the heat of the day.

We got up early the next morning (or would have gotten up if any of us had been able to sleep) and went bird-watching, an activity I don't understand. Watch birds *what?* The birds of the Amazon have wonderful names, however:

Undulated Tinamou
Horned Screamer

Laughing Falcon
American Finfoot
Wattled Jacana
Plumbeous Pigeon
Mealy Parrot
Common Potoo
Ladder-tailed Nightjar
Pale-tailed Barbthroat
Gould's Jewelfront
Black-eared Fairy
Spotted Puffbird
Lanceolated Monklet
Yellow-billed Nunbird
Red-necked Woodpecker
Ocellated Woodcreeper
Pale-legged Horneo
Common Piping-Guan

And these are very useful if, for instance, you're writing an epic poem about the Bush administration cabinet secretaries and need a rhyme for "Manuel Lujan." But don't ask me which birds are which. And don't ask anybody else either. There's always the horrible chance that they'll be able to tell you. And seventeen hundred species of birds are found in Peru alone:

Cinnamon-rumped Foliage-gleaner
Black-spotted Bare-eye
Ash-throated Gnateater
Screaming Piha
Amazonian Umbrellabird
Lesser Wagtail-Tyrant
Black and White Tody-Flycatcher
Golden-crowned Spadebill
Bright-rumped Attila

Social Flycatcher
Violaceous Jay
Orange-fronted Plushcrown
Coca Thrush
Giant Cowbird
Short-billed Honeycreeper
Variable Seedeater
Purple-throated Fruitcrow

I did like the flocks of parrots. They'd all sit together in a tree saying, in unison, "I'M A PRETTY BOY!" No. But I don't see why, with patience, they couldn't be trained to do so. Even the beautiful things in nature can be made interesting if you put your mind to it.

It was strange to see parrots, toucans, macaws, and cockatoos flying around without perches, cages, or a jungle covered in newspapers. Actually, the toucans and macaws weren't *that* wild. They were hanging around the lodge, squawking and begging and acting like New York homeless. A macaw ate the shutter release off Shelley's camera, and one of the toucans stuck its huge beak into Michael's coffee cup, slurped the contents, and got jittery and irritable.

When we came back (a bit irritable ourselves) from bird-watching, Julio found a sloth for Shelley. It was in the top of a cecropia tree reading a letter from Bill Clinton asking it to come to Washington and help reinvent government. Really, it was doing even less than that, although it was doing it upsidedown, which I think should count against the sloth's slothfulness. I find even *getting* upside down fairly laborious and nibbling tree leaves from that position a difficult task.

Shelley had never seen a live sloth. They can't be kept in captivity because, although sloths eat the leaves from some thirty kinds of trees, any given sloth will eat leaves from only a couple of those kinds, so you'd have to take thirty giant rain forest trees around everywhere with your captive sloths. Tom had a telescope, we set this on a tripod, and Shelley looked through the lens. "Oh, he's beautiful!" she said. She was wrong. The sloth had a long, awkward, gawky body of the kind basketball players had before steroids were discovered. Julio gave a sharp whistle, and the sloth turned its chalky face—very slowly—in our direction. A green smear of leaf slobber was spread around its mouth.

Sloths move at the speed of congressional debate but with greater deliberation and less noise. Shelley's sloth stared at us for half an hour and, having decided we were a surprise, headed for cover. One triumvirate of sloth claws came unhooked from a tree branch and a sloth leg swung down like fudge batter dripping from a spatula until another tree branch was languidly encountered and methodically grasped. Then a second sloth limb repeated these motions, then a third, until at last the sloth had all its appendages located elsewhere and thereto the sloth head and body proceeded at a stately pace.

Our notions of grace have been so influenced by slow-motion videotape that sloths seem to be graceful. In fact, they're just slow. But Shelley disagreed. She wants to start a Sloth Circus. "This is a circus strictly for adults," said Shelley, "very soothing—Windham Hill calliope music. The clowns are all dressed in business suits. They don't fall down, they get tripped up by little clauses in contracts. And all the stunts are leisurely. On a high wire in the center ring, the circus sloths sleep late on Sunday morning, then read the *New York Times.*"

We, too, had a leisurely morning, although Julio had a long list of experiences we'd never forget and were supposed to be having. We finally consented to go in a small speedboat to look for dolphins. There are two kinds of dolphins in the Amazon. Estuarine dolphins look like slimmed-down versions of the Sea World type, as if Flipper'd been doing extra laps and had given up leaping for fish between meals. Amazon River dolphins, however, are terrifying. They're pink, a too-vivid parody of flesh, like the Crayolas of that name or the plastic that Barbies are made of. You don't get a good look at pink dolphins because they don't jump. They just roll to the surface, presenting an indistinct mass of plump tissue, like a drowned and bloated corpse given unnatural animation, a scuba zombie. The *ribereños* say that the pink dolphins sometimes take human form and appear as beautiful maidens who entice young men ("Want to go out for sushi?"). The dolphin maiden lures her prey to the riverbank. Then the fellow disappears forever. The *ribereños* consider it bad luck to kill Amazon River dolphins. And even worse luck to date them.

The estuarine dolphins travel in pods and are more inclined to Greenpeace fund-raising antics. Unfortunately, we couldn't find any estuarine dolphins, and after a couple of hours on the river we resorted to desperate measures. And here is some bad news about our friends, the aquatic mammals—they actually *do* like Judy Collins. Michael started it. He sang "Who Knows Where the Time Goes," and three dolphin fins appeared. Tom and Susan and I tried "Someday Soon," and there was a blowing and bubbling astern. Michael and Shelley sang "Suzanne," and a minute later, thirty yards off our bow, two dolphins launched themselves into the air with excellent hang time.

We tried "Smoke Gets in Your Eyes" by the Platters. Nothing. "Can't Help Falling in Love" by Elvis. Nothing. "Alley-Oop" by the Hollywood Argyles. Nothing. But, when all six of us (Julio knew the words in Spanish) warbled "Both Sides Now" . . . If dolphins had Bic lighters or a way to hold them or anything to stand up on, the dolphins would have been standing up holding Bic lighters and singing

fromupanddownandstillsomehowitscloudsillusionsIrecall

in squeaky, fast-forward voices.

Dolphins may be equal to us in intelligence, but they have a long way to go with taste. This is a tragic phenomenon that occurs elsewhere in nature, such as at the White House. However, we were unable to scientifically determine whether dolphins have even worse taste than the president because we couldn't bring ourselves to sing "People."

"Time for a civilization hike!" said Michael. "Enough of bugs! Birds! Great big fish! We've got to get away from this hustle and bustle of nature and spend time in restful human society—get in touch with our *outer* selves." Julio took us to meet a friend of his, José, a man in his seventies who lived on a farm along the banks of the Amazon. José had a few acres of sugarcane and a few acres of pasture for cows and water buffalo. He grew mangoes and bananas. And he had chickens and relatives everywhere underfoot.

Ribereño dwellings are built on posts about grandchild-high. Sometimes there is an enclosed room, but usually the home is open on at least three sides—all porch and no house. One interior wall separates kitchen from parlor. The construction materials are rough boards and tin sheets. There's only a little furniture: a table, a bench, a couple of stools, and maybe an heirloom mantel clock. There is always, however, a framed marriage photograph hand-tinted in Amazon River dolphin-ish color.

The kitchen stove is just cement or stones with palm wood burning on top and a grill propped over the coals. A catfish the size of a golf bag is normally roasting on this grill. The smoke goes any which way. There is no chimney. Tethered out front will be two or three dugout canoes of a pattern begging to be made into a coffee table and sold at Crate and Barrel. And, if the family is well-off, there will be a square-sterned, factory-made canoe or johnboat with an outboard motor.

Julio's friend had a yet more prized possession, a fifty-year-old sugarcane press set up in a shed next to his house. The press was operated by a water buffalo pushing a tree-limb crank in a circle around the floor, the water buffalo being lured in this orbit with offerings of pressed sugarcane. The cane juice was collected in a bucket and the bucket was emptied into an enormous copper pan, the shape of a backyard television satellite dish and fully as large—probably the largest piece of metal this side of Iquitos that wasn't a roof. The pan nestled atop a circular stone forge or oven burning at a temperature I estimated to be almost as great as that inside my mosquito netting at night at the lodge. As the cane juice boiled down, José skimmed the impurities with an old spaghetti colander. What was left was molasses, a huge amount of it.

Molasses has only so many uses. I didn't figure the locals were *that* fond of pancake syrup. I asked Julio a discreet question. And, yes, José did make bootleg rum, a huge amount of it. We could get some for a dollar a liter. We did.

After a long nap we went on an Indian Embarrassment Tour. We hiked ten minutes through the jungle to a muddy clearing. Here the tour company had paid members of the once-fierce Yagua tribe to build a traditional communal house. It was a fifty-foot long, twenty-foot-high, loaf-shaped construction thatched all the way to the ground. It looked like a big pile of leaves. There were no windows. The inside looked like the inside of a big pile of leaves. The Yagua were wearing skirts that looked like piles of leaves, too, sort of vegetable dirndls. They had streaked their faces with Max Factor, donned fish-bone and parrot-feather necklaces, and stuck Indian-type things in their hair. The women covered their breasts with something that resembled a large baby's bib, made of cotton and not, I think, part of the original Yagua dress code.

We were supposed to "trade" with the Yagua. The tour-company brochure had been firm on this point. We were encouraged to bring "trade items" such as clothing, fish hooks, pocketknives, and the like. But we weren't supposed to try to give the Yagua money. "Money is not of much use on the river," said the brochure in a palpable untruth. We consulted among ourselves and discovered we'd all brought stupid T-shirts. I'd gone to my local gun-nut store and gotten some with big Stars and Stripes across the fronts and mottoes such as TRY TO BURN *THIS* FLAG, ASSHOLE! The Yagua brought balsa wood carvings and decorated gourds and various items of jewelry made from parts of animals that hadn't been, our brochure was careful to assure us, killed or anything like that. "They do not kill animals for this purpose," said the brochure, "but use the leftovers from their kitchen."

The Yagua were bored. So, for that matter, were we. Michael grew up on the Texas border and speaks Spanish, or used to. He said his vocabulary had evaporated with years of living in New York and using his Spanish for nothing but reading the cigarette and hemorrhoid medication ads on the subway. Michael told a half-dozen small Yagua children that Tom and Susan and Shelley and I were *"bestias—no humanos."* He said they could tell because we were so big and old and still could not speak one word that they could understand. We came from a frightening place with little bitty rivers *("poquitos mini-ríos")*. It was very far away and filled with T-shirts. And we ate—nouns failed him—cigarettes and hemorrhoid medication.

One old man had pulled out all the stops in the authentic-dress business. He had a grass skirt so elaborate he was lucky he hadn't been declared an endangered ecosystem from the waist down. The old man produced an eight-foot blowgun and some darts made from thin wooden splinters as long as a hand, with a little cotton wool wrapped around one end and the other end dipped in a poison frog—devil's Q-Tips. The blowgun itself was crafted from a thin, ruler-straight sapling that had been split and hollowed and bound back together with rattan. The old man took the blowgun, aimed it at a tree, and missed six times. Tom said he'd like to try and hit the tree on first puff. Then we were truly embarrassed. I only hope the Yaguas cheated us hugely on the T-shirt deals. As we left, the children lined up and waved happily. *"¡Adios, no humanos!"*

We walked around the corner to where the Indians really lived—in wood and tin houses like everyone else. A radio playing mariachi music was hooked up to a car battery. They were all wearing stupid T-shirts.

The next morning we took our big thatched boat, our water-borne Trader Vic's, and went downstream to the town of Orellana at the mouth of the Napo River. Orellana was named for Francisco de Orellana, one of Pizarro's captains and the first European to travel the length of the Amazon. He left the Andean foothills of Ecuador in 1541, made his way down the Napo to the main river, and reached the Atlantic over a year later, having a terrible time the whole trip. The members of Orellana's expedition nearly starved to death, which means they must have been bad wing shots, inept nut-gatherers, and remarkably poor fishermen. Or maybe, being good Catholics, they thought they were supposed to eat fish only on Fridays. Anyway, they raided Indian villages for food. Orellana's tales of village women who fought back (he made them out to be very large women, inasmuch as they managed to kill some of his soldiers) are the basis for the river's "Amazon" name. The Spaniards were eventually reduced to eating the soles of their boots "boiled with herbs," and they should have been glad Nikes weren't invented.

The town of Orellana has a population of four hundred, electricity for a couple of hours a day, a muddy plaza with a concrete monument to shoe-nibbling conquistadors, an ugly modern clay brick church, and a few stucco buildings painted with the same swimming-pool paint they had in Bangladesh. In the plaza a dozen men were cutting boards from jungle hardwood, or, rather, one man was cutting while eleven or so watched. A log fifteen feet long and a yard in diameter had been laid on the grass and a chain saw had been turned into a handheld lumber mill. One horizontal lengthwise cut was taken off the log. Then a series of parallel lines about two inches apart were drawn on the level surface. The chain-saw operator began to take fifteen-foot-long slices off the log, freehand. The other men stood around holding their noses. The log was from a moena tree, a relative of the rosewood, and it smells like a fart when it's cut.

The moena is not, for obvious reasons, one of the trees causing the rain forest to be cleared by greedy lumber companies. Interesting that a tropical plant should equip itself, probably hundreds of thousands of years ahead of time, with a defense mechanism against Danish modern furniture makers.

The real industry in Orellana is gathering tropical fish. The rain forest is the principal source of kissing gouramis, neon tetras, marbled hatchetfish, and such-like. It is a little-known fact that the bottom of the Amazon is covered with small plaster castles, toy treasure chests, and miniature deep-sea divers who make bubbles.

Michael and Tom and I discovered more bootleg rum. There's a great variety of rum in the Amazon—there's *trago* and *agua ardenté* and *cachasa* and *mezchal del caña de azucar*. Sometimes the rums are flavored with fruit juices and vine saps. The specialty of Orellana was a rum mixed with fermented wild honey. This makes an alleged aphrodisiac called *rompe calzon,* or "bust-underwear." Maybe it was my age or maybe the damp, prickly, rash-inducing nature of the underwear that was supposed to be busted, but *rompe calzon* had no effect on me, though I tried it in ample dosage.

After another long nap (the boat having meanwhile traveled up the Napo and into the Sucusari river), we arrived at the tour company's second camp. Here a really sophisticated effort at simplicity had been made. The camp was nothing but one large, wobbly bamboo platform with a roof of palm leaves. Narrow mattresses lay on the platform with a little tent of netting over each. And there was a poison frog in the washbasin ready to be photographed for a brochure.

It was a male frog, said Julio. He could tell because of the eggs. The eggs of the poison frog are carried on the male's back. It's a nineties, caring kind of poison frog.

The Sucusari camp was decorated with twee balsa plaques carved by previous tourist groups. (Balsa *isn't* a tropical hardwood. It's very soft.) The plaques bore the names of the travelers and memorialized principal incidents of their travels—"Remember the time the canoe tipped over!"—and often contained brief poems on the order of:

> *Though the bugs made noise,*
> *Our trip was full of joys,*
> *Because the monkey howls,*
> *And the wise owl hoots,*

Taught us that it's,
Bad to pollute.

A pet capybara named Margarite was kept at the camp. The capybara is the world's largest rodent, a four-foot-long, hundred-pound member of the guinea pig family. Notice, however, that no one ever claims he is being "used as a capybara." Margarite also had about as much personality as a guinea pig. Although the camp cook said that sometimes when visitors were swimming in the river Margarite would jump in the water and nip female tourists on the rump.

"Last one in gets to live to maturity!" said Michael. Margarite didn't molest Susan or Shelley, and Julio assured us that the piranha of the upper Amazon aren't really dangerous. They hardly ever eat anybody, he claimed. Indeed, at Orellana we'd seen half a dozen kids swimming in the river. Of course, we don't know how many kids there were to begin with. Another rare thing, said Julio, was an attack by the Candiru catfish. This is the famous tiny, spined catfish which swims right up a part of the male anatomy that just thinking about makes me wince too hard to type, and it can only be removed by surgery. "That almost never happens," said Julio. He didn't get in the water himself.

Tom and I tried a dugout canoe, a small one—a difficult craft to maneuver, especially since, with two well-nourished North American males aboard, the whole thing was underwater. A dugout is much superior to a conventional manufactured canoe because you can get soaking wet without bothering to capsize it.

But we were coming perilously close to having fun, and that is not the point of eco-tourism. So we went to the Orejón Indian village and I got chiggers.

III

Chiggers are a kind of mite or, rather, the larvae of a mite, and they are only a hundredth of an inch long. It's hard to keep an eye out for them. They crawl on your body and find some hot, damp spot (which, in the Amazon, is every place) where your clothes are tight (I have apparently grown too fat for my socks) and there they release an enzyme, the evolutionary purpose of which is to make you tear your Friends of the Earth membership card into small pieces, these being what the chigger larvae actually feed upon.

The only thing you can do about chiggers is not scratch them. And you can drink three six-packs of beer and not take a whiz while you're at it. No Sirens calling to Ulysses, no Lorelei enticing Rhine boatmen to destruction, no pink dolphin maiden breathing heavy through her blow-hole at the local swains ever produced a desire as wild and overpowering as the yen to scratch a chigger bite. By comparison, a sailor in port after six months at sea has a mere partiality to feminine companionship. Madonna has half a mind to get some publicity. And politicians are this way/that way about getting re-elected. And never has there been such delight in surrendering to a temptation or achieving a goal. The next thing you know, you've been scratching for two and a half hours and your legs are blood salad.

Chiggers are supposed to drop off after about four days. But mine seemed to migrate north instead and establish themselves in a less socially acceptable area for scratching. And my chigger itches persisted for weeks so that, when I was back in the real world, engaged in the ordinary activities of adulthood—giving a speech, visiting a museum, serving as an usher at a friend's wedding—I would be suddenly overwhelmed by an uncontrollable desire to thrust both hands down the front of my trousers and make like I had a bad case of Arkansas pants rabbits.

I blame my chiggers on Theocritus, who invented the pastoral poem in the third century B.C. Theocritus was from Syracuse, the large, urbane Greek colony in Sicily, and he spent his career in Alexandria, the most cosmopolitan metropolis of the ancient world, the capital of arts, ideas, and sophistication, the Seattle of its day.

Theocritus was a city boy, but as a youth he lived for a while on the Aegean island of Cos. A school of medicine had been founded there by Hippocrates in the fifth century B.C., and various cultural institutions had grown up around the school. Cos was, in effect, a college town. Like many of us who went to college in a cute place, Theocritus had fond memories of amusing locals, of young love in wholesale quantities, of long, gabbing walks in the woods with friends, and of how idyllic everything looks when you're supposed to be in chem lab. Hence:

> *Ah, sweetly lows the calf,*
> *And sweetly the heifer,*
> *Sweetly sounds the goatherd with his pipe,*
> *And sweetly also I!*
> — *"Idyll IX"*

This type of lyric, with its remarkable lack of percipience about barnyard noises, folk music, and self, was brought to full development in the first century B.C. by Virgil:

> *Oh, if you'd only fancy life with me in country poverty . . .*
> *And shepherding a flock of kids with green hibiscus!*
> *Piping beside me in the woods you'll mimic Pan*
> — *"Eclogue II"*

From Virgil a line of direct descent runs for two thousand years to John Denver.

Virgil had, at least, grown up on a farm, though not an unprosperous one, and actual labor was done by the slaves. He spent most of his adult life as a court favorite of the emperor Augustus.

Successful men of affairs (or, in the case of the modern ecology movement, their children) customarily spout nostalgia for simple times and places—catching bullhead with dough balls on bent pins, sprawling in the hayloft atop the milkmaid, running through meadows barefoot, stepping in things. To this piffling wistfulness, Virgil added the element of utopian idealism. He envisioned a pastoral Eden:

The carrier too will quit the sea, no naval tree masts
Barter their goods, but every land bear everything,
The soil will suffer hoes no more, nor vines the hook.
The sturdy plowman too will now unyoke his team,
And wool unlearn the lies of variable dye.

— *"Eclogue IV"*

Christians have traditionally interpreted "Eclogue IV" as predicting the birth of Christ and the new age that will follow (hence Virgil's role in Dante's *Inferno* as the only good pagan in hell). But advocates of a very different kind of New Age like Virgil's idea even better. Edward Abbey wrote a novel, *The Monkey Wrench Gang,* about pro-bucolic activists who wreck construction machinery to stop progress and stuff. Abbey would be a saint to environmentalists if saints got recycled instead of going to heaven. In 1986 Abbey said that he had "hope for the coming restoration of a higher civilization: scattered human populations, modest in number, that live by fishing, hunting, food gathering . . . that assemble once a year in the ruins of abandoned cities for great festivals of moral, spiritual, artistic and intellectual renewal . . ."

Of course, Theocritus, Virgil, and people who put sugar in bulldozer fuel tanks don't hold Western civilization's majority brief on nature. At least they didn't used to. There are 305 mentions of wilderness in the Revised Standard Version of the Bible, none of them laudatory. In the Old Testament, six Hebrew words are translated as *wilderness*. The literal meanings of the words are "a desolation," "a worthless thing," "a sterile valley," "an arid region," "a haunt of wild beasts and nomads," and "an open field." In the New Testament the two Greek words for *wilderness* both mean "lonely place."

The terms we have inherited for paradise don't indicate that our ancestors had any inclination toward eco-tourism after death or even in their daydreams. *Paradise* has its root in the Old Persian word for "enclosure." *Eden* comes from the Hebrew "delight." *Valhalla* is

"Hall of the Slain." *Olympus* is a ninety-eight-hundred-foot mountain in Thessaly that nobody had bothered to climb or they would have known the gods weren't up there. *Heaven* doesn't have anything to do with earth at all; it's the firmament. And, to borrow a term from one of those non-Western cultures that's supposed to be so in tune with the ecosystem, *nirvana* means "extinction."

While paradises tend to be alfresco, they are not at all wild, except for Valhalla, which is wild but indoors. The traditional Muslim seven heavens sound like a visit to Van Cleef and Arpels followed by an encounter with paparazzi flash cameras: (1) Silver, (2) Gold, (3) Pearl, (4) White Gold, (5) Silver and Fire, (6) Ruby and Garnet, and (7) Divine Light Impossible for Mortal Man to Describe.

Until very recently ordinary people spent most of their time outdoors—farming, hunting, gathering nuts and berries, pillaging the countryside in armed bands. The more contact people actually have with nature, the less likely they are to "appreciate" it in a big mushy, ecumenical way. And the more likely they are to get chiggers.

James Fenimore Cooper was the son of a wealthy land agent. He went to Yale. He lived most of his life in Scarsdale except for seven years spent as the American consul at Lyons. Cooper wrote the Leatherstocking Tales idealizing pioneer life and particularly the life of that pioneer ideal Natty Bumppo. In Cooper's 1827 book, *The Prairie,* Bumppo says, "They scourge the very 'arth with their axes. Such hills and hunting grounds as I have seen stripped of the gifts of the Lord, without remorse or shame! . . . how much has the beauty of the wilderness been deformed in two short lives!"

Cooper's contemporary, President Andrew Jackson, was an actual backwoodsman. Jackson, in his 1829 inaugural address, says, "What good man would prefer a country covered with forests and ranged by a few thousand savages to our extensive Republic, studded with cities, towns, and prosperous farms, embellished with all the improvements which art can devise or industry execute."

The concept of "nature" is itself, so to speak, artificial. Are Ring-Dings elf food? Is Wal-Mart part of the spirit world? For people who live in what we would call "the state of nature"—for Yaguas, Orejóns, *ribereños,* me when I'm fishing in Michigan—nature is nothing in particular. It's meat locker, wastepaper basket, patio, and toilet.

Perhaps I should say nature is nothing *in general*. Man alone in the wilderness—with nothing but a camperback pickup, a cooler full of Bud Light, and a cellular phone between him and the raw power of the elements—is not thinking of nature as an abstraction. His interest in the natural world is highly specific: "Shit, I'm out of ice."

When those who have a purpose for being outdoors encounter those who are outdoors because of how earthy the earth is, some conflict of interest ensues. Witness the strained relations between loggers and owl enthusiasts or between k. d. lang and pot roast. At the very least the lover of shrubbery will get kidded. Roderick Frazier Nash (author of *Wilderness and the American Mind,* eminent environmentalist scholar, prominent spokesman for ecological ethics, and a man so devoted to nature that he read enough James Fenimore Cooper and presidential inaugural speeches to find the quotes I used above) was fed a line and swallowed the hook, the worm, and the bobber:

> I had the opportunity to talk, through an interpreter, with a man who hunted and gathered in the jungles of Malaysia. I tried without success to discuss wilderness. When I asked for an equivalent word I heard things like "green places," "outdoors," or "nature." Finally, in desperation, I asked the interpreter to ask the hunter how he said "I am lost in the jungle." . . . The interpreter turned to me and said with a smile that the man had indicated he did not get lost in the jungle. The question made as little sense to him as would asking an American city dweller how he said "I am lost in my apartment."

Personally, I have been lost in my apartment any number of times. I have a friend, Gilbert, who is a hunting guide in New Brunswick and a member of the Micmac tribe. One day he and I were lost in a vast alder bog on one of those overcast days without shadow to give bearing. Gilbert turned to me and said with a smile, "Indians never get lost—although sometimes the *path* wanders."

For most of history, mankind has managed to keep a reasonable balance between thinking nature's adorable and thinking it wants to kill us.

Virgil's soppy lyric to his true love aside, the original Greek Pan was born completely covered in hair, with a goat's beard, hooves, and horns. His mother, the nymph Callisto, was so frightened that she ran off and left him to the care of whatever welfare agencies Olympus had. A sudden spasm of fear in the wilderness is supposed to be caused by a glimpse of Pan, hence the word *panic*. Many of the traditional attributes of Satan are traceable to Pan. Our image of Pan as a frolicsome, pipe-tooting gadabout in need of a leg wax is a late classical invention. And the notion of Pan, as a nature deity, being more or less the God of Everything—"pantheism"—is the result either of a misidentification with the Egyptian god who created the world, ram-headed Chum, or of etymological confusion between the name Pan, which means "pasturer," and *pan,* the neuter form of the Greek word *pas,* meaning "all" or "everything." Pan's actual position in mythology was something akin to baby-brother-of-the-president-during-Democratic-administrations.

The wild Anglo-Saxons were, if anything, less fond of wildness than the Greeks. In *Beowulf* the monster Grendel and his rather more monstrous mother are said to "dwell in a land unknown, wolf-haunted slopes, wind-swept headlands, perilous marsh-paths, where the mountain stream goes down under the mists of the cliffs . . ." We'd declare it a national treasure and lobby to have it protected under the Wilderness Preservation Act. Loss of habitat is threatening endangered monster species everywhere.

Our own pilgrim forefathers didn't enjoy camping, were not exhilarated by fresh air, and found little fascination in contact with indigenous cultures. Pilgrim leader William Bradford, in his *History of Plimoth Plantation,* writes of arrival in the New World:

They had now no friends to welcome them nor inns to entertain or refresh their weatherbeaten bodies; no houses or much less towns to repair to, to seek for succour. . . . what could they see but a hideous and desolate wilderness, full of wild beasts and wild men . . .

Gardens provide a clue to a society's attitude toward nature. The first mention of a garden in Western literature is in the *Odyssey,* where Homer describes the palace grounds of King Alcinoüs of Phaeacia. These seem to have been covered entirely in fruit trees, grapevines, and vegetable plots—more a greengrocer's than an arboretum. The early Greeks didn't garden. They farmed, but not for fun. Cimon planted the first pleasure garden in Athens in the fifth century B.C. The early Romans didn't think much of herbaceous borders either. In the third century B.C. Cato the Elder recommended growing cabbages. Nothing like a "naturalistic" garden would be seen in Europe for another two millennia.

Art, also, gives us some idea of what people consider worth noticing in the world. Pure landscape painting was known to the Romans, but apparently as a novelty. Pliny, in his *Natural History,* goes out of the way to mention a painter in the time of Augustus who introduced a style that included "sacred groves, woods, hills, fishponds, straits, streams and shores, any scene in short that took his fancy." But pictures without people, gods, or important animals in them didn't recur in Europe until Dürer made some watercolor sketches in the fourteenth century, and it was another three hundred years before anybody sold a lumpy mountain prospect, an overdressed sunset, a big wave getting a rock wet, or a quaint stretch of cart-track mire with gnarly tree nearby.

From the very beginning of the Renaissance, however, there were dangerous stirrings in that wild, untamed segment of nature, the intelligentsia. In 1336 Petrarch hiked up Mount Ventoux, near Avignon. Supposedly, no one before him had made such a trip just to see the view. Once on top, Petrarch opened a copy of St. Augustine's

Confessions (obviously, a different kind of climbing gear was carried in the trecento) and happened upon the passage where Augustine rails against those who "go about wondering at mountain heights . . . and to themselves they give no heed."

Suitably abashed, Petrarch scuttled back downhill. But during his brief sojourn upon the Ventoux peak, the poet stood astride the medieval and modern ages—the first European to climb a mountain for the heck of it and the last to feel like a jerk for doing so.

A mush-pot sentimentality about things natural was growing. Loon-June-moon infected the best minds. By the 1500s Montaigne was raving about the natives of lately discovered America, calling them "men fresh sprung from the gods."

Montaigne had a servant who had gone as a soldier or a seaman to Brazil and probably to the Amazon basin. The Indians' dwellings are described as "very long, with a capacity of two or three hundred souls, covered with the bark of great trees, the strips fastened to the ground at one end and supporting and leaning on one another at the top . . . whose covering hangs down to the ground and acts as the side." This is the communal house that the Yagua don't want to live in anymore. And the servant says he never saw Indians who were "palsied, bleary-eyed, toothless or bent with age." Probably true enough. In Stone Age societies in the tropics such venerable folks are what we'd call dead.

The rest of the information from Montaigne's source sounds like wishful thinking or a crib from "Eclogue IV":

> This is a nation . . . in which there is no sort of traffic
> . . . no name for a magistrate or for political superiority,
> no custom of servitude, no riches or poverty . . . no
> occupations but leisure ones. The very words that signify
> lying, treachery, dissimulation, avarice, envy, belittling
> . . . unheard of.

The whole day is spent in dancing.

They live in a country with a very pleasant and temperate climate.

And Montaigne believed every word. He says:

> What we actually see in these nations surpasses not only all the pictures in which poets have embellished the Golden Age and all their ingenuity in imagining a happy state of man but also the conceptions and the very desire of philosophy.

From this bosh it is but the jot of a pen nib to the twaddle of Jean-Jacques Rousseau. In his *Discourse upon the Origin and Foundation of the Inequality among Men* (1754), Rousseau converts Primitivism from a telling of tall tales into a theory of political science. "Let us begin therefore, by laying aside facts, for they do not affect the question," says Rousseau with a frankness rare among modern political scientists. Rousseau then gives us a picture of *au naturel* man "satisfying the calls of hunger under the first oak, and those of thirst at the first rivulet . . . laying himself down to sleep at the foot of the same tree that afforded him his meal; and behold, this done, all his wants are completely satisfied." Not only are all his wants satisfied, he's taking great care of his body. "Man . . . in a state of nature where there are so few sources of sickness, can have no great occasion for physic . . ." Since the complete requirements of human health and happiness can be provided by a tree and a creek, Rousseau concludes that the whole rest of history has been a waste of time: "It is evident . . . that the man, who first made himself clothes and built himself a cabin, supplied himself with things which he did not much want."

Shack and shift are bad, says Rousseau, because we become convinced we can't live without them even though he, Rousseau, has just proven to us that we can and that we don't like getting dressed or going indoors anyway. Therefore all progress and even thought is wrong. "As there is scarce any inequality among men in a state of nature, all that which we now behold owes its force and its growth to the development of our faculties and the improvement of our understanding."

Nobody likes to take responsibility for himself. Our troubles are always someone else's fault. Rousseau perfects this idea. It wasn't just another person who did us dirt, it was *every* other person since the foundation of Ur. Civilization is to blame.

Does anyone need to be told that this is puerile and absurd? Yes. John Davis, editor of the *Earth First!* magazine, does. In a book called *Green Rage: Radical Environmentalism and the Unmaking of Civilization* by Christopher Manes, John was quoted as saying, "Many of us in the Earth First! movement would like to see human beings live much more the way they did fifteen thousand years ago as opposed to what we see now." Christopher voices his approval of John's thought and adds one of his own. "Indeed, many radical environmentalists see themselves as part of a tribe rather than a political movement, as a resurgence of primal culture that has been quiescent since the Neolithic." Chris, Johnny, we need to have a talk. And wipe your feet before you come in the house.

Any person who has spent time outdoors actually doing something, such as hunting and fishing as opposed to standing there with a doobie in his mouth, knows nature is not intrinsically healthy. Kill an animal and inspect its hide and innards. You'll find it has been prey to ticks, lice, fleas, and all the other things that, at the beginning of this chapter, I predicted would assail a naked suburbanite. You'll see that it has been the victim of injuries and diseases as well. Nor are people who live in places without electricity, sewage treatment plants, penicillin, and dental checkups as Rousseau's imagination or Montaigne's household help would have them. European male oppressors may have brought smallpox and VD to the Third World, but they did not bring malaria, yellow fever, sleeping sickness, river blindness, plague, or chiggers. And what kind of person sleeps under an oak tree filled with ripe acorns, spending the whole night being pelted with rock-hard nuggets falling from fifty feet in the air? As for eating those missiles, my encyclopedia says, "The Acorns of the oak possess a considerable economic importance as food for swine."

William Rose Benét, scholar, essayist, and founder of the *Saturday Review,* defined *primitivism* as

> a persistent tendency in European literature, art, and thought since the 18th century . . . to attribute superior virtue to primitive, non-European civilizations . . . Later primitivism expanded to include among the objects of its enthusiasm the violent, the crude, undeveloped, ignorant, naïve, non-intellectual or sub-intelligent of any kind, such as peasants, children, and idiots.

It's interesting how many of these words—other than "violent"—apply to Henry David Thoreau. Montaigne was a naff and Rousseau, a screwball. But it's Thoreau who's actually taught in our schools. And it is into the wet, dense muck of *Walden* that Roderick Nash, Edward Abbey, John Davis, Christopher Manes, and the party of ten loud women have dipped their wicks.

Thoreau took the bad ideas and worse ideals of the primitivists, added the pitiful self-obsession of the romantics, and mixed all of this into transcendentalism, that stew of bossy Brahmin spiritual hubris.

The transcendentalists were much devoted to taking the most ordinary thoughts and ideas and investing them with preposterous spiritual gravity. They saw the divine in everything, even in long, boring lectures about how everything is divine. Any random peek into the essays of Ralph Waldo Emerson will show you the method by which "Don't Litter" has been turned into an entire secular religion.

In 1845 the twenty-eight-year-old Thoreau (having failed to read Rousseau closely enough) built himself a little cabin near Walden Pond in Concord, Massachusetts. The land was owned by Emerson and was about as far out of town as the average modern driving range.

Thoreau frequently went to dinners and parties in Concord, and, according to his list of household expenses in *Walden,* he sent his laundry out to be done. Thoreau lived in his shack for two years devoting his time to being full of baloney:

> I had three pieces of limestone on my desk, but I was terrified to find that they required to be dusted daily, when the furniture of my mind was all undusted still, and I threw them out the window in disgust.

> I have always been regretting that I was not as wise as the day I was born.

Or maybe he was on drugs:

> My head is hands and feet.

We have here the worst sort of person, the sanctimonious beatnik. Thoreau is the progenitor of the American hipster arrogance we've been enduring for the past century and a half. And he is the source of the loathsome self-righteousness that turns every kid who's ever thought "a tree is better looking than a parking lot" into Saint Paul of the Recycling Bin.

> But I have since learned that trade curses everything it handles; and though you trade in messages from Heaven, the whole curse of trade attaches to the business.

> Our inventions are wot to be pretty toys, which distract our attention from serious things . . . We are in great haste to construct a magnetic telegraph from Maine to Texas; but Maine and Texas, it may be, have nothing important to communicate.

The New Hollander goes naked with impunity, while the European shivers in his clothes. Is it impossible to combine the hardiness of these savages with the intellectualness of the civilized man? [Thoreau died of TB.]

All of the above is from the first hundred-odd pages of *Walden* and I defy any thinking adult without an airsickness bag to go further.

Being pathologically high-minded can have unfortunate side effects. The painter George Catlin, who traveled in the American West in the 1830s, was one of the first advocates of creating large national parks. But Catlin was so fond of things just the way nature made them that he thought Indians should be put in the parks, too.

One hundred and sixty years later, in a Sierra Club book called *Lessons of the Rainforest,* Kenneth Iain Taylor is arguing that the Indians of the Amazon should be subjected to the same zoo-animal treatment. "For the wisdom necessary to save the rainforests is contained only in the complete traditional systems that these people practice," claims Taylor. "Nor can we expect these ancient ways of forest preservation to be continued by acculturated, integrated, or assimilated people stripped of their traditions and crashing around the forest with firearms and chainsaws and outboard motors." Waterskiing tournament at three. No natives need apply.

In 1989, twenty-two years after Roderick Nash wrote *Wilderness and the American Mind,* that thoughtful book about our national attitude toward the outdoors, he wrote another book called *The Rights of Nature* in which he was thinking too hard entirely. *Rights* owes a good deal to the "process philosophy" of Alfred North Whitehead, who decided that the total universe is a completely interdependent great big whole thing and therefore every bit of it has equal right to existence—bug, turd, and Alfred North Whitehead. As a moral precept this is as useful for telling right from wrong as Whitehead's work with Bertrand Russell, *Principia Mathematica,* is for keeping score at golf. For further insight into Nash's frame of mind it is worth examining the dedications in his two books. *Wilderness* is "For My Mother and in Memory of My Father" while *Rights* is inscribed "For Honeydew, liberator of marmots and dancer with the elk." I suggest sturdy shoes, Honeydew.

Because Nash has become so high-minded that he can no longer tell whether it's a cowboy or a nine-hundred-pound antlered ruminant who's doing the two-step with his significant other, he is free to begin comparing Nature Conservatory contributors and Humane Society members with the people who fought to end human slavery. Nash extols the work of turn-of-the-century ethicist (and Clarence Darrow brother-in-law) John Howard Moore, who said, "The same spirit of sympathy and fraternity that broke the black man's manacles and is today melting the white woman's chains will tomorrow emancipate the working man and the ox." It's not a sentence I'd care to stand on a table and recite to a bar full of men who work, especially if any of them work with oxen.

Nash quotes some other wig-out as saying, "The animal rights issue is at the same place now as the slavery issue was fifty years before Abolition." "In fact," Nash goes on to claim, "most of the ingredients that sparked the Civil War presently exist. There is what many construe to be the denial of natural rights to exploited and oppressed members of the American ecological community. Ownership, what some even call the enslavement of nonhuman species and of the environment, is again the explosive issue."

I wonder how Louis Farrakhan likes being called a "member of the American ecological community." Yes, we may have to give the environmentalists a Fort Sumtering, but, since Nash and his type are typically devoted to gun control, who's going to shoot back?

IV

Not least among the unfortunate side effects of high-mindedness is the Amazon ecology tour, which Michael and Shelley and Susan and Tom and I were still on. And we were thinking deeply about the whole business of suffering extreme discomfort in the interests of personal pleasure. Psychology has a name for this.

Julio was meanwhile pointing out that the rain forest is upside down. That is, jungle vegetation is so dense that sunlight, growing space, nutrients in the form of decomposing plant matter, and even rain itself are most available at the top of the rain forest, in the canopy. Usually, if you want to see a profusion of disgusting life forms, you look under a rock. In the jungle you climb a tree. Plants called hemiepiphytes germinate in the treetops, then send roots down to the earth instead of branches up to the sky. Epiphytes never touch ground at all. Their roots just dangle in the air creating a messy snarl and collecting detritus—making their own potting soil. This humus may get thick and rich enough to host a colony of earthworms, and the tree upon whose limb this natural windowbox is sitting will sprout roots from its branch (grow a foot on its arm like Thoreau had heads on his feet) to take advantage of the soil. Orchids are epiphytes. If we lose the rain forest, we'll lose the earth's principal source of prom corsages. Think of all the poor girls getting bouquets of lettuce and celery pinned to their spaghetti straps.

With such profuse herbage occupying the sky, snakes, lizards, bugs, and the more agile mammals have moved there too. And Julio was determined that we should see them. Some well-meaning foundation (not the American Acrophobia Association) has built a system of platforms and rope bridges in the jungle canopy. We hiked for an hour from the Sucusari camp and arrived at a great big tree with a staircase around it, the kind of thing Scarlett O'Hara might have descended in *Gone With the Planet of the Apes*. At the top of these stairs was the first platform. It was about high enough above the ground to test the thesis that a cat always lands on its feet if you didn't care about the cat. From here we were supposed to walk a rope bridge sixty or eighty feet long to another big tree with stairs, climb these, cross a second rope bridge, climb more stairs, traverse another bridge, and so forth until we were

120 feet in the air and consumed with nausea, vertigo, terror, and the nagging worry "Is it sweat or have I wet myself?" I say "we" but just Susan and I were doing the worrying. Altitude didn't bother Michael, Tom, Shelley, or Julio. And they had that kind sympathy and solicitous attitude that people who aren't afraid of heights always show to those who are:

"See how the ropes wiggle when I do the boogaloo!"

"Ever read *The Bridge of San Luis Rey?*"

"If you look straight down, you can see the puke from the last group that was up here."

Mankind is supposed to have evolved in the treetops. But I have examined my sense of balance, the prehensility of my various appendages, and my attitude toward standing on anything higher than, say, political principles, and I have concluded that, personally, I evolved in the backseat of a car.

"Ninety percent of the rain forest's photosynthesis is taking place here in the canopy," said Julio. Susan and I were certainly green. "More than half of the rain forest's species live in the canopy." But I didn't see any. All I saw were two carefully placed feet—my own—and ten white knuckles gripping things. "Twice as many insect species are found here compared to ground level." Which is great news when you haven't got a hand free to swat them.

Our tour company had a third jungle camp near the canopy walkway, and as soon as we got there, Michael, Tom, and especially I began looking for more bootleg rum. This time we turned up something called *haya huasca* instead. It came in an old Coke bottle with a wooden plug in the top and was made from herbs and bark and such. Michael said that, as best he could translate, it was supposed to "make us throw up and see the future."

We didn't get sick and we certainly didn't see the future, or I would have kept my eye on yen fluctuations and would be rich. It was a mild drug, producing just a few sparks of light and some glowing auras at the edges of the field of vision and delivering a minor inner bliss, a little psychic wet kiss. That is, I thought it was a mild drug until Susan and I began urging everyone to climb back to the top of the canopy walkway and "dig the sunset."

And it's amazing up there when you're looking at something besides your fingers and shoes—like swimming through the tops of trees, like riding green surf. Sure the rope bridges sway, but so do Mother's arms. I even looked down, though there was nothing to see. The jungle is so thick, I don't think you could fall through it. (I was talked out of trying.) If you did fall, you'd probably become a epiphyte human with all your roots—wife, kids, the mortgage—dangling in the air.

I went so far as to examine how the canopy walk was constructed, that's how filled with courage I was. Each rope bridge was made, not with ropes, really, but with four steel cables—two to form the footpath and two to be used as handrails. Rope crossties ran between the cables, at intervals, like ribs in a ship hull. Nylon mesh netting was strung between the crossties, then ordinary cheap Home Depot aluminum ladders were laid flat between the footpath cables with wooden planks over the ladder rungs, and that was it. The cables were attached to the trees by half hitches and clove hitches, oregano hitches, sheet and pillowcase bends, and knots you couldn't get ZZ Top beards into. It looked like hippie engineering to me. I'm a veteran of the *Whole Earth Catalog* era, and I've watched a lot of geodesic domes and yurts and such lay over on their sides and go *fttttt.* But with *haya huasca,* who cared?

Besides, there was a sunset the color of eco-tourist hiking shorts. And, with dusk, all those species Julio had been talking about arrived: fat, black lizards with butts shaped like canoe paddles; big yet nearly invisible Esmerelda butterflies with perfectly clear wings; iguanas the size and shape of scaly green dachshunds; a thousand tree frogs saying "Wyatt Earp"; dragonflies as lacy and complicated and rather larger than Victoria's Secret lingerie; and hummingbirds that could actually carry a tune. Well, maybe that last was the *haya huasca.* I'll bet

Thoreau really *was* on drugs. It certainly is the easy way to make the ecosystem better, at least to look at. And drugs would excuse sentences like "I have always been regretting that I was not as wise as the day I was born."

I was beginning to get a few insights of that type myself. I started looking at the multitude of insects, the astounding number of them, the great smacking gobs and oodles, the scads and lashings of bugs galore. They wandered all across each other and every surface and right through the air across no surface at all and all over me. I decided that God had created the world for bugs. Whatever we have in the way of Old and New Testament and so forth was plagiarized from some original buggy text. It was bugs who lived in the Garden of Eden (full of *rotten* fruit and *dead* animals). And the bugs had probably eaten . . . everything, the whole damn tree of knowledge included. By sheer weight of numbers they are obviously God's chosen creatures. There had, no doubt, been a little bug Moses. What would the Ten Bug Commandments be? "Go forth and multiply," certainly. Maybe, "Thou shalt find a porch light and bump into it for hours." And there had been a bug Jesus Christ, nailed to a small and rather complicated cross.

About then the *haya huasca* began to wear off. This was probably a good thing. Unfortunately, it wore off before Susan and I managed to get down from the canopy walk. And there we were in the pitch dark, frozen in terror like a pair of reverse suicides with the whole police and fire departments (Shelley and Michael and Tom) urging us to step out on a ledge.

Haya huasca made me believe strange things but no stranger than the things more sensible Americans believe cold sober. Susan and Shelley were excited to discover that one of the Orejón Indians who had helped build the canopy walkway was a *brujo*, a male witch or shaman. Shelley's family had been Jewish for five thousand years, and Susan's, Christian for two thousand. About these creeds they were reasonably skeptical, but the *brujo* they'd met ten minutes ago. . . . I'm being unkind. The *brujo* seemed to be a nice man, very dignified with sad and common-sensical eyes. I'm sure he was, in his way, as pious and devout as ever was Reverend Lackland, the incredibly boring pastor of Monroe Street Methodist Church, which I attended as a child in Toledo, Ohio.

In fact, the *brujo*'s spiritual cleansing ceremony was at least as tedious and lengthy as Methodist Sunday school. Most religious services seem to be so. Is ennui the sacrifice God wants us to make to Him? Is He pleased by an offering of fidgets, guilty dozings, and daydreams of releasing white mice in the choir loft? Wouldn't we better glorify God by enjoying the blessings of His creation, by, say, getting on the green in three and two-putting? Of course, there aren't many golf courses in the Amazon.

The *brujo* sat each of us on a stool. Then he took a little bouquet or broom made of dried leaves of the *shacapa* plant and flicked us all over while softly whistling something that reminded me only a little of Simon and Garfunkel. He finished by blowing cigarette smoke all over our persons. Susan and Shelley looked blissful, though they are ardent nonsmokers.

What we had experienced was "like a dry shower," said the *brujo* later, Julio translating. The fellow had been a *brujo* for thirty-five years. You become a *brujo* by altering your diet, by "leaving out all pleasure foods," and by fasting. "Your visions become your lunch" was Julio's literal translation. Also, you drink *haya huasca*.

Julio said he'd fallen into the Amazon once while wearing knee-high rubber boots. The boots had filled with water and pulled him under, and he'd nearly drowned. He went to a *brujo* who cured him of being frightened of the river, a cure that apparently lasted longer than my cure of being scared of heights. Of course, I was using *haya huasca* without professional supervision. Also, said Julio, his mother had once begun to lose weight, and a *brujo* informed her that Julio's father had secretly married another woman and that the second wife was putting a curse on Julio's mom. I'd think a secret second wife would be pretty much a curse in its own right. Anyway, the *brujo* removed the curse, and I bet he was cheaper than my divorce lawyer. A team of *brujos* could do no harm in matters like the Woody Allen–Mia Farrow custody case or Hillary Clinton's health care reform plan. Although I understand Hillary has removed all the ashtrays from the White House.

The next morning, spiritually dry-cleaned and tuned in to that great National Public Radio station which is nature, we went for a last peek at the ecology. We took one of the square-sterned canoes equipped with a small outboard and half-paddled, half-motored up a narrow inlet to a lake with water the color of espresso (decaf, it is to be hoped, since Amazon tourist types are very health-conscious).

The jungle loomed over us in the most looming jungle sort of way. We saw some disgusting insects and some awful lizards and a snake, albeit a small and phlegmatic snake. Snakes are my least favorite thing, not counting rope bridges 120 feet in the air. Tom was contemplating a spider the size of a Bass Weejun. "Nothing dies of old age around here, does it?" said Tom.

"These black water areas are the habitat of electric eels," said Julio. "They grow to be six feet long and can generate six hundred volts of direct current at about one-half to three-fourths ampere, enough to stun a horse." We are all hoping for the development of wind- and solar-powered eels soon.

"Julio," I said, "does the Amazon have any legendary monsters—Yeti, Bigfoot, Nessie, the Jersey Devil, anything like that?"

"No," said Julio. So maybe the Amazon natives recognize the essential benevolence of nature even in this most violently competitive and sanguinary biological niche. Or, maybe when you've got six-foot electric eels and tiny catfish that swim up your pecker, you don't need legendary monsters.

And yet I was surprised again by the unscary, nonmysterious, subthreatening nature of the rain forest. The fake-seeming safari noises, the floral arrangements growing on tree branches, the Disney World–like lack of odors, the angelfish in the minnow nets, and now, looking around, I realized the jungle was filled with houseplants. Most of the greenery on our windowsills was bred from tropical stock. Terror is difficult to experience surrounded by ficus trees, dumbcane, Christmas cactus, spider plants, philodendrons, and Boston ferns as though you were visiting the overheated apartment of a maiden aunt.

On the lake we motored between lily pads two yards across. According to my guidebook, these can "support the weight of a small child," although there are certainly laws about trying that. Then we crossed a dozen acres of white water hyacinths, our outboard prop getting thoroughly tangled in beauty and fragrance. Several trees along the shore were filled with the hanging nests of *oropéndolas,* a tropical oriole that makes its own birdhouses from woven vines and twigs. And they are no better at it than kids taking a crafts program at summer camp. *Oropéndola* nests look like sheep scrotums. Another tree was full of saddle-backed tamarind monkeys bouncing around like flying puppies. It seems the more evolved an animal is, the more time it spends playing. Which does not explain why I'm at the typewriter, unless it does. Or maybe we don't know what worm fun and snail recreation look like. They may be having a riot. And in one more tree we saw a pair of speckled owls, perched on a branch, asleep with their heads leaned together, cuter than thrift-shop salt and pepper shakers. Then came the best sight of all, a blue morpho butterfly, a big hand-span of a butterfly in an indescribable tint—a Day-Glo pink of a blue, an international-signal orange of a blue. Eco-tourists in the Miami airport wouldn't wear this blue. A color not found in nature was finding itself in nature right in front of us, floating in that scatterbrained way butterflies do, just beyond our bow.

We came back from the lake and down to the mouth of the Sucusari river and out into the mile-wide Napo. Here black drapes of rain approached in the sunshine. Wide fields of clear sky appeared between vast storm clouds. There were lightning strikes and a rainbow at the same time. It was an encyclopedia of weather.

The rain swept toward our canoe, and we made for the nearest house. It was a one-room shack but a big one, and this was a good thing because it was a big family that owned it, and all of them had run inside, too. Thirty of us must have been in the shack, and "rain" does not describe what was happening outside. The difference between a downpour in the temperate zone and a downpour in the tropics is the difference between stepping into the shower and being thrown into the pool. Or, rather, having the pool thrown on you. Imagine yourself standing in the deep end and all the water is on the high board.

The shack was humble even by *ribereño* standards. The only furniture was a table. A few newspaper ads decoated a wall. But they had rum, and Michael and I had cigarettes. And they also had a liquor called *clabo huasca,* made from some vine. It was not quite as potent as *haya huasca,* but it did cast a happy glow upon the scene. The kids brought out their pets to show us: a bat (cute as bats go, certainly cuter than those we'd seen in the bat professor's hands), some puppies, a baby peccary that looked like a cross between a hamster and a wart hog, and a flock of chachalacas, noisy little jungle turkeys. The parents beamed. The young men turned on a boom box. The young women flirted a bit. We drank more rum and *clabo huasca* and smoked more cigarettes and had a little fiesta until the sun came out.

Our hosts were migrants from the impoverished and rebel-bothered mountains of Peru. They'd come as squatters and cut a little homestead from the jungle. Julio's parents had come to the Amazon for the same reason and so had many *ribereños,* and many more are on the way. It is these decent, hardworking, hospitable, pleasant people who are destroying the rain forest. They are not doing it in quite so rapid or spectacular a manner as the timber companies or the big Brazilian ranchers. But there are a lot more poor people in South America than there are well-capitalized corporations. Knotty pine will make a comeback and mahogany will go out of fashion. Everybody will die of high cholesterol from eating too many hamburgers and beef prices will go down. The timber companies and the ranches will disappear, but the poor will still be there.

I have a photograph taken in 1887 showing my grandfather, his parents, and his nine siblings lined up in front of a one-room unpainted shanty on a forty-acre dirt farm in Lime City, Ohio. The roof was made of wooden shingles instead of corrugated tin, and due to climatic differences, the shack my great-grandad built had more in the way of walls, but other than that, the old O'Rourke plantation was indistinguishable from the mansion of our hosts on the Napo.

I'm sure great-grandfather Barney O'Rourke would have liked to move to a passive solar bungalow in the Berkeley Hills, carefully recycle his trash, use only appropriate technology in his certified organic garden, and bicycle to his job at the university teaching a course in Sustainable Development. But it wasn't an option. Among other things, I don't think Barney could read.

The rain forest is an interesting, if sticky, place for rich people to visit. But it is a dreadful place to live. The *ribereños* and the employees of the ranches and timber companies and, for that matter, lots of the Yagua and Oréjon wouldn't be there if they had another choice. The rain forest could then fester away in ecologically invaluable peace. But in Latin America, as in most of the world, you have to be born at the top to get to the top or even to get to a point where you own a refrigerator. Or you have to be impossibly lucky or ruthless. Not that the ruling oligarchy in these parts hasn't made an attempt to aid the underclass. As early as Spanish colonial times there was a law in Peru that specifically forbade calling an Indian a dog. But unalienable rights, security of property, rule of law—these have not been much tried.

V

When we were back in the Iquitos airport, waiting for our plane to Miami, the ten loud women reappeared. I gathered from their loud chat that they'd been on a tour boat docking at various places along the river, probably the same places we'd seen. They seemed to have had a meaningful time, full of auras and so forth, and heck, we'd seen some auras ourselves. But one of the women was carrying a polished wooden box with a glass front, and inside the box was a dead and mounted blue morpho butterfly. I looked again, to make sure my imagination wasn't creating a too-perfect journalistic irony. But Michael, Shelley, Tom, and Susan saw it, too. "Oh, yes," said Julio, "the ecology groups are always bringing back snakeskins, animal pelts, caiman skulls, all those sorts of things."

Theocritus, Virgil, James Fenimore Cooper, Montaigne, Rousseau, Edward Abbey, Henry David Thoreau, John Denver, and ten loud women—quit pestering your mother.

5 ECOLOGY

We're All Going to Die

I

Mankind has done harm to nature, at least if looks and smell are anything to go by (and they are in the rest of life). But the environmentalists can shut up. Everybody's a radical Green now. I've had an impoverished Haitian in Port-au-Prince tell me he was worried about the Creole alphabet. "It has too many letters," he said, "we must conserve resources." And a writer in the January 1994 issue of *Audubon* magazine reports that her six-year-old daughter criticized the nursery furniture, saying, "They killed trees to make my bed."

Few people doubt the earth's ecology is in awful shape or have qualms about the price of fixing it. CBS News and the *New York Times* took a poll in 1989, and 80 percent of the respondents agreed with this statement: "Protecting the environment is so important that requirements and standards can't be too tight, and continuing environmental improvements must be made regardless of the cost."

"Regardless" would seem a bit strong if people thought about it. But the fact that they don't think about it reflects a near consensus that humanity is making a horrid mess of this world. For a very average example of modern reasoning on this subject take Vice President Al Gore's book *Earth in the Balance,* which has sold nearly half a million copies as of this writing. The flyleaves of the paperback edition contain words of high praise from the *Christian Science Monitor,* the *Washington Post,* the *Los Angeles Times,* the *New Republic,* and M. Scott Peck—in short, from everyone who matters.

Earth in the Balance presents no original research, and, though it has a chapter at the back called "A Global Marshall Plan," it proffers no new solutions. *Earth in the Balance* is really just a compendium of all the ecological frets and dreads that have been accumulating in our minds since the days when James Thurber's grandmother worried about electricity leaking out of empty lightbulb sockets. What's interesting is the book's casual—almost unconscious—assumptions, made evident in hundreds of judgmental word clusters scattered through the text like something you didn't order in a pizza topping:

> the global ecological crisis
>
> a rapidly deteriorating global environment
>
> the dangerous truth about what we are doing to the earth

Musty logic-choppers of the Aristotelian ilk would call these phrases petitio principii, or "begging the question." It is a famous old logical fallacy to assume as true ("the global ecological crisis") that which is to be proven by argument (an ecological crisis is being suffered by the globe).

But logic is so annoying. And what's logical thinking ever gotten us anyway except things like the atomic bomb? When Gore says things like "Our ecological system is crumpling as it suffers a powerful collision with the hard surfaces of a civilization speeding out of control" (which summons mental images of a hundred-mile-per-hour Guggenheim Museum putting a huge dent in Mt. Rainier), he's not just being full of shit, he's indicating that the disputation is over. The debate, if there was one, about whether the earth is a filthy wreck, has been decided. This orb upon which our brief mortal span is tred—what a dump.

When viewing some of the dumpier parts of the earth, it is hard to imagine that there might be arguments in favor of pollution. And yet there are. By any standard of measurement the majority of people on earth are now richer, healthier, and longer-lived than they ever have been. So say the Organization for Economic Cooperation and Development, the World Bank, the UN Food and Agricultural Organization, et cetera. These improvements in the human condition came with the industrial revolution, which created most of our pollution. Robert Kates, director of the World Hunger Program at Brown University, estimates that the production of goods and services on our planet has increased by 500 percent just since 1950.

The countries that are most industrialized and hence, one would think, most polluted have the best morbidity, mortality, and income statistics. National well-being might almost be said to be a by-product of pollution. Figures compiled by the Nobel laureate economist Simon Kuznets in his book *Economic Growth of Nations* show that our modern comfort is borne aloft on a dense cloud of factory smoke. From the end of the seventeenth century until the last quarter of the eighteenth century, the per capita gross national product of agrarian England and Wales grew at an average rate of 1.9 percent a decade. From the middle of the nineteenth century until the 1960s, industrialized Great Britain's per capita GNP grew, per decade, by 13.4 percent. Likewise, the U.S. per capita GNP, between the 1840s and the 1960s, grew by 17.5 percent per decade. And Japan's, between the 1870s and the 1960s, grew by an average of 32.3 percent each ten years.

You can say, "Yes, but all these good things will be bad for mankind in the long run." And I can quote John Maynard Keynes, " 'In the long run we're all dead.' " You can say, "We're poisoning the earth for future generations." And I can say, "I thought you were in favor of population control." You can say, "All this pollution may be fine for man, but we're destroying the rest of nature." And I can say, "There's always one fox who thinks burrowing should be abandoned because it makes life so hard on the hounds." And you can say, "Fuck you." And so forth. But the question of ecological ruin *is* debatable.

The people who believe that, as a result of industrial development, life is about to become a hell, or may be one already, are guilty, at least, of sloppy pronouncements. On page 8 of *Earth in the Balance,* Al Gore claims that his study of the arms race gave him "a deeper appreciation for the most horrifying fact in all our lives: civilization is now capable of destroying itself." In the first place, the most horrifying fact in many of our lives is that our ex-spouse has gotten ahold of our ATM card. And civilization has always been able to destroy itself. The Greeks of ancient Athens, who had a civilization remarkable for lack of technological progress during its period of greatest knowledge and power, managed to destroy themselves fine. On page 3 of *EITB,* Gore says that after encountering Agent Orange in Vietnam "I started to feel wary of all chemicals that have extraordinarily powerful effects on the world around us." Ten pages later Gore tells how his concern for the environment and other global issues was intensified by the near death of his young son. And I believe him. Love and a sense of life's fragility can make us all better or, anyway, more conscientious people. Yet how wary was Gore of the anesthetics, antiseptics, and antibiotics that saved his son's life?

But let us, for the time being, leave the vice president to the indignity of his office, surely punishment enough for his rhetorical sins. *Earth in the Balance* is popular, but *50 Simple Things You Can Do to Save the Earth* has become a kind of *Thomas the Tank Engine* for the environmentally minded. Citing various odds and sods of sources and often no sources at all, *50 Simple Things* comes forth with some wonderful statements. "Every year in the U.S. we lose 7 billion tons of topsoil— an area the size of Connecticut," says a tiny page 89 subscript, the kind that used to run in the margins of *Mad* magazine. Connecticut has a land area of 5,544 square miles. We've been farming most of America for 150 years; 831,600 square miles should be gone. That's the whole Midwest. And come to think of it, I haven't heard anything lately from my sister in Cincinnati.

Another subscript, on page 18, claims, "The average annual energy bill for America's hot tubs is $200 million." Okay, but try seducing someone on a compost heap.

On page 17 yet another unattributed subscript says, "About 75% of the water we use in our homes is used in the bathroom." Thank goodness. Think of the mess it would make in the den.

Ecology types seem a bit obsessed with water, maybe because so many of them live in California where the water is fizzy and comes with lime slices. They're worried about how long it will be until Lake Michigan goes flat and earth's citrus quarries are depleted. Someone named Karina Lutz, managing editor of something called *Home Energy* magazine, contributed an essay to *50 Simple Things* in which she avers, "Every drop of water wasted is a drop less of a wild and scenic river, a drop less of a salmon run, a drop more in a dam filling a glorious valley." Perhaps. But most of the water we use ends up going pretty much where it was headed anyway, even if in temporarily icky form. It's not as though we're hoarding the stuff in the attic or filling jerry cans and running over to Hoover Dam to dump them into Lake Mead.

A careful reading of *50 Simple Things* leaves you wondering whether you're going to die from environmental disaster or intellectual annoyance. Failing either, you can worry yourself to death. On page 81 the book flatly states, "All milk sold in the U.S. today contains pesticide residue." I put some beer into the baby's bottle (or would have if I had a baby) and called the Food and Drug Administration. "Well," said Catherine Carnevale, director of the Office of Constituent Operations, "that's probably one of those statements that someone can make without fear of being contradicted because measurement only goes so low." Dr. Carnevale explained that the limit of detection in chemical tests for pesticide contamination is .01 parts per million. She said that in 1992 the FDA had checked 558 milk samples representing sixty major dairy-producing areas of the country. And, indeed, 48 percent of the samples did have detectable residues. But these were traces of breakdown products from the DDT family of bug killers, none of which has been used for a decade. (So it's the milk you drank with Bosco while watching *Sky King* that's killed you already.) And the highest level of 1992 milk contamination found by the FDA was .04 parts per million, that's $\frac{3}{100,000,000}$ths more than what's technically known as "none." Dr. Carnevale stated she felt this had "no toxicological significance."

I'd barely gotten over this panic when, on page 40 of *50 Simple Things,* I found the sentence, "Baby powder, for example, often contains asbestos." I quickly changed Junior, poured cake mix down his diaper, and called the FDA back. "Around fifteen years ago," patiently explained Dr. John Bailey, acting director of the FDA Office of Cosmetics and Colors, "there was concern that talcum powder, as it was mined, could be contaminated with the type of asbestos that's associated with lung disease. Considerable research was done by the FDA and by cosmetics companies. Contamination was found to be either very low or nonexistent. The type of asbestos involved was not of a health concern. From our perspective it's not an issue."

Remember, FDA employees are serious about fear. We pay these people to panic about an iota of rodent hair in our chili, even when the recipe calls for it. FDA employees are first-class agonizers, world champions at losing sleep. When Meryl Streep got hysterical about Alar, they actually checked the apples instead of Meryl's head. And let's assume that FDA employees are also human. The more things they can find to be anxious about, the bigger their budget is going to be. They've got every incentive to tell us to run for our lives. So, no matter what it says about asbestos in *50 Simple Things You Can Do to Save the Earth,* don't use your kid as an oven mitt.

‖

Ecology is the science of everything. Nobody knows everything. Nobody even knows everything about any one thing. And most of us don't know much. Say it's ten-thirty on a Saturday night. Where are your teenage children? I didn't ask where they said they were going. Where are they really? What are they doing? Who are they with? Have you met the other kids' families? And what is tonight's pot smoking, wine-cooler drinking, and sex in the backseats of cars going to mean in a hundred years? Now extend these questions to the entire solar system.

There is confusing evidence and contradictory argument about every major ecological issue. For instance, about the pesticides that "all milk sold in the U.S. today" contains. Some pesticides do cause cancer in laboratory animals. But the test doses are massive to the point of travesty. According to economist Ben Bolch and chemist Harold Lyons in their self-explanatorily titled book *Apocalypse Not* (Cato Institute, 1993), the research that set off the Alar scare used so much Alar that to do the same experiment on humans would require each subject to eat fifty thousand pounds of apples a day for life. (Alar isn't actually a pesticide, it's a growth retardant; but it's man-made and it gets on food, so it's, you know, yucky.) The original Alar research was done by Bela Toth at the Eppley Institute in 1977. Subsequent research by independent laboratories and by Uniroyal, the manufacturer of Alar, cast some doubt on the Toth findings but did implicate an Alar breakdown product in the growth of mouse blood vessel tumors when the mice drank the equivalent of nineteen thousand quarts of apple juice a day. This may explain why laboratory mice so frequently have to ask to be excused to go to the little mouse's room.

In 1990, Sanford Miller, dean of the Graduate School of Biochemical Sciences at the University of Texas at San Antonio, told newspaper columnist Warren Brookes:

The risk of pesticide residues to consumers is effectively zero. This is what some fourteen scientific societies representing over 100,000 microbiologists, toxicologists and food scientists said at the time of the ridiculous Alar scare. But we were ignored.

Everything is a poison in sufficient dose. Try drinking nineteen thousand quarts of apple juice if you don't think so. Or have someone hold your head under pure water for half an hour. And being locked in a tiny cage and stuffed with agricultural chemicals by giant creatures in white coats and unfashionable eyeglasses probably isn't good for you either. In *Apocalypse Not* Bolch and Lyons point out, "The presumption that the laboratory procedure is not itself carcinogenic is increasingly suspect." They cite an August 1990 article in *Science* by Bruce N. Ames and Lois S. Gold that questions the health effects of repeatedly filling lab animals with the maximum tolerable amount of *anything*.

Ames is a professor of biochemistry at the University of California at Berkeley and the inventor of the most widely used scientific procedure for determining the mutagenic effects of chemicals, the Ames test. He knows his cancer. He also knows that a distinction between "man-made chemicals" and "natural chemicals" is spurious. "It is probable that almost every plant product in the supermarket contains natural carcinogens," he and Gold said in a letter to *Science* in May 1989.

In an attempt to bring some perspective to toxin scares (or maybe just as a cruel stunt), the American Council on Science and Health publishes a pamphlet called "Natural Carcinogens in Your Holiday Menu." The mixed nuts contain aflatoxins, among the most potent mutagens known. More mutagens, called furan derivatives, are found in the onions. Lima beans, when chewed, release cyanide from cyanogenetic glucosides. (Personally, even as a child, I'd suspected as much.) There's carotatoxin, a nerve poison, in carrots. Mushrooms come with hydrazines, many of which are animal carcinogens. Other

animal carcinogens—quercetin glycosides and hydrogen peroxide—
lurk within tomatoes, as does tomatine, which interferes with nerve
transmission. Human carcinogens, psoralens, taint celery. Broccoli is
host to goitrin and glucosinolates, which harm the thyroid. And the
potato is a regular Chernobyl among vegetables. Within the dread spud
we find solanine, chaconine, amylase inhibitors, and isoflavones—
which, respectively, cause gastrointestinal-tract irritation, harm your
nervous system, interfere with digestive enzymes, and mimic female
sex-hormone activity. An extra helping of au gratin and you're a
toilet-bound neurasthenic hermaphrodite with gas. If you live that
long. Potatoes also contain arsenic.

These are just the foods that are good for us, the foods we're
supposed to eat more of. I haven't even mentioned things like alcohol,
a known divorcogenic which interferes with the body's car-wreck
defenses.

50 Simple Things You Can Do to Save the Earth says, "Fortunately, there are effective natural alternatives to chemical pesticides."
In *Apocalypse Not,* Bolch and Lyons say, "Given the furor about synthetic pesticides and the lack of excitement over natural carcinogenic
pesticides, plant growers are busy breeding crop strains that are naturally resistant to pests. Some of the new strains are so toxic to human
beings that in one case (a new type of celery) the plant causes contact
dermatitis among produce workers." Revenge of the salad bar.

Man damages the environment. Kids damage the carpet. Does
it matter? Is it worth it? Depends on the kids. Depends on the carpet.
Even when the greatest degree of ecological caution is being exercised,
humans wreck havoc. So do cow farts. "The world's 1.3 billion cows
annually produce nearly 100 tons of methane—a powerful 'greenhouse
gas,' " claims *50 Simple Things.* The environment itself plays hell with
the environment. A storm will ravage a beach no matter how elo-
quently the Sierra Club argues that the shoreline should be left in
pristine condition. Lightning will strike a stand of old-growth timber
with ever so many endangered owls roosted therein. Coyotes in Cali-

fornia have been exposed to *50 Simple Things* and *Earth in the Balance* and know they should be eating lower on the food chain, but they'll still gnaw the guts right out of Bambi. No amount of self-righteousness will turn the bloody tooth and claw of nature from tearing flesh to catching Frisbees.

Of course, that is not an excuse for running a speedboat through a family of manatees or paving Monument Valley and building a Six Flags amusement park there. Fervent ecologists argue that we should be nice to the earth because animals, plants, rocks, and such have as much right to be here as we do. They are our equals. This is exactly wrong. We are endowed with a moral capacity that animals, plants, rocks—and many fervent ecologists—lack. We should not be dirty, wasteful, or cruel. To do so harms others. That's wrong. Therefore we don't disembowel Bambi live the way coyotes do, we shoot him first.

As legal scholar Peter W. Huber has pointed out, "Getting facts right is a fundamental requirement of morality." Mankind is accused of numerous and grave environmental crimes. Each of these alleged felonies must be thoroughly investigated and fairly judged. Otherwise we won't know how large a fine to levy upon ourselves, which type of community service we should sentence us to, or what kind of prison we should all lock each other up in.

III

Some ecological scares are frauds. The earth is not running out of things. In 1980 University of Maryland economist Julian Simon made a well-known wager with several times aforementioned jerk Paul Ehrlich. Simon bet that the average inflation-adjusted price of natural resources would decline. Ehrlich bet the contrary. Simon let Ehrlich choose the time span and the resources. Ehrlich decided on ten years and picked copper, chrome, nickel, tin, and tungsten. The two men figured out how much of this stuff $1,000 would buy and agreed that in 1990 they'd figure out how much all of it would sell for in 1980 dollars. If the price went up, Simon would pay the difference to Ehrlich. If the price went down, Ehrlich would pay the difference to Simon. In October 1990 Ehrlich sent Simon a check for $576.07.

Every metal had fallen in price, tungsten by 78 percent. In fact, between 1980 and 1990 prices fell for all strategic minerals except manganese and zinc. (Expect the Franklin Mint to issue commemorative tubes of zinc oxide sunblock soon.)

Inflation-adjusted energy prices have also fallen since 1980. As of the early nineties coal was down 91 percent and crude oil, 35 percent. Gasoline prices were 6 percent lower in 1991 than they were in 1972 before the OPEC embargo and a full one-fourth less than they'd been in the Buick-filled, boron-splurging year of 1963. (Again, this assumes constant dollars, though personally I've found my dollars to be a bit flighty.) And, Stephen Moore of the Institute for Policy Innovation says, if we perform the mathematical task of adjusting for inflation by indexing prices to wages, we'll find that what the average person pays for oil has been declining since 1870, when the average person didn't even know what to do with the stuff and wasn't about to put it in his horse.

When a resource gets scarce, as oil did twenty years ago, we become more efficient in our use of it. Pretty soon there's more oil than we need. The price comes down. And OPEC nations, we observe with satisfaction, go broke. If there is a permanent scarcity of a resource, we change resources. My sentence "The earth is not running out of things" is actually as much of a lie as anything you'll read in *Earth in the Balance* or *50 Simple Things You Can Do to Save the Identical*. We run out of things all the time. We're way out of whale oil. Also, out of whalebone for corsets. Fortunately, the government of 150 years ago didn't have presidential commissions, congressional committees, Al Gore, and the other apparatus of worry our present government possesses, or Washington might have foreseen this. Whale oil would have been rationed. A black market would have been created. Whale oil prices would have soared. All the whales would have been killed immediately. And today we'd live in a dim, lampless world where Judy Collins sang duets with tuna fish and everybody had a waistline like Golda Meir. Instead, gaslights, petroleum-based whale-oil substitutes, electricity, and control-top panty hose were invented. When we ran out of whale oil, no one even noticed.

Having mentioned electricity, let me also point out—to you and Thurber's grandmother—that electricity *doesn't* run out of empty lightbulb sockets. It doesn't drip off high-tension wires either. We're not all dying of horrible cancers resulting from electromagnetic fields generated by our IBM PCs, our house current, and our girlfriend who insists on cranking up the electric blanket in July. Americans have been slathered in wiring for three generations. Surely we'd notice if this was killing us (other than when we use the hairdryer in the bathtub or are a black person convicted of murder in the South). At the very least, we'd notice the remarkable health and longevity of the people in the smoky, dark, impoverished, hungry, unelectrified parts of the world. Besides, the earth's own electromagnetic field is more powerful than most man-made kinds. If it weren't, every time we went hiking in the woods our compass would take us to the microwave in somebody's summer cottage. If electromagnetism is lethal, it's a few billion years too late to do anything about it.

Still, power lines *could* have some effect upon our health. That's perfectly true. The problem with this truth, however, is it can't be proven false. It's a two-headed coin. My phone is ringing. That *could* be Uma Thurman asking if she can come over and give me a back rub. Nope. It's the bank again. They've made another one of their errors in arithmetic concerning my checking-account balance. But it *could* have been anyone. There is no scientific method by which the complete absence or total impossibility of a thing can be proven. And there are too many scientific methods by which an impression of cause and effect can be generated.

Watch as I create "statistical evidence that power-line locations affect cancer rates." I can do this despite the fact that I know nothing about electricity or medicine and not much (says my bank) about math. Power lines are found all over the country arranged in an orderly fashion aptly called a grid. Cancer occurs more randomly. Random, of course, does not mean evenly spread. Randomness comes in blots and clusters. Flip a penny a thousand times, and you'll see some long streaks of Lincolns as if that coin did indeed have two heads. Now give me a map of the power grid and a map of cancer occurrences. I will find groups of cancer victims near high-tension lines. I will also find groups of cancer victims near bookstores where Paul Brodeur, author of *Currents of Death: Power Lines, Computer Terminals, and the Attempt to Cover Up Their Threat to Your Health* made promotional appearances and signed books.

IV

Some ecological scares are scary. Splitting the atom has destroyed two fair-sized Japanese cities and caused other distressing phenomena such as poorly groomed antinuclear activists and numerous last-person-on-earth *Twilight Zone* episodes. And biotechnology is a worry. What if they take genetic material from wet noodles and blowfish and splice it into politician chromosomes and create a Clinton administration?

But to get the full thrill of fear from Three Mile Island, milk containing bovine growth hormones, or Hillary, you have to unedu-cate yourself, engage in a pursuit of ignorance, immerse your intellect in nonlearning. Ronald Bailey, author of *Eco-Scam* (St. Martin's Press, 1993), a book devoted to quelling environmentalist hysteria, points out that in the early days of genetic engineering geneticists themselves were frightened by what they were doing. In 1974 a committee of promi-nent biochemists including James Watson, who with Francis Crick discovered the structure and function of DNA, wrote a letter to *Science* magazine proposing a moratorium on the kinds of gene splicing con-sidered most dangerous. Nobody wanted a variety of anthrax bacteria able to disguise itself as a free Kool-Aid sample and mail itself to your house. And, following the publication of the *Science* letter, molecular biologists did indeed observe a worldwide voluntary moratorium that lasted two years. Bailey calls it "the first self-imposed ban on basic research in the history of science." In 1976 the National Institutes of Health were called upon to create safety guidelines to ensure the quarantine of all gene-splicing experiments. And in 1977 Congress (with then representative, you guessed it, Al Gore in the lead) nearly passed legislation limiting the methods by which scientists were allowed to learn about the fundamental elements of life.

But, by the late seventies, scientists were beginning to discover that exchange and interpolation of genetic material happens all the time in nature. Bacteria are particularly inclined to homemade gene splicing, and there is nothing that Congress, the NIH, or the *Science* magazine letters column can do about it. And bioengineering itself turned out to be less like a Dr. Frankenstein's lab and more like a very precise version of the traditional selective breeding of plants and animals—without weeds to pull or manure to shovel. Man has been breeding livestock for ten thousand years and has yet to come up with a monstrous sheep that can trample buildings and graze a whole golf course for breakfast.

According to Bailey, James Watson later said, "Scientifically, I was a nut. There is no evidence at all that recombinant DNA poses the slightest danger." Bacteriologist Winston Brill told Bailey, "No one has gotten even so much as a sniffle from biotechnology." And biophysicist Burke Zimmerman, who in the seventies testified before Congress about the dangers of gene splicing, says in his 1984 book *Biofuture,* "In looking back it would be hard to insist that a law was necessary, or, perhaps, that guidelines were necessary."

Biotechnologists could still come up with something awful by accident, not to mention on purpose. Nature does it all the time. Nature is forever inventing things like the bubonic plague, though whether intentionally or not is a question too deep for this state college graduate. But, in the meantime, we've got a four-billion-dollar biotech

industry that produces cheap insulin, accurate medical tests for everything from pregnancy to colon cancer, new vaccines, the diagnostic
process that keeps the nation's blood supply free of AIDS and hepatitis,
and hundreds of other products, with thousands more on the horizon—a small price to pay for an occasional giant sheep.

Atomic power would seem to have a similar benefit-to-panic
ratio. Why is a nuclear reactor considered so much more terrifying than
any other large, complicated thing that gets hot? In 1991, 54,659
Americans were injured by ovens and stoves. But we're so scared of
atomic power that people living in the vicinity of the Three Mile Island
reactor accident may have suffered an increase in cancer occurrences
not from radiation but from worrying about it. And this is not something made up by Lyndon LaRouche geeks selling CHAPPAQUIDDICK 1,
THREE MILE ISLAND 0 bumper stickers in airport lobbies. The worry
hypothesis was put forward as the result of a study conducted by
Columbia University and the National Audubon Society. As reported
in the May 27, 1991, *Washington Post:*

> Jan Beyea, senior scientist at the Audubon Soci-
> ety, said the higher rates of cancer among people living
> nearest to TMI [Three Mile Island] could not be at-
> tributed to radiation exposure. "This increase has occur-
> red both in areas where there was radiation exposure and
> where there was not," he said . . .
> "We can't say it's definitely stress, but it's sugges-
> tive of stress," Mervyn Susser, a Columbia University
> epidemiologist who was the principal investigator for the
> study, said in an interview.

Reactors are dangerous. About thirty-two people died in the
immediate aftermath of the Chernobyl disaster and many more have
died since and will die in the future. But each year about sixty-five
people are killed mining coal in the United States and plenty of other

coal miners will die from black lung disease. Walk through the audience at the MTV Awards and find the NO COAL buttons. Is radiation especially fearsome because it's invisible? Would we feel better about it if we could see it coming the way we can see the cars and trucks which squish flat forty-five thousand of our countrymen per annum?

There *is* the matter of nuclear waste, of which no one is fond. But what's left over when we burn fossil fuels isn't very appetizing either, and there's lots of it. *50 Simple Things* says that in 1986 "6.5 million tons of hydrocarbons and 8.5 tons of nitrogen oxides" were dumped into the atmosphere by motor vehicles alone. (Who weighs these things and how they get nitrogen oxides onto the bathroom scale, I have no idea.) *Apocalypse Not* states that all U.S. nonmilitary atomic reactors would, with fuel reprocessing, "produce an annual volume of high-level wastes equal to about 35 feet on a side." (And who figures this out I don't know either, nor would I care to hold the tape measure.) Assuming some degree of accuracy in such large and loopy quantifications, atomic power would seem to make a smaller, if more permanent, mess. A hundred years of national power generation would leave us with approximately three acres of awful stuff stacked about as high as a New York City brownstone. I can think of a number of areas in New York where three acres of nuclear waste would make the neighborhood safer to walk around in than it is now, and better lit.

Thousands of Americans drown every year. Imagine—with the present age's terror of hazards and enthusiasm for government protection therefrom—if water had just been invented. The Brady Bill would have included a five-day waiting period for above-ground pools; only licensed adults would be allowed to bathe, and children under fourteen would be required to wear life jackets when using squirt guns.

V

Ecological problems are scientifically messy. This is true even when unanimity seems to rule. Things Sting might hug George Bush about

(and George write Sting a thank-you note for) are, in fact, too complicated for either of them to understand. Those of us with the normal
amount of brains can't comprehend them. Anyone who studies the
ozone hole, for instance, soon feels himself out in that ozone indeed.
An immense article on this matter (or the lack of it) appeared in the
April 15, 1993, issue of the *Washington Post*. The author was Boyce
Rensberger, a fellow who seems to have been paying attention in
college science classes while the rest of us were scribbling test answers
on our shirt cuffs. But midway through the text, Mr. Rensberger
throws his hands in the air:

> While there is evidence that the ozone damage is
> happening, it has proven impossible so far to detect any
> resulting increase in [ultraviolet light] reaching the
> ground. . . .
>
> "The amount of increase that the theory says we
> could be getting from ozone depletion is smaller than the
> error of our best measuring instruments," said John E.
> Frederick, an atmospheric physicist at the University of
> Chicago.
>
> "People get all excited about a few-percent
> change in UV, but it's nothing to get a 20 percent in-
> crease naturally," Frederick said. "If an increase of 20
> percent were going to be so damaging, there should be
> no life in Florida. . . ."

Which may explain Epcot Center.

Even obvious and uncontestable ecological harms must be
subjected to ethical consideration and cost/benefit analysis. That is,
they must be if we put any value on human well-being, and we'd better
because name another animal that thinks twice about the environment.
There is nothing the public abhors more than an oil spill. Yet we
cannot move around large quantities of necessary fluids without spilling
them occasionally. Those of us who drink have proven this by experi-

mental method. And here comes the Congressional Research Service—federally funded, bipartisan, and all that—with a July 1990 report by James E. Mielke, *Oil in the Ocean: The Short- and Long-Term Impacts of a Spill*. Mielke says the damage from even a horrendous splash of crude in the briny is "relatively modest and, as far as can be determined, of relatively short duration."

The CRS report based its conclusions on a number of disgusting seaside snafus including the 1976 *Argo Merchant* catastrophe on the Nantucket Shoals that nearly got the Kennedy Compound greasy and the 1969 Santa Barbara offshore oil-well blowout that gave us the original of that late twentieth-century ecological photo Pietà: the tarred—and, of course, feathered—seagull. Of particular interest is the case of the *Amoco Cadiz,* which ran aground off the coast of France in 1978. The ensuing spill was six times as large as the *Exxon Valdez*'s; 1,635,000 barrels of oil wound up on the beaches, birds, oyster beds, fisheries, and Bretons of Brittany. Several thousand avians died, but no long-term effect on bird population has been discovered. Fish died too, but, again, the effect was temporary—if not for the specific fish, for fish in general. Two years after the spill scientists found "little evidence of histopathological and biochemical damage" to the oysters. This being science talk, I think, for "nothing a little Tabasco sauce won't fix." Soap cleaned the Bretons, wave action cleaned the beaches, and the saltwater marshes repaired themselves. They did so better, in fact, than man was able to do. The CRS noted that marshes where no attempt was made to remove the oil were "restored by natural processes within 5 years, whereas in cleaned areas, restoration took 7 to 8 years." A slew of lawsuits later, total damage to France and its minions and wards was determined to be $115.2 million.

But in 1978 the art of making the public abhor oil spills was in its nonage. Not now. Exxon had to spend $2.2 billion cleaning up after the *Valdez*. It paid an additional $800 million to Alaska and the federal government and, as of this writing, still faces $1.5 billion in civil lawsuits. That's $4.5 billion Exxon could have spent reducing the price of home heating oil for the poor or sending somebody at its gas stations out to—speaking of cleanups—clean up the damn bugs on my windshield.

Those bugs, after all, are victims of the petroleum industry, too. And species extinction is another subject of harmonious general angst. We are losing species faster than car keys, umbrellas, clip-on earrings, small pieces of paper with important phone numbers written on them, and camera lens caps put together. Naturalist Norman Myers, in his 1979 book *The Sinking Ark,* claimed the earth could "lose one-quarter of all species by the year 2000." The World Wildlife Fund has used as a flag- (and fund-) raising cry: "Without firing a shot, we may kill one-fifth of all species of life on this planet in the next ten years." And in 1989 even the General Accounting Office felt compelled to break its historical silence on the subject of biodiversity and, abandoning its usual duties of toting up government pillage, issued a report professing, "The Earth is nearing a stage of extinction of species unequaled since that of the age of the dinosaurs."

We are losing species. And no one likes to take the position of "Have you looked under the couch cushions?" But a layperson might want to ask one or two questions. Are we talking rhinos and tigers, or are we talking shower-curtain mold and windshield bugs? Are we really opposed to every single extinction? I don't recall donating to Save the Smallpox.

And a scientist might want to make more technical queries such as "What the fuck's the Government Accounting Office talking about?"

One reason we are losing so many species is that we've decided there are so many more species to lose. According to an article by Charles C. Mann in the August 16, 1991, issue of *Science* (and I love citing *Science*—anything so hard to read must be deeply wise), taxonomists used to think the earth had three or four million distinct kinds of living things. Then, in the 1960s, tropical rain forests were brought to taxonomy's attention. These wet, steaming locales proved to contain a terrific (you can take my word for it) profusion of life forms. Says Mann, "On the basis of new sampling techniques, Terry Erwin of the U.S. National Zoo calculated that there are 30 million species of insects; recently, mycologist David Hawksworth reckoned that there are 1.5 million types of fungi. And no scientist has even a guess at how many microorganisms remain to be added to the tally . . ."

Some biologists now think the total number of species may be nearly 100 million. However, to date, only about 1.4 million of these have been captured, looked at, and named. "As a result," says Charles Mann, "those who prophesy the end of half the world's species find themselves in the awkward position of predicting the imminent demise of huge numbers of species nobody has ever seen." Several of which might cure cancer, of course. And several of which might cause it.

Then there is the matter of whether our theories about species extinction bear any relationship to real life, that is to say, death. Most of the research about species extinction has been conducted on islands because islands are controlled environments and scientists can get drinks with little umbrellas in them there. But the earth is an island only in the greeting-card-on-recycled-paper aphorism sense. And species that suffer loss of habitat on islands do not have the same options as species that suffer loss of habitat on landmasses do, such as moving to the suburbs and raiding our bird-feeders. Island logic also tells us that an increase in habitat size means an increase in number of species. But it doesn't necessarily. You can build your bed as large as you like and still get very few people to sleep with you.

Current research also takes for granted that habitat loss is permanent. It's politically and economically difficult to get Benetton, Bloomingdale's, and Blockbuster Video to tear down the mall, dig up the parking lot, and run a hose in the ruins to return the site to its original wetland conditions and get the shower-curtain mold and windshield bugs growing again. But according to the U.S. Department of Agriculture, fifty million acres of new forest have sprung up in the eastern United States since 1920. This in the most crowded part of our country during a period of great population growth and blowout urban sprawl. The National Wilderness Institute says, "Most wildlife is more abundant today and more widespread on both private and public lands than in 1900."

One of the best-studied areas of habitat loss and regeneration is Puerto Rico. It's an island, so the scientists can get mai-tais and frozen mango daiquiris. It's tropical, so there's lots of life and not just in the bars. And Puerto Rico is one of the few rain-forest sites where long-term biological records have been kept. Charles C. Mann, in that *Science* article of his, notes that Puerto Rico is thickly forested now but had been "almost completely stripped of virgin forest" ninety years ago. "Yet it did not suffer massive extinctions," says Mann. "Even birds lost only seven of 60 species." We don't want to lose seven species of birds—New York City pigeons, my aunt's horrible canary, the kind of chicken that's served at hotel banquets. . . . Maybe we *do* want to lose seven species of birds, although probably not the seven that went for scrambled eggs in the denuding of P.R. But, anyway, the point is living creatures are reasonably resilient or they wouldn't be living, and in some places at least, man is giving them a chance to resile.

One more consensus issue which some people find less than fully consensual is recycling. I have a friend, Jerry Taylor, who is the director of natural resource studies at the Cato Institute. Cato is a libertarian think tank and an excellent, brilliant, and nobly run institution (I happen to be a research fellow there). Libertarians are great believers in voluntary human behavior, the free marketplace being a good example. Jerry pointed out that when used items—Ferraris, for instance—have real value they don't need to be "recycled," they get sold. "If recycling is so great," said Jerry, "how come no private individual will pay you to do it?"

"Sex is great," I said, "and no private individual will pay me to do that." Jerry said he wasn't surprised.

Jerry Taylor wrote a paper about recycling for the American Legislative Exchange Council, an organization devoted to state government concerns. The title of the paper was (Jerry's one of those people who love to carve out common ground and create mutual good feeling among antagonistic groups) "Three Cheers for the Throw-Away Society!" Here Taylor presents figures showing that fast-food packaging—about which people are always complaining between Big Mac bites—makes up just one-tenth of one percent of municipal waste.

Taylor points out that if you measure trash by weight (and anybody who has to take out the trash wouldn't measure it any other way), we're using less packaging per person than ever before.

Taylor argues that the packaging we do use cuts down on food waste. He cites the work of Dr. William Rathje, author of *Rubbish! The Archaeology of Garbage* and head of the University of Arizona Garbage Project. (One can't help wondering what Dr. Rathje's Ph.D. is in; journalism is this author's guess.) Dr. Rathje excavated landfills in the United States and Mexico and discovered that Americans discarded twice as much food packaging but Mexicans discarded three times as much food.

Taylor praises the little foil and plastic-laminate juice boxes, "aseptic containers," that have been banned in some places because they are hard to recycle. They *are* hard to recycle, but they require fewer natural resources to make, less energy to fill and transport, and no energy to store. Plus there's all the money that's saved when they can't be recycled. As Taylor's colleague at Cato, Senior Fellow Doug Bandow, wrote in a 1992 newspaper column, "Most recycling programs are financial disasters. Even in the Northeast, with the highest collection and disposal costs, curbside recycling programs usually run at least twice as much as the cost of disposal through either landfills or incineration."

You can throw paper recycling in with the rest of the garbage, and you don't have to sort out the color advertising supplements. "Fully 87% of our paper stock," says Jerry Taylor, "comes from trees which are grown as a crop specifically for the purpose of paper production. Acting to 'conserve trees' through paper recycling is like acting to 'conserve corn' by cutting back on corn consumption." To cap the argument Taylor presents a National Wildlife Federation study show-ing that recycling one hundred tons of newspaper produces forty tons of toxic sludge. "Thirteen of the 50 worst Superfund hazardous waste dumps were once recycling facilities," says Taylor.

I asked Jerry if he could defend Styrofoam cups, those little guilt goblets that have caused so many moments of shame during coffee breaks at environmentalist conferences. Taylor rummaged in his files and produced the work of chemist Martin Hocking, who figured out that making a paper cup requires 36 times as much electricity as making a Styrofoam cup and generates 580 times as much waste water. Green types need no longer have burned fingers, lukewarm java, or decaf dribble stains on the fronts of their DON'T BUNGLE THE JUNGLE T-shirts, unless they want them.

The heck with biodegradability, too. Taylor quoted George Proios, executive director of the New York State Legislative Commis-sion on the Water Needs of Long Island (just a splash, George, but plenty of ice): "If biodegradable products end up in landfills, they will break down and form leachate and methane gas, the two major prob-lems with all current landfills. Non-biodegradable materials, such as plastics, are therefore far more desirable in landfills than biodegradable materials."

Jerry Taylor went so far as to have a kind word for the card-board boxes CDs are sold in. He reminded me that manufacturers never spend more money than they have to. All that junk around a Red Hot Chili Peppers recording is there to facilitate display, provide space for sales copy, and protect against breakage and loss. And it's also there, let me add, to keep the little bastards who protest that CD boxes waste the earth's resources from shoplifting the things.

Everyone agrees earth is swell compared to, say, Neptune or Washington, D.C. But, ecologically speaking, that's all everyone agrees on. I can find people to say good things about dirty air. "Measurements from Austria, Finland, France, Germany, Sweden, and Switzerland show a general increase of forest resources. The fertilization effects of pollutants override the adverse effects at least for the time being," claim Pekka E. Kauppi, Kari Mielikäinen, and Kullervo Kuusela, who must have some pretty advanced college degrees just to spell their names. That's from an April 1992 article titled "Biomass and Carbon Budget of European Forests, 1971 to 1990" appearing in, one more time, *Science* magazine.

Or DDT. In her book *Trashing the Planet* (HarperCollins, 1992), Dixy Lee Ray—zoology professor, past chairman of the Atomic Energy Commission, and former governor of Washington State—calls the charges against this famously pestilent pesticide "unsubstantiated." And Ray maintains that, by not using the stuff, we're causing a huge increase in worldwide mosquito-borne disease. She gives the example of Sri Lanka, which had 2.8 million cases of malaria in 1948. Then DDT spraying started. By 1963 there were only 17 malaria cases. Then DDT spraying stopped. And Sri Lanka had a million cases of malaria by 1968. The United Nations Department of International Economic and Social Affairs 1986 publication *Determinants of Mortality Change and Differentials in Developing Countries* (a fun read) doesn't quite agree with Dixy. The UN says Sri Lankan malaria cases did number in the teens until DDT use was abandoned but went up only to about *half* a million in the late sixties. And, by the early eighties, the annual infection rate was down in the 50,000 range. The Sri Lankans have been shooting each other a lot. Maybe the noise scared the mosquitoes away. Personally, I think DDT breakdown products wear out their bio-welcome—all that stuff from the *Silent Spring* era still hanging out in my café au lait. And Dr. Carnevale of the FDA, who was so generally reassuring on the moo-juice question, said she thought so, too. Still, 17 malaria cases in a tropical hole like Sri Lanka is impressive.

And even the worst specimen of our society's consumerist madness and capitalist profligacy, a product that fairly stinks of waste, has its defenders. Patricia Poore, editor and publisher of *Garbage, the Practical Journal for the Environment,* uses Pampers on her kid.

VI

Environmentalists do not like all this contradiction and complexity and wish it away when they can. Al Gore will brook no argument about the greenhouse effect. In *Earth in the Balance* he says, "The theory of global warming will not be disproved." A 1992 Gallup poll of four hundred meteorologists and geophysicists found that 60 percent thought global temperatures had risen in the last century, but only 19 percent attributed this to man-made causes. Greenpeace itself surveyed four hundred Greenpeace-picked scientists, and just 13 percent deemed runaway global warming probable. This does not deter Al. Says he, "Scientists concluded—almost unanimously—that global warming is real and the time to act is now."

And never mind that only a few years ago global *cooling* was real and the time to act was *then*. Anna J. Bray of the Heritage Foundation gathered a number of chilling pronouncements from the cool disco era:

> Meteorologists disagree about the cause and extent of the cooling trend. . . . But they are *almost unanimous* [emphasis almost unanimously my own] in the view that the trend will reduce agricultural productivity for the rest of the century.
>
> —Peter Gwynne, *Newsweek,*
> April 28, 1975

> [T]he threat of a new ice age must now stand alongside nuclear war as a likely source of wholesale death and misery for mankind.
>
> —Nigel Calder, *International*
> *Wildlife,* July 1975

> The cooling has already killed hundreds of thousands of people in poor nations. . . . If it continues, and no strong

measures are taken to deal with it, the cooling will cause world famine, world chaos, and probably world war, and this could all come by the year 2000.

        —Lowell Ponte, *The Cooling,* 1976

The global freeze that killed us then and the global boil that will kill us soon are both caused, of course, by technological progress.

The continued rapid cooling of the earth since World War II is also in accord with the increased global air pollution associated with industrialization, mechanization, urbanization, and an exploding population.

        —Reid Bryson, *Global Ecology:*
        Readings Towards a Rational
        Strategy for Man, 1971

An increase by only a factor of four in global aerosol background concentration may be sufficient to reduce the surface temperature by as much as 3.5 degrees Kelvin . . . sufficient to trigger an ice age.

        —Dr. S. I. Rasool and Dr. S. H.
        Schneider, *Science,* July 9, 1971

And—here the reasoning truly escapes me—we were supposed to do the same things to stop the earthly shivers that we're now supposed to do to halt the planetary sweats.

At this point, the world's climatologists are agreed on only two things: That we do not have . . . tens of thousands of years to prepare for the next ice age, and that how carefully we monitor our atmospheric pollution will have direct bearing on the arrival and nature of this

weather crisis. The sooner man confronts these facts
. . . the safer he'll be.

—Douglas Colligan, *Science
Digest,* February 1973

World-savers are chefs with only one recipe. Toss the salad.
Toss the steak. Toss the coffee. And hurry up about it, says Albert
Gore: "The insistence on complete certainty about the full details of
global warming—the most serious threat we have ever faced—is actually an effort to avoid facing the awful, uncomfortable truth: that we
must act boldly, decisively, comprehensively, and quickly, even before
we know every last detail of the crisis."

Put this together with other Gore statements:

Vast amounts of unused information ultimately become a
kind of pollution.

[C]oping with all that data will be extremely difficult, not
least because most of it will never enter a single human
brain.

If, when the remaining unknowns about the environmental challenge enter the public debate, they are presented as signs that the crisis may not be real after all, it
undermines the effort to build a solid base of public
support for the difficult actions we must soon take.

And we must boldly, decisively, comprehensively, and quickly conclude the vice president is a nut.

Some of the vice president's co-opinionists are worse than
nuts. There is Jonathan Schell, who is most famous for his book *The
Fate of the Earth* about "nuclear winter." Not that Schell doesn't believe
in global warming, too, but *The Fate of the Earth* concerned the sad
results of an H-bomb exchange between the United States and the

Soviet Union. Schell described, in harrowing detail, the awful effects of an atomic war we weren't having. He scared the Birkenstocks off the kind of people who were, incidentally, no help whatsoever in getting rid of the USSR. *The Fate of the Earth* depended, for its frightfulness, on masses of seemingly objective, supposedly scientific ratiocination. But here is Schell in the October 1987 issue of *Discover* magazine telling us what value he truly places on objectivity and the scientific method:

> [W]e need to act on theory alone, which is to say on prediction alone. It follows that the reputation of scientific prediction needs to be enhanced. But that can happen, paradoxically, only if scientists disavow the certainty and precision that they normally insist on. Above all, we need to learn to act decisively to forestall predicted perils, even while knowing that they may never materialize. We must take action, in a manner of speaking, to preserve our ignorance.

Dixy Lee Ray and her collaborator, Lou Guzzo, have made a collection of such damning quotes. Another comes from atmospheric scientist and global-warming alarmist Stephen Schneider, as cited by Schell in the article above. This is the same Dr. Schneider whom we just noted going on about spray cans and ice ages. Schneider has made a career of telling the public that the climate is going to change drastically any time now, and indeed every spring and fall he's been right. Dr. Schneider, if Schell quotes him accurately, is a self-admitted liar and knave:

> [W]e have to offer up scary scenarios, make simplified, dramatic statements, and make little mention of any doubts we may have. Each of us has to decide what the right balance is between being effective and being honest.

For Schneider, Schell, Gore, et al., science is daytime TV with no facts, just emotions, opinions, and themselves as Geraldo Rivera. What do the ignorance mongers expect to gain from this?

People with a mission to save the earth want the earth to seem worse than it is so their mission will look more important. In fact, there's some evidence that these people want the earth to *be* worse than it is. Michael Fumento, author of *Science under Siege* (William Morrow, 1993), has compiled additional damning quotations. Fumento notes that in 1990, when cold-fusion nonsense briefly promised an infinite supply of bargain-priced, ecologically harmless energy, environmentalist pest Jeremy Rifkin called this, "The worst thing that could happen to our planet." This is not a new position among the pesky. In a 1977 issue of *Mother Earth,* Amory Lovins wrote, "It would be little short of disastrous for us to discover a source of clean, cheap, abundant energy because of what we might do with it." And in 1978 the inevitable Paul Ehrlich said, in the Federation of American Scientists' *Public Interest Report,* "Giving society cheap, abundant energy . . . would be the equivalent of giving an idiot child a machine gun." (Not a meal, a bath, some toys, and a warm bed or anything like that.)

Ronald Bailey, who besides being the author of *Eco-Scam* is also the producer of the PBS series *TechnoPolitics,* believes that environmental advocates enjoy the idea of living in apocalyptic times. Their drab existences—spent sorting through trash, wearing lumpy handknits, attending indignant meetings, and trying to get the photocopier to work with recycled paper—are made exciting by the imminent end of the world. Said Stewart Brand in the *Whole Earth Catalog* of yore:

> We have wished, we ecofreaks, for a disaster or for a social change to come and bomb us into the Stone Age, where we might live like Indians in our valley, with our localism, our appropriate technology, our gardens, our homemade religion—guilt-free at last!

We were all pretty well bombed into the Stone Age, back then, as I recall. But in "homemade religion" Brand may have a point. Worshiping the earth is more fun than going to church. It's also closer. We can just step off the sidewalk. And sometimes we can get impressionable members of the opposite sex to perform sacramental rites with us. "Every drop of water wasted is a drop less of a wild and scenic river, Jennifer. We'd better double up in the shower."

The specter of biosphere doom serves the mystical needs of people too sloppy and self-indulgent for regular religion. And it is a scary story to tell in the (energy-conserving) dark. But the ultimate appeal of ecological catastrophe has to do with politics rather than Yahweh or Rod Serling.

Ecological utopias could be achieved only by massive political coercion. Said David Foreman in *A Field Guide to Monkey Wrenching:*

> We must . . . reclaim the roads and the plowed land, halt
> dam construction, tear down existing dams, free shackled
> rivers, and return to wilderness millions and tens of mil-
> lions of [acres of] presently settled land.

Just who is this "we"?

Again, in *Earth in the Balance,* the proposed solutions to environmental problems would require a huge increase in political power over individuals. Says Al Gore:

> Human civilization is now so complex and diverse, so
> sprawling and massive, that it is difficult to see how we
> can respond in a coordinated, collective way to the global
> environmental crisis. But circumstances are forcing just
> such a response.

The whole dreadful history of twentieth-century politics has been made up of "coordinated, collective" responses to supposed threats that were always said to be "complex and diverse" and "sprawl-ing and massive." Nazis, Fascists, Bolsheviks, Maoists, Islamic Funda-mentalists, and my silly commune in Baltimore in 1970 responded "in a coordinated, collective way" to the Jews, the bourgeoisie, private property, class enemies, decadent Western culture, and the pig cop on the local beat. The results were universally horrendous (except at my commune, which got busted for marijuana).

VII

If increased political power over the individual is the answer to envi-ronmental difficulties, then let us go examine ecological conditions in a region that had half a century of coordination like Billy Hell and collectivity in carload lots.

There was no shortage of political power in Eastern Europe's Communist bloc. And, when it seemed as though government regula-tory influence over individuals might be slipping—such as it did in Hungary in 1956 or Czechoslovakia in 1968—the helpful Soviet Union sent tanks.

In the territory once occupied by that Communist bloc, where the borders of ex–East Germany, the erstwhile People's Republic of Poland, and former Czechoslovakia meet, there is a region known as the "Black Triangle." Here the landscape is full of fuming smelters, malodorous chemical factories, and enormous power plants burning coal of such a low grade that the swamp muck of the Carboniferous period can still be whiffed in the smoke. On bad days no smoke is visible; it can't be distinguished from the air. On good days the atmo-sphere is the color of used bathwater. The buildings are stained with soot. Nature is grimy to the touch. The breeze has texture, like grit in a sandwich when the lettuce hasn't been washed. Inhaling is bad breath in reverse. A drag on a cigarette cleanses the lungs.

In the Czech Republic portion of the Black Triangle is the drab villiage of Chabarovice, and in Chabarovice is a horrible toxic

waste dump. How horrible, no one is quite certain. But Czech journalists assured me it is so horrible that whenever Czech journalists are
doing stories about horrible toxic waste dumps they immediately go to
Chabarovice and tell how horrible it is. Horrible things have been
dumped here: all sorts of lethal contaminants from communist factories
plus, some say, Russian chemical weapons from World War II, and, say
others, German poison gas from World War I. When scientists came
to analyze the dump, it was so horrible that their instruments worked
horribly, and they couldn't even tell what kind of horrible stuff they
were analyzing.

Chabarovice is an hour and a half north of Prague. I drove
there in September 1993 with two Czech friends of mine, Ivanna
Husák and Martin Weiss. We'd heard Chabarovice had been ruined by
the dump, but the Sudetenland-era fake Bavarian concrete town hall
and the pokey socialist terrace houses covered in mildew-colored
stucco didn't need ruining. We'd heard people were fleeing Chabarovice, but it seemed as though everyone with the wit or ability to move
had done so already. We tried to find the mayor. His secretary said he
was at home. His wife said he was at the office. In Italy or France this
would mean His Honor was having an affair. In Chabarovice it probably meant he'd run off to be a busboy in Stuttgart. A crippled drunk
man gave us directions to the dump.

Ivanna and Martin went off to see if they could find anything
in the environs that glowed or had two heads. I climbed a wobbling
six-foot chain-link fence that had been erected when the dump was
closed in 1991 and that bore what I assumed was a warning sign:
STREZEN PSY.

One immediately evident horrible thing about Chabarovice
was that the toxins hadn't been buried or even left on the ground; they
had been, in fact, exalted. The Chabarovice site was an artificial hill of
strip-mine tailings maybe forty feet high and covering a couple dozen
acres. A hole two hundred yards wide had been scooped out of the top
of the hill, and into this crater liquid toxins had been poured to form

a sort of miniature Lake Titicaca of hazardous slime. The road up to the dump was littered with metal pipe and pieces of boiler machinery, not from anything nuclear, I hoped. The scum basin itself wasn't very big, no larger than the skating rink in Central Park. It seemed to have been receding, the contents evaporating out into the stuff I was breathing or seeping down through the rusty-looking, munched-up bedrock rubble and into someone's dinner cabbage. A wide beach of chemical residue the color of an old dog bone surrounded the pond. Whatever filled this reservoir was also subdued in tint. I guess I expected the malignant hues of party-of-ten-loud-women Patagonia jackets, but the goo was cloudy, curdled, grayish green-beige. These were natural colors—that is, the colors things naturally turn when they're very sick or dead. Indeed, no living item was visible in any direction. Other than me—and how long I'd stay viable was a question.

A wooden ramp ran out from the shore of the ooze lagoon so that fifty-five-gallon barrels could be rolled to a liquid grave. The ramp was the size and shape of a small boat dock, giving the scene the look of everybody's nightmare about what might happen at the summer cottage if we don't do something about the environment soon.

On the other side of the gunk, opposite the wooden ramp, was a field of steel drums and plastic sacks, all of which seemed to be leaking something with an unhealthful appearance. Interspersed among these were chunks of strange fibrous matter of the kind that erupts from the worn-through places in cheap upholstery or dribbles out the seams of bargain winter parkas. And here and there was some regular trash, friendly and reassuring by comparison.

A wind sock was mounted on a pole beside the pond. I guess when the wind sock pointed in the direction of downtown Chabarovice, the villagers were supposed to scram. Of course the villagers would have to be in the dump to see the wind sock, so they'd probably want to scram anyway. I was careful to keep the breeze at my back. But there was still plenty of smell—industrial solvent, mostly, the odor of model airplane glue. This brought back memories, though not nostalgic ones. I was fourteen or fifteen, a little too old to be building model airplanes but down in the basement fiddling with a Stuka dive-bomber or an F4U Corsair, staying out of the way of a hectoring stepfather and wishing I were fiddling with girls, if I knew how, or smoking cigarettes, except my folks would sniff that as easily as I now sniffed the Chabarovice dump. And I knew I was just going to take the model airplane out behind the garage and burn it as soon as I'd finished it—for kicks, although not very good ones.

I walked down the mound of strip-mine junk and climbed back over the fence. Ivanna and Martin were waiting by the car. "What does *Strezen Psy* mean?" I asked. "Patrolled by guard dogs," said Ivanna. So there's one good thing about East bloc toxic waste—dead Doberman pinschers.

VIII

Czechoslovakia was a socialist country. The nation wasn't ruled by a few plutocrats who just wanted to shackle rivers, plow land, and so forth for their own selfish ends. No, the state was run in a coordinated, collective way for the benefit of all Czechoslovakians. Indeed, since Czechoslovakia was part of the great international socialist movement, it worked for the benefit of everyone everywhere.

Of course you can argue, as European Greens do, that communist countries were polluted because a clean environment was not a communist priority. The Communists cared only about development, about increasing industrial output, about building a workers' paradise. And they did all of those things so well.

The Communists had the same success creating workers' paradises as they had creating safe landfills. In fact, all over Eastern Europe, the landfills and the workers' paradises are nearly indistinguishable. The grand effects of Al Gore's dream of infinite government planning for the good of all mankind can be seen the moment you cross what used to be called the Iron (a recyclable material) Curtain.

I'd driven to the Czech Republic from Frankfurt. I was motoring at 120 miles an hour on the autobahn through the rolling Hesse countryside. But this wasteful and polluting exacerbation of the global environmental crisis came to an abrupt halt at Eisenach on the old East German border. From there on I was persuaded into more ecologically responsible behavior by the fact that every single kilometer of road was under repair. And needed it. And so did everything else I could see. The houses were shabby when there were houses at all. More often there were concrete "worker flats," shabbier still. These eight- or ten-story vertical root cellars were built midst ample land for Fremont, California–style private homes with gardens and lawns. But that would be inefficient. "An acre of lawn needs more than 27,000 gallons of water every week," says *50 Simple Things.*

Germany is a seriously clean country. A friend of mine was riding a train to Stuttgart once, and, looking out the window, he saw a farmer on a ladder washing the windows of his barn. But in former East Germany there was actually litter along the highway. And worse than litter, whole Trabant automobiles (products of East Germany's coordinated, collective response to its citizens' transportation needs) had been abandoned by the side of the road. Trabants that were still working wobbled and smoked and shuddered around me with the equally ill-built and awful-running East German Wartburg cars and IFA trucks and Czech LIAZ semis, Skoda sedans, and Jawa motorcycles. The whole of the traffic in the East seemed like something that should be crushed at a county fair by a pickup truck with giant tires.

Empty factories, forsaken ore breakers, and slag heaps dominated the scenery. The smell of burning lignite penetrated my air-conditioning system.

Dresden needs to be bombed again and done away with for good. The road from there to Prague ran beside a rail bed. An unpleasant little coal-fired narrow-gauge locomotive lurched along the tracks, spewing stink. It would have caused the most stolid of nine-year-old boys to leave off model railroading and go play with dolls. I stopped for fuel at a small garage in Dippoldiswalde and there encountered the most un-German thing imaginable. The restroom was dirty.

The East German political system, like the Dippoldiswalde septic system which survives it, didn't work. Getting a mass of people to labor, will-they, nil-they, toward abstract goals for the sake of people in the mass doesn't work. It can be done temporarily in dire emergencies such as last-minute decoration of the gym for the prom or during famines or when Nazis invade. Even the Soviet Union worked while Nazis were invading it. But on the morning after V-E Day, the proletariat was sloshed on the job again, Stalin was back to killing people, and the peasants were hiding their pigs.

In Prague I was given a tour of the Tatra streetcar factory by Ivan Husák, director of marketing and sales and father of my friend Ivanna. The plant looked like one of those WPA arts project murals from the 1930s where brawny men snuggle drill presses and hug rivet guns in a bower of levers and gears lit only by the romantic glow of a welder's torch. The plant also looked like it hadn't been swept or dusted since the WPA was disbanded. The old brick machine sheds were full of oily soot, caked grease, rusted iron filings, and general grime. The Tatra factory was a Miss Havisham's wedding cake of socialist realism.

Lack of greedy capitalists siphoning away corporate profits hadn't done Tatra much good. Nor had lack of greedy capitalists done much for Tatra workers. They make between $360 and $430 a month. Executive compensation may be a big issue in the United States, but I doubt Tatra workers feel better because their bosses get a maximum per month of $640.

There's nothing very wrong with the Tatra product. The factory is ancient and shabby, but what's made there is well crafted. The workers work harder than I'd work for $2.25 an hour. The streetcars have a 1970s box-it-came-in modern look but are fairly comfortable. Hundreds of them, including quite ancient models, are reliably whirring and clanging around Prague. Tatra mechanical designs are straightforward, what's known in manufacturing as "proven technology." The equipment is built to be operated with low maintenance in tough climates. "They work in *Russia,*" said Mr. Husák. The problem is competition. Tatra had been selling to a captive market. I looked at a sales map showing where Tatra streetcars were in use. Dots appeared all over the old Soviet bloc plus one lone dot in Cairo.

Tatra is hoping to finish a new factory, hoping for deals in Brazil, Manila, Oslo. But production is down, from a thousand street-cars a year before the Communists were overthrown to only two hundred now. Mr. Husák told me this in the company's modest conference room while a very slow electric kettle boiled water for tea.

Various German companies make more sophisticated street-cars. And Tatra itself may be bought out by the German affiliate of Westinghouse. And do people really want streetcars anyway? I liked Ivan Husák too much to ask that, but few urban mass-transit systems operate at a profit anymore. People would rather drive themselves. Although *A Dodge Minivan Named Desire* isn't much of a title for a Tennessee Williams play.

IX

If collective, cooperative enterprise can't succeed in building streetcars, how is it supposed to provide clean water and air, remove toxins from our food, save endangered species, prevent deforestation, and cool (or, as it may be, warm) the globe?

It can't. And the Communists left behind a wretched mess. In 1991 the Ministry of Environment of the newly free Czech Republic published *Lights and Shadows,* a report on the country's ecological situation. It is a government document of unlikely frankness and says, in the charming diction of the English-language version, "As it follows out of analyses made by the most varied research institutes, in respect of principal environmental quality indicators we are the worst country in Europe."

According to *Lights and Shadows,* energy use per unit of net income is, in the Czech Republic, 30 percent higher than the world average. "One-third of agricultural land suffers water erosion." Forty-eight and a half percent of the nation's forests "are distinctly and permanently damaged." (No matter what Kauppi, Mielikäinen, and Kuusela may say about smog being good for the firs.) And Czechs discard "35 metric tons of solid refuse per person per year." I hope that includes strip-mine tailings because we famously wasteful Americans produce only .8 metric tons per person. A paltry 5 percent of Czech garbage is recycled. And that's the good news, if the Cato Institute's Jerry Taylor is right about recycling economics. Czechs might have wound up with thirty-five metric tons of cans, bottles, newspapers, and mine waste neatly separated and stacked on their back porches with nobody willing to come pick it up.

"The water quality," says *Lights and Shadows,* is jeopardized in almost all water sources," and "sewage treatment is eleven years behind water supply development." This means, I think, that you have to run the faucet for 132 months before you fill the Mr. Coffee. And, says *Lights and Shadows,* air pollution measurements "rank our republic among the worst on the world scale." For instance, in 1988 the Czech part of former Czechoslovakia produced 840,000 metric tons of atmospheric particulate matter—pieces of junk in the air. That's 28.3 tons per square mile, compared to only 2.3 tons per square mile in the continental United States. I can understand why the Czechs have trouble breathing. What I can't understand is why they aren't squashed flat.

There are health consequences to this contamination. *Lights and Shadows* estimates that in Teplice, one of the most polluted regions of the Czech Republic, 13.6 years are cut from the average life span. I can't vouch for the figure, but I did visit Teplice, and I'd trade a few years of my life to never smell the place again.

Lights and Shadows argues that a grimness in nature has grim social effects, too. "According to a set of selected indicators . . .. the region below the Ore Mountains [that is, the Black Triangle] is the worst region in the Czech Republic." The report goes on to cite such statistics as 50 divorces per 100 marriages in the deforested Sokolov District, .32 suicides per 1,000 population in the strip-mined Chomutov District, and 76.2 abortions per 100 live births in the Ústí nad Labem District where the wretched town of Chabarovice is located. (A sad tally, but it does leave one wondering what blue-skied and eco-conscious America's excuse is. Our divorce rate is about the same as Sokolov's, our white males 65 and over kill .45 per thousand of themselves a year, and black women in the United States get 63.8 abortions for every 100 kids they have. Could sexual liberation, Social Security, and welfare be as dangerous as atmospheric particulate matter?)

Lights and Shadows has an afterword by Václav Havel in which that worthy says, "There are many reasons why the environment in our country is in such a catastrophic state. One of the reasons is the fact that the previous establishment was founded on a sort of proud ideology which proclaimed that Man was the final, though mortal, master of the Earth." But do things get better when that establishment thinks Man is Earth's final, though mortal, wet nurse?

I drove north to have a look at the Chomutov strip mining and found a big hole in the ground. Irony-proof Marxists had named it "Czechoslovak Army Mine." The hole down the road was called "Defenders of Peace." I climbed a mound of greasy brown rocks and stared into a sixty- or eighty-foot-deep pit that was certainly not abysmal. That is, it had a bottom. It had too much bottom. From where I stood to as far as the eye could see, everything looked like the bottom of a pit.

The landscape left behind by strip mining has been called "lunar" and "Martian," but it is, of course, "earthly." This is what our planet looks like if we strip off all the waste and litter of organic life. This is true wilderness, not only untamed by man but undomesticated by amoeba or lichen.

Out in the middle of the pit was a large, skinny piece of machinery with the appearance of an erect mechanical centipede. Excavating buckets moved along its length like undulations of body segments. The buckets were scooping up rock at one end and dumping it out at the other. This parody of digestion must have had something to do with the search for or seizure of coal. But it was hard to tell, everything in the hole including the mechanical centipede being the same dull, rusty shade. Later I examined a lump of the brown coal being mined in Chomutov. It crumbled in my fingers and looked to be about as puissant a fuel as old linoleum or rotted wine corks.

There is a strong aesthetic element to the environmentalist movement. Most modern people who have been to college will call any view without man-made features beautiful. The fact that they would rather be in a motel than on an ice floe doesn't make them liars. They do think the ice floe is prettier. The "exterior decorator" motive behind ecological activism is so prevalent that it has led Jerry Taylor to say, "Environment is a luxury good."

But, personally, I like strip mines. The Czechoslovak Army Mine looked like a swell place to hold a Led Zeppelin concert, put the members of the U.S. House of Representatives, contemplate the vanity of, as it were, earthly ambition, or stage that enormous Demo Derby to which the rattletrap motor vehicles of the ex–Soviet bloc seem so perfectly destined.

I didn't care that the mine was ugly. I did care that no one knew if it was profitable. Environmentalist organizations usually have strong opinions about everything. A Greenpeace Czechoslovakia report on these mining regions said, "The material being removed from the top of the mining sites has a greater value than the coal below." But the same report also said this undervalued coal allowed the local electric power plants to make 10 billion Czech crowns (about $357 million) "of tax-free profit a year." And Dr. Antonin Mucha, a physical scientist working with the Greenpeace-associated organization Children of the Earth, disagreed with both these positions, telling me, "It's very difficult to say the brown coal is not economical. But . . . there is no sense in using it for energy production."

Petr Pakosta, chief of the Department of Environment in the Most District—a place where there's so much strip mining that the entire city of Most had to be moved out of the strip mines' way—said, "If the coal were used as a chemical material, it would be worthwhile to mine it. But since it's used to heat, 80 percent goes up the chimney, so it's useless." Or maybe it's useless. Mr. Pakosta lacked the only real means of discovering such things. The free market takes a lot of abuse, especially from environmentalists, but they might as well protest against tablespoons and yardsticks. Price is just a measurement. A measurement is information. And without information it's impossible to make informed decisions. "It's a law that coal belongs to the state," said Pakosta, "so there's no price to it."

OKD, the Czech national coal company, has—even with such a priceless advantage—managed to get itself into high-priced trouble. According to the financial page of the *Prague Post* (September 15–21, 1993), OKD is nearly one billion crowns in debt. Under the Communists, the company was able to sell twenty-four million tons of coal a year. Now it can find buyers for only fourteen million tons. And still OKD goes looking for more coal.

I went to a village near Most, Libkovice, which was being demolished to make way for the digging of needless coal. I asked Stanislav Brichcek, who would have been the mayor of Libkovice if there'd been a Libkovice to be mayor of, if this vein of coal could be worth "the material being removed from the top of the mining site." He said, *"Not* taking into account the destruction of the village, the mining will be"—he wobbled the flat of his hand in the international sign for dubious undertakings—"so-so profitable."

That's a big *not*. According to Greenpeace, ninety-six historical villages and all of ancient Most have been obliterated by strip mining, and the Czech Republic has a thousand square kilometers of open mine pits, none of which have been restored with topsoil or used for

Led Zeppelin concerts. A thousand square kilometers is four hundred square miles, an area nearly as big (and nearly as useless) as Los Angeles in a nation smaller than South Carolina. This is too much strip mine even for me. Environment may be a luxury good, but don't luxury goods make life worth living?

One good imperiled by the mine company was luxurious indeed, a whole castle. At least, it had been luxurious. Schloss Eisenberg, as the stately pile is called when Germans rule the Black Triangle, or Jezeri Castle, as it's known when Slavs do, is a few miles north of Most. During World War II it was used as a Nazi POW camp for French military officers. (Very different from the camp in *Stalag 17* but, anyway, all French tunneling was probably done toward the wine cellar.) In 1948 it was taken over by the communist military, who used it, to judge by the state of the décor, for indoor grenade practice and bachelor parties. But the outside of the palace was still splendid and the inside had all the great halls, vaulted ceilings, fireplaces as big as two-bedroom New York apartments, sweeping staircases, tower keeps, secret passages, and gloomy dungeons that this type of residential real estate demands.

Jezeri Castle was built in 1720 on foundations dating to the Middle Ages. The style is late baroque and highly theatrical. Huge grotesques support the front door lintel. There are no symmetrical façades. Two hundred rooms form a floor plan as complex as paisley. The architectural details are dense and fluid, and the roof is a flood of ogee curves. Every view of Jezeri Castle seems intended for representation on china plates and souvenir ashtrays. In America a thing like this would be worth its weight in water slides. The parking concession alone would bring in more than all the strip mines in the Czech Republic (and probably take up the same space). But, under the coordinated, collective economic system of Eastern Europe, Jezeri was going to be torn down. A coal pit comes to within a few feet of the château walls. It is as if, later in life, the dwarves had a falling out with Snow White and claim-jumped her castle.

Jezeri was rescued by the efforts of an artist couple, Jaroslav and Vera Stejnych. During the 1980s they moved into the abandoned property as combined squatters and preservation committee. They staved off the mining company with the connivance of a Communist Party official who was having an affair with a friend of theirs. Jaroslav said he wants to restore half of the castle, the half that looks toward the birch woods of the Ore Mountains, and leave the other half, the half that faces the coal pit, as a "monument to communism."

The village of Libkovice had no such fortunate sex scandal, although it was a romantic enough place for one. Until recently Libkovice was beautiful. Half-timbered cottages, hundreds of years old, sat in their gardens along gravel lanes. A dollhouse Chartres of a church faced the common. Grain fields rolled away toward the mountains. Put this within Lexus and Acura range of New York and think of the orthodontists, personal injury and accident lawyers, advertising executives, and people who are occasionally mentioned in "Suzy Says" who'd be snapping up weekend getaways. Of course, that, too, would mean displacement for the villagers of Libkovice, but at least they would have soaked some Manhattanites before they went. As it was, the flowerbeds were overgrown, fruit was rotting on the trees in the dooryards, the houses were gutted, the church was stripped, and angry graffiti appeared on the walls around town. STOP THE MADNESS said one message. STOP THE EXCESSIVE RATIONALIZATIONS LEFT OVER FROM A MORIBUND CENTRALLY CONTROLLED ECONOMY would have been more to the point but harder to spray-paint.

Ivanna Husák, Martin Weiss, and I drove to Libkovice on a drizzly, chill autumn morning. A few miles from town we saw an old man with one eye standing beside the road. He was waiting for the leftover, moribund centrally controlled bus. We gave him a ride. His house in Libkovice had been expropriated, and he'd been forced to move to another village. He was alone in the world except for his dog. But he wasn't going to let the government have his home without a fight. So he left the dog to guard the empty house, and every day he took the bus to Libkovice to bring the dog food.

The house had been built by his family. It was a hundred years old "but newly reconstructed," said the old man with a rustic's proud disinterest in the antique. It had six rooms, outbuildings, and a yard. And he had a firm idea of what the place was worth. He'd wanted 374,000 crowns ($13,400), but the government compensation had been only 109,000 crowns ($3,900).

The Czech Republic has yuppies, too. And we were a mere fifty miles from Prague. What would somebody who, for example, had just gotten the new McDonald's franchise in Wenceslas Square pay for an authentic Bohemian peasant cottage (we'd met the authentic Bohemian peasant) in a quaint village like Libkovice? (And didn't the place just scream "Central European Peter Mayle"?) Ivanna and Martin agreed that 600,000 crowns (over $21,000) would be the minimum. In Prague itself, they said, six-room houses went for a million crowns.

The old man took us to one of the last occupied homes in the village, which the ex-mayor refused to leave. I could see why nobody had tried to make him. Stanislav Brichacek was a gangling man, no longer young, but with big raw hands and a fierce set to his features. It wouldn't have surprised me if, somewhere under the cluttered farmyard at the back of his house, guns had been buried to fight the Communists and the Nazis before them and the Sudeten Germans before that.

Ex-mayor Brichacek explained how all the mineral rights in the Czech Republic belong to the state, and so does the coal company. Under the Communists, the coal company could tear up any village, farm, or town it wanted. This had changed. Sort of. The new government said that whether a village was to be destroyed for the sake of coal was up to the mayor of that village. But then the new government said that so many people had been forced out of Libkovice that it was no longer large enough to have a mayor. Brichacek had written letters of protest to the Department of Interior, Department of Environment, the Parliament, the president, the Council of Europe in Strasbourg. "I have written everywhere except to the main railway station," he said. He'd received no answers.

"The law is flexible according to the miners' wish," said Brichacek. He then explained how the government figured compensation for expropriated property. The bureaucrats would make a reasonably fair appraisal of a house but then "depreciate" it by subtracting 1 percent of the value for each year of the structure's age. Thus a $20,000 home would go for $19,800 if it was one year old, $19,602 if it was two years old, $19,405.98 if it was three years old, and so forth. This kind of mathematics would put Versailles or the White House within the range of most pocketbooks.

X

Ivanna, Martin, and I drove to Most to have lunch with the district environment department chief, Petr Pakosta, the man who'd pointed out that Czech coal has no real price. Most is all high-rises built of cement slabs, with as few windows as prison blocks. In fact, the only way to tell that these apartments aren't prison blocks is that there are no ACLU lawsuits trying to close down Most. One monument had been saved from the historical town site, a cathedral that the Communists had somehow put on wheels and moved for miles and deposited in the middle of a highway interchange.

An old lady directed us to the government offices, another cement-slab high-rise. "Go to the 'carousel,'" she said, making, I guess, a joke about government runarounds or maybe about the architecture, which couldn't have been less carnival-like.

"It is panel-concrete technology abandoned by the British in 1962," said Pakosta. A form of modern architecture too lousy for the British is an awful thing.

Pakosta was a rounded, bearded man, his blond hair going gray. He had a jolly look and an engaging manner—Santa's younger brother who'd gone into politics. Pakosta said the Most District, one of forty such administrative districts into which the country is divided, had 550,000 dumps. About 30 of the dumps were very bad. How many were as bad as Chabarovice? Who knew? In Most the coal company owned 75 percent of the land (and counting) and paid no taxes on it. And Most had all those bad health and worse social statistics mentioned in *Lights and Shadows*. And other problems besides: There used to be 112 pubs in the old city of Most, Pakosta said with signal regret.

It took all lunch to pry these items from Pakosta. He didn't want to talk particulars. And not because of bureaucratic caution or official reticence. Pakosta was perfectly forthcoming. But, when I asked him about environmental practice, he answered me with ethics and philosophy. "Mainly it is a moral devastation," said Pakosta, "that started with German liquidation of Czechs. Then the significant influence of superpowers, such as the Soviets, deciding about our borders gave Czechs inferiority and feelings of helplessness. State control and state property make people indifferent to the place where they're living, losing both positive and negative interest. It's not a matter of communism or socialism but a matter of all big complexes where people are losing their identities." And their pubs. We were having lunch in a dreary restaurant on a high-rise first floor.

For a while, I was exasperated with Pakosta. "More specifics, please," I kept saying, reporter-like, wanting ugly facts and scary numbers about communist eco-flubs. But Czechs have suffered from enough "big complexes," from enough nationalism, Bolshevism, and fascism, to know that the damage done by the bad specifics of pollution is nothing compared to the damage done by the horrible generalizations of political theory. Even at the Greenpeace office in Prague I'd heard about the benefits of "identity," of individualism. Dr. Mucha from Children of the Earth had told me that the ecological damage in the Czech Republic was "not a problem of the planned or open economy but a problem of ownership. Everything belonged to all of us and to nobody." In an American Greenpeace office someone would have thrown a plant at his head. (The plants in the office of Greenpeace Czechoslovakia, incidentally, needed watering.)

And yet the idea of coordinated, collective action persists. Ivanna, Martin, and I drove back to Prague for more interviews. It is the only big city in Europe never destroyed by fire or war (or political theory either). The damage that Nazis, Communists, and "Marxists with human faces," as the reformers of 1968 liked to call themselves, did to Prague was the infliction of a grayness, partly of soot and partly of spirit. The outer boroughs of Prague are still gray. But the center has changed. There are brightly lit shops, billboards, and real cars from Western Europe. The streets are full of active, busy working men and women (and working girls, too, since some of Prague's newfound commerce is conducted at night in fishnet stockings). Tourist flash-bulbs pop. Video screens flicker. Neon tubes glow. Prague is being colorized. And not everyone is happy about this.

The Czechs are so mired in the experience of huge ideologies that even freedom—just people doing what they like in a world of legal equality—seems to be a huge ideology. "Advertising is a kind of terrorism," said Vojtěch Kotecky, eighteen and a half years old and a member of the Rainbow Movement.

"Huh?" I said.

"Very hard advertising creates an air in which we must consume so much," explained Vojtěch, who told me that the Rainbow Movement was trying to ban nuclear power and protect the ozone layer—which seem large tasks to undertake before finishing high school. Vojtěch thought that maybe advertising should be illegal.

Did he want a return to the former government? I asked. No, definitely not, he said. The old regime was all about centralized control, resulting in problems such as the destruction of Libkovice. He and his fellow Rainbow Movement members had gone to Libkovice and stood on the roofs of buildings to try to stop the demolition by the coal company. One fellow was nearly killed when a house was knocked out from under him.

But, I said, how could advertising be banned without the kind of centralized control that the Communists had?

A law could be passed. "This government refuses to use the democratic process," said Vojtěch.

"This government *is* the democratic process," I said. The Czech Republic has, in the past few years, had its only free elections in six decades.

"There is a false dichotomy between communism and the West," said Vojtěch. "All is based on a centralized economy." He suggested a "decentralized and self-sufficient economy."

(". . . where we might live like Indians in our valley . . .") The Rainbow Movement must still be on the *Whole Earth Catalog* mailing list (". . . with our localism, our appropriate technology, our gardens, our homemade religion—guilt-free at last!"), even though the thing went out of business before they were born.

How, I asked Vojtěch, could such decentralization be enforced without a great deal of centralized control?

Vojtěch, in a very non–American-adolescent way, said he didn't know. He was also clean, well barbered, and pleasant.

Vojtěch took me to the Czech Parliament building to meet a sort of mentor to the Rainbow Movement, Pavel Seifer, an MP and deputy chief of the Labor Social Union Party. Seifer didn't think the Czech government was very democratic either. (His party had lost most of their Parliament seats in the last election.)

Seifer was a hip MP. He wore a little gray goatee, a dark shirt with a light tie, and one of those fashionably large sport coats that practically have room in them for two Labor Social Union Party members. Seifer claimed that the free market championed by the present Czech government was ideological while the environmentalism championed by him was not. "What we hate most about the current political situation is this ideological edge," he said. "We expected that with the death of a regime based on ideology there would be an end to ideological argument. The way to democracy is through democratic instruments, not ideology." He said he "hadn't heard any successful U.S. or British politician saying they are going to build up capitalism." And, lately, of course, he's right.

Seifer explained his program for fixing environmental problems. He would do it as Vojtěch would, by passing laws. This in contrast to the government's program. "The premier is saying, 'First we have to make money to protect the environment,' " sniffed Seifer.

The Czech premier, Václav Klaus, has actually said much worse than that. "Ecology is the whipped cream on a piece of cake" is one quote attributed to him. But Václav Klaus may be as foolish as he likes and this doesn't make Pavel Seifer worth taking seriously.

"Is the ecological situation worse now than it was under the Communists?" I asked Seifer.

"Objectively, yes. In some areas it's not worsening, but only because of reducement of production," said Seifer. "There are not so many factories but more trucks and cars."

"Would the Rainbow Movement have been allowed under communism?"

"Only illegally," said Seifer. I grunted. He added quickly, "With the present government such organizations are allowed but subsidies are being eliminated, thus they are suppressed."

"Wait a minute," I said. "If environmentalism is so democratically and nonideologically popular, why do environmentalists need government money to lobby the government?"

"They need," he said, "offices, phones, and ways to send letters—a way to exist as an organization."

Or, as Václav Klaus might say, "First we have to make money . . ."

And Premier Klaus would get no disagreement from Petr Gandalovič, his deputy minister in the Section of Technical Protection of the Environment. Ivanna and I met Gandalovič for a late dinner. He was an energetic young man who seemed to be about out of energy. Gandalovič talked about what a financial and legal tangle it was trying to reprivatize the Czech Republic, trying to give everything an owner again. Each piece of property has to have a person or group of people with a direct and real interest in making sure that property doesn't get covered with soot, buried in chemicals, deforested, demolished, eroded, irradiated, or turned into a strip mine. Unless, of course, the owners want a strip mine, in which case they have to argue with their neighbors.

"The trouble with righting old wrongs is in the setting of precedents," said Gandalovič. If one problem is fixed, then everyone else with that problem wants the same fix immediately and that's expensive. For example, he said, the strip mines are being privatized, but they're hard to sell because the expropriation of surface property is no longer a matter of government-enforced eminent domain. "Now owners of mining claims must negotiate with landowners."

"In that case," I said, "um, what's going on in Libkovice?"

Gandalovič looked like a man sent to empty a bathtub with a teaspoon. "It's still under the old laws," he said. And he summed up the coordinated, collective environmental problems of the Czech Republic. "The air will blow away, but the system will remain."

"Speaking of air blowing away," said Ivanna, "we were at the dump in Chabarovice."

"Yes," said Gandalovič, "there are eighteen thousand such chemical dumps in the country. About five percent—nine hundred or so—are dangerous. To properly seal Chabarovice, to put a clay layer beneath it, would cost fifteen billion crowns [about $536 million]. The whole Czech budget is only three hundred sixty billion crowns." So, if the Czechs spent all of their tax dollars on nothing but dump repair, they could have the worst of the problem under control in just thirty-seven and a half years. "With Chabarovice we had various options," said Gandalovič, "from the highest tech to fencing and guarding with dogs."

I said, "I've got some bad news about the dogs."

6 SAVING THE EARTH

We're All Going to Die Anyway

I

The people of the United States have made enough money to protect the environment. We can do something better for nature than set dead mutts to guard the mess we made in it. We are a rich country. In America in 1991, $31.1 billion was spent on shoes, mostly by my ex-wife. Between 1980 and 1992, 5,683 new beverage brands were launched (5,685 if you count the return of Coca-Cola and the reintroduction of Perrier with the remarkable new miracle health ingredient, water). In the same period, 1,750 new pet products were offered to the public. And if one of these had happened to be Canine Green Cards$_{TM}$, it would have been a boon to the late hounds of Chabarovice.

We can afford the cost of environmentalism. And there's that 1989 *New York Times*/CBS poll where 80 percent of us said, "Continuing environmental improvements must be made regardless of cost." So we don't care if we can afford it or not. Money is no object. Great. Now what do we do?

Possibly we should spend less of that money. According to the

Environmental Protection Agency's own figures, the bill for pollution control in the United States in 1990 was approximately $115 billion. That year the average price of farmland was $668 an acre. For $115 billion we could have bought Kansas, Nebraska, Iowa, Missouri, and 16,600 square miles of Illinois. In fact, at $115 billion per annum, we could buy all the agricultural land in America in a little more than half a decade. This would give us a fine nature preserve. Of course we'd have to get all our food from Canada, so we'd be living on a steady diet of maple candies and round, funny bacon. And our cities would be pretty dirty. Like they're not already.

Or maybe we should spend all of that money and more; $115 billion is only $460 apiece. This is hard on the homeless—they have to go without crack for several days. Generally speaking, however, we can stand the charge. But should we allow government to decide how the money's spent?

The U.S. government has been a terrible steward of the environment. We don't need a nature preserve the size of four and a quarter midwestern states because the federal government already owns 30 percent of our nation's land. In the past the government used the land it owned mostly as a place to chase Indians out of. Also a lot of federal land was given away so that people like my family could have homesteads. This resulted in awful cousins downstate and other ecological problems.

Then, in the early 1970s, environmental consciousness erupted among voters, and Washington began spending piles on such things as signs with owls saying GIVE A HOOT, DON'T POLLUTE. Yet in the 30 percent of the environment that the government controlled directly, merry hell was being played.

While the rest of America was hugging trees, the U.S. Forest Service was selling them at throwaway prices and allowing clear-cutting in places where ecological damage would be extreme and reforestation almost impossible.

The Bureau of Reclamation was damming rivers, turning

scenic canyons into motorboat parking lots, and leaving salmon with no place to have sex. The electricity produced by these dams and the water collected behind them were sold at below-market prices, permitting cities to grow where cities shouldn't and allowing farmers to irrigate land they oughtn't. The land suffered salinization: The cities trembled, burned, and got covered in mudslides. And disaster relief was paid with our tax dollars.

The Department of Defense used more of those tax dollars to dump hazardous wastes on public land. There are between five and ten thousand federal-property dump sites. Having paid for them once, we'll pay for them again. In September 1991 the *New York Times* estimated that cleanup costs will be between 75 and 250 billion dollars.

Meanwhile the Army Corps of Engineers was traipsing around draining wetlands and mopping up flood plains so that if we're ever invaded, our enemies won't get their feet wet.

And the Bureau of Land Management was abetting the degradation of thousands of acres of rangeland by leasing grazing rights to ranchers dirt cheap—dirt being about all that would be left when the subsidized cattle got done hoovering welfare grass.

The Political Economy Research Center (PERC) is a think tank based in Bozeman, Montana. It is run by avid environmentalists who also possess avidity for free markets, property rights, and individual liberties. PERC has published a book, *Taking the Environment Seriously* (Rowman & Littlefield, 1993), edited by law and economics professor Roger E. Meiners and business professor Bruce Yandle. Herein is gathered the work of a number of market-oriented environmental scholars. The chapter "Environmental Harms from Federal Government Policy" was written by PERC Senior Associate Jane E. Shaw and by Richard L. Stroup, who is an economics professor at Montana State University and was the director of the Office of Policy Analysis at the U.S. Department of the Interior under Reagan. Stroup and Shaw work to discover some logic behind Washington's crap on the public weal.

The U.S. Forest Service is not, they point out, operated by people with a pathological hatred of redwoods and sequoias or by people whose brothers-in-law own the chain-saw industry. Most members of the U.S. Forest Service joined because they had a mission to grow trees. But, in order to grow trees, they need a richer and more powerful Forest Service. And, because of various laws passed by idiot Congress, the only way for the Forest Service to become richer and more powerful is to cut the trees it grows. When the Forest Service manages a forest for recreational purposes, the recreational fees go to the U.S. Treasury. But the Forest Service gets to keep a portion of revenue from logging and gets appropriations from Congress to manage land that's logged. The results are unfortunate. In the Tongass National Forest in Alaska, it costs the Forest Service $100 in access roads, environmental impact studies, and so forth to get a tree ready to be cut. That tree then sells for $2. In the real world this would be a $98 net loss. But for the Forest Service it's a $102 gain to the budget.

Students of government call such things "perverse incentives." But a little perversion in the woods would only scare the animals instead of destroying their habitat at great expense to the taxpayers. Various environmental groups are willing to pay to romp naked in national forests while leaving the trees alone. But the Forest Service is forbidden by law to sell timbering rights to people who actually like timber. If you get a government logging contract, you've got to cut the logs no matter what it costs you, the nation, or the spotted owl.

The same is true of grazing rights. Environmental groups would like to lease federal rangeland and keep that land untouched, but the Bureau of Land Management will sell grazing rights only to real cowboys. You can't just go in wearing a big hat and get a bunch of cheap land unless you mean to wreck it.

When resources are controlled by government instead of by an individual, the disposition of those resources is no longer guided by common—or any other kind of—sense. Bureaucracies have their own agendas and so do special interests such as loggers, ranchers, and, for that matter, environmentalists. Bureaucrats want bigger bureaus. Special interests are interested in whatever's special to them. These two groups bring great pressure to bear upon politicians who have another agenda yet: to cater to the temporary whims and fads of the public and the press.

For example, the elk herd in Yellowstone National Park needs culling. But elk hunts cause uproar from the kind of people who think they'd like an elk for a pet. So all summer the elk eat everything in reach, destroy the Yellowstone ecological balance, and, come winter, they gruesomely starve.

For another example, thousands of acres of federal land that aren't being ruined by the overgrazing of sheep and cattle are being ruined by the overgrazing of wild burros and horses. There's nothing indigenous about wild burros and horses and nothing exotic either. They're just farm animals that escaped from Spanish Conquistadors. But they're too cute to shoot. It's a good thing the Spaniards were more careful with their poultry, or roads all over the American West would be slick and deadly with broken yolks from herds of wild chickens.

When bureaucrats, special interests, and politicians coalesce, they form what PERC calls an "iron triangle." And what then happens to the mere individual is what happened to him in the "Black Triangle" of East Germany, Poland, and Czechoslovakia.

Nor is government mismanagement limited to the land it owns. The government also mismanages the land you own, or, rather, it convinces you to do so, the great felon here being the Department of Agriculture. DOA has been paying crop subsidies since 1927. The subsidies are production based. The more you grow of something nobody wants, the more the government pays you for growing it. Thus farmers have been encouraged to heap their land with fertilizer and soak their crops in pesticide, and damn the costs, ecological or otherwise. Production subsidies also make it worthwhile to farm marginal land, to clear woods and thickets and run the plow through swamps and marshes depriving Daffy and Bugs and Rocky and Bullwinkle of their homes. The Agricultural Stabilization and Conservation Service has made direct payments for draining wet soil, and the Farmer's Home Administration has given out cheap loans to buy the equipment to do it. And if the corn won't grow because the land's too soggy, too parched, too ugly, or whatever, there's subsidized crop insurance to make sure you don't care.

The government has another method of keeping food prices high, through acreage-reduction programs. The Department of Agriculture gives you cash for staying in bed and planting nothing. But, in order to get paid for not farming a piece of land, you have to prove that you used to farm it. So woods were cleared and swamps were drained anyway, to get money for leaving them alone later. And acreage-reduction programs also mean that whatever land is left in production will be squeezed for maximum yield and slathered with truly massive amounts of bug spray and synthetic poop.

Government subsidies can be critically analyzed according to a simple principle: You are smarter than the government, so when the government pays you to do something you wouldn't do on your own, it is almost always paying you to do something stupid.

Government improves the environment about as well as government does most other things. Government usually doesn't work. It doesn't work because it's political. People who are wise, good, smart, skillful, or hardworking don't need politics, they have jobs. The difference between the political process and an honest life is the difference between parading around waving picket signs while hollering catcalls in front of the White House and getting up in the morning to go make a living.

Government also doesn't work because of the problem of concentrated benefits and diffuse costs. Say Congress is considering legislation to give people with nose rings free Pearl Jam CDs for life. Citizens with an extra hole in their schnozzle will be phoning and faxing and E-mailing pro–Pearl Jam sentiments to their congressmen and senators. We people with normal faces will oppose the bill. But nothing very terrible is going to happen to us if it passes. It's pocket lint compared to what health-care reform will cost. So we won't bother to lobby against free CDs. We'll just wonder what happens when those people kiss and she gets her nose ring tangled in his mustache hair, and then we'll turn off the news and fix dinner.

When government does, occasionally, work, it works in an elitist fashion. That is, government is most easily manipulated by people who have money and power already. This is why government benefits usually go to people who don't need benefits from government. Government may make some environmental improvements, but these will be improvements for rich bird-watchers. And no one in government will remember that when poor people go bird-watching they do it at Kentucky Fried Chicken.

Government is not in the business of producing results. Government is in the business of producing government: passing laws, changing rules, setting up bureaucracies. This is why government is always more interested in problems than solutions. A good problem lets congressmen get news coverage for introducing high-minded and noble-sounding legislation, provides the EPA with justification for an expanded budget, and gives Al Gore a campaign speech. A good solution benefits the general public—by no means a protected species.

Government programs fail. There's no shame in this. Lots of things in life fail, as anyone who's over forty-five and has body parts knows. But government failures refuse to go away. When a private entity does not produce the desired results, it is (certain body parts excepted) done away with. But a public entity gets bigger. Activists say the program was underfunded; pundits say it was poorly structured; and Bill Clinton says intransigent Republicans stood in the way.

The Federal Water Pollution Control Act of 1972 was estimated to cost, as of the late 1970s, twenty-one billion dollars a year in government outlays and compliance expenses. A 1982 EPA study said, "The broadest statistical analysis of water quality trends found no clear nationwide improvement over the period 1974 to 1981 . . ." Robert H. Nelson, a senior policy analyst with the U.S. Department of the Interior, says, in *Taking the Environment Seriously,* "Although there have been a few notoriously dirty rivers cleaned up and some other conspicuous exceptions, the decade of the 1980's on the whole does not seem to have been significantly different."

So the Federal Water Pollution Control Act of 1972 was scaled back. Ha. "EPA is now projecting costs of more than $60 billion per year in the year 2000," says Nelson.

There is a problem with letting government buy us the things we want, such as a cleaner, more diverse, more environmental environment. The problem is worse than political, it's psychotic. The government has a deranged method of spending money. This was first pointed out by Milton and Rose Friedman in their 1980 classic text on economic liberty, *Free to Choose,* which was on the bookshelf at the Grameen Bank in Bangladesh but which not one person in the Clinton administration seems to have read. The Friedmans describe the four ways money is spent:

1. You spend your money on yourself. You're motivated to get the thing you want most at the best price. This is the way middle-aged men haggle with Porsche dealers.
2. You spend your money on other people. You still want a bargain, but you're less interested in pleasing the recipient of your largesse. This is why children get underwear at Christmas.
3. You spend other people's money on yourself. You get what you want but price no longer matters. The second wives who ride around with the middle-aged men in the Porsches do this kind of spending at Neiman Marcus.
4. You spend other people's money on other people. And in this case, who gives a shit?

Most government spending falls into category four. Which is why the government keeps buying us Hoover Dams, B-1 bombers, raids on Waco cults, and 1972 Federal Water Pollution Control Acts.

■■

If we're going to improve the environment, the first thing we should do is duck the government. The second thing we should do is quit being moral. Screw the rights of nature. Nature will have rights as soon as it gets duties. The minute we see birds, trees, bugs, and squirrels picking up litter, giving money to charity, and keeping an eye on our kids at the park, we'll let them vote.

Neither is "clean environment" a political right of humans. Rights must be free, as are the rights of speech, assembly, religion, petition, et cetera. You have the right to bear arms. You don't have the right to take a gun without paying for it.

Pollution control is not free. According to Robert Nelson, "the total social burden for environmental protection measures will be approaching $500 billion per year by the year 2000." And Nelson cites an EPA-funded study which claims that in 1990 clean air and clean water regulations reduced the American gross national product by almost 6 percent. Six percent of the 1990 U.S. GNP is enough money to provide jobs with salaries of fifty-thousand dollars to 6,651,480 unemployed people. In America in 1990 there were, by the way, 6,874,000 people unemployed.

The environment turns out to be the "luxury good" that Cato Institute's Jerry Taylor said it was. If you're unemployed, you might even think, like Václav Klaus, that "Ecology is the whipped cream on a piece of cake." Not what you want most when you're short of meat.

But our government persists in acting as though an immaculate earth were a God-given right instead of a taxpayer-purchased benefit. Says Nelson in *TTES:*

> The Clean Water Act of 1972 set a goal to eliminate all water pollution by 1985, regardless of costs. The Endangered Species Act directs that an action of a government

> agency cannot put the survival of a species in doubt, no
> matter what the burdens imposed. . . . The Clean Air Act
> of 1970 required the Environmental Protection Agency
> to set air quality standards to avoid any adverse health
> effects, again without allowance for costs incurred.

This recklessness with public funds has led to such things as the new federal hazardous-material landfill regulations. In theory, these regulations will lower the incidences of chemically caused cancers. But the Office of Management and Budget and the EPA itself calculate that twenty billion dollars will be spent for each case of cancer averted. Of course you, personally, might be willing to spend twenty billion dollars not to get cancer. But, assuming you had twenty billion dollars, how would your wife and kids feel about you spending it this way? You can hear them saying, "Dad, it's just a lump," and "Honey, who cares about a sudden change in a wart or mole?"

The Council of Economic Advisors has pointed out one EPA rule, concerning wood preservatives, that is estimated to prevent a single occurrence of cancer every 2.9 million years at a cost of five trillion dollars per life saved.

There are very moral reasons for this immoral waste. Current ecological philosophy does not regard pollution as a cost—a cost of being alive, a cost of being employed, a cost of all the goods and services man needs and enjoys. Instead, pollution is thought of as a crime, a vice, a desecration. It's easy to be rational about keeping costs down, but it's hard to be rational about committing just the right amount of sin. "Great car!" "Yeah. And we got it for a false witness, a little adultery and dishonoring mom and dad—a real bargain."

Presenting pollution as a form of sacrilege is good for environmentalists, if not for the environment. Ecological concerns are made more urgent and important by wrapping them in sacramental vestments. If it's just a dead whale, then all it does is stink up the beach.

But if it's a martyred icon . . . Well, for starters, it outweighs Jesus by twenty thousand pounds.

Nature worship allows its devotees to see themselves as something more than folks who are right that oil slicks hurt seagulls. Every time an environmentalist says a bunny is cute, he is sanctified and made holy. And Green piety is also a form of job insurance for Greens. If every bit of pollution is wicked, then, even if pollutants are carefully controlled, there will still be evil in the world.

By making the environment out to be priceless, environmentalists are—as the word says—depriving it of price, just as the Communists deprived everything of price in Czechoslovakia. "The laws of economics tell us what to expect when a zero price is attached to a scarce and valuable asset," say Meiners and Yandle in the preface to their book.

Rather than getting up on a high horse and finding ourselves faced the wrong way, we should treat ecological problems simply as problems and solve them as well as we can. The best problem solvers are individuals. Many people acting independently are more intelligent than a few people acting as a group. It is the difference between Princeton University and the Princeton University football team. Anyone who has been involved with even the smallest and most informal committee knows individuals make better decisions. A date is a kind of committee. Choosing what movie to see can be a herculean task for even the brightest couple, let alone ordering Chinese afterward.

Relying on the individual means relying on the free market. The price system is the only method by which large numbers of independent people can tell each other who wants what and how much he wants it. The news that we get from prices is an enormous real-time *MacNeil/Lehrer NewsHour* about everything everywhere. Though the fact that price is just information can be hard to swallow when you're paying your credit-card bills. The temptation is to call VISA and tell them there's a court-ordered news blackout at your house.

The free market will not work perfectly, but it will work better than most types of government regulation. The private is preferable to the public. Which is safer, your yard or a city park? Which is cleaner, your bathroom or the pissoirs of Paris? Which is more palatable, the dinner you cook or school lunch? If you're a male bachelor under twenty-five, skip the last two questions.

A pleasant natural environment is a good—a luxury good, a philosophical good, a moral goody-good, a good time for all. Whatever, we want it. If we want something, we should pay for it, with our labor or our cash. We shouldn't beg it, steal it, sit around wishing for it, or euchre the government into taking it by force.

If, for instance, we want more of an endangered species, we should do the decent thing and buy some. That is, we should pay bounties, from charitable donations or earmarked tax funds, to people who preserve that species—the same way we used to pay bounties to people who killed species we didn't want. We could pay bounties for the number of the desired creatures observed on someone's land or bounties for keeping or creating the kind of habitat the creatures like or bounties for eliminating whatever's making the creatures so rare. (In the case of whales, we'd pay Michael Crichton for Japan bashing.)

This is almost the opposite of the way the current federal Endangered Species Act works. In a paper for the Political Economy Research Center, Richard L. Stroup describes the act's provisions: "The owner must sacrifice any use of the property that federal agents believe might impair the habitat of the species—at the owner's expense. Furthermore, if the owner either harms the species or impairs its habitat, severe penalties are imposed." This, argues Stroup, is tantamount to a law requiring that anyone who discovers an Old Master painting in his attic "cannot own it but must keep it on the premises and make sure that it is not stolen or damaged; whatever the expense . . . A federal agency will check regularly to see how well the owner carries out that obligation." And Stroup asks us to imagine the fate of any newfound Leonardo da Vincis under this system. Crumple up that *Mona Lisa: The Early Years* and start the grill. How do you want your whooping crane cooked?

And that's about the way the Endangered Species Act has worked. Since 1973, when the act was passed, 632 species have been officially listed as endangered. Only 17 species have been taken off that list, and 8 were removed because they'd become extinct.

If our desire to preserve the environment is real, then we should make that preservation provide economic benefits. Some people will baby-sit nature for purely altruistic reasons, but don't bet the red cockaded woodpecker on everybody doing it. The stockholders of a big timber corporation such as International Paper Company would not take kindly to a gross excess of altruism with their savings and investments. But they don't have to. Economist Terry L. Anderson and natural resources expert Donald R. Leal, in their book *Enviro-Capitalists,* point to International Paper's fee-based recreational program as a method of fostering wildlife for profit:

> As the revenues from the program grew, IP's regional forest managers began managing their forests differently. They began leaving large corridors of trees . . . for wildlife to travel through safely. They began leaving clumps of trees uncut while younger stands next to them grew, thus creating greater age diversity. They began reducing the size of cut areas and making them more irregular in shape thereby making them more conducive to a greater variety of wildlife. . . . They began discovering new ways of protecting endangered species such as the red cockaded woodpecker.

International Paper leases land to hunting clubs and sells permits for hiking, camping, fishing, canoeing, and standing around ogling and going "awwwww" at the trees. Four million acres of IP's forests are now being managed in the above-described manner, and between 1983 and 1990 the company garnered ten million dollars in recreational revenue by doing so.

If paying people to help improve the environment is right, then so is putting an end to uncompensated takings. Changes in federal land-use rules decided by regulatory bureaucracies, rezonings conducted by legislative fiat, building permit applications that are labyrinthine of process and Methuselahean in duration . . . The result of all these is simply what the Czech coal company was doing to the villagers of Libkovice.

When we ask landowners to change—for our benefit—the way they're using their land, and that change costs the landowners money, we have to foot the bill. This is fair. It also encourages landowners to cooperate. Plus it gives us an honest accounting of the price of our wonderful and virtuous concern for nature. When we get an actual invoice for the $460 apiece that we're spending on the environment, we may decide we want a VCR instead. Then we can watch the red cockaded woodpecker's final days on videotape.

Besides paying people to create environmental goods, we should pay people to accept environmental costs such as garbage landfills. In the vast space of America there is no shortage of places to put landfills, but there is a shortage of people willing to have landfills put next to them. The answer is to pay these people. You say you don't want a landfill in your neighborhood no matter how much money you'd get? How about $250,000,000 in cash, tax-free? And all that your fellow countrymen had to do to change your mind was kick in a buck each.

Clark Wiseman, a visiting fellow at the Resources for the Future think tank, has calculated that all the U.S. municipal solid waste of the next thousand years would fit in a hole 44 miles square and 120 feet deep. That's about from Malibu to San Bernardino and from Pasadena down to Disneyland, and what a good idea.

We can pay people for improving the environment, and we can charge people for screwing it up. The easiest way to bill polluters is to put a fee or tax on effluents—the more hazardous the waste, the higher the fee. Say chlorofluorocarbons destroy the ozone layer. It's not absolutely certain that they do, but many scientists think so, and the media (and hence politicians) are convinced of it. So make the CFC fee very large: one hundred dollars per whatever unit chlorofluorocarbons are measured in, call it one hundred dollars per vowel. Manufacturers will have an incentive to reduce or eliminate CFC emissions and will be free to do so by whatever means is most economically efficient. The marketplace results will tell us whether what we're doing makes sense.

Maybe there's no good substitute for CFCs in hair spray. Maybe hair spray will go up to five hundred dollars a can. Then we'll have to decide whether to lower CFC fees to appease angry crowds of Miss West Virginia contestants, female impersonators, and other people with beehive coiffures or whether to raise CFC fees even higher to appease angry crowds of nude sunbathers who think they've got cancer.

This will be entertaining. Also, certain absurdities will be avoided. Tom Gable, chairman of the Gable Group public relations firm, represents a number of pharmaceutical companies. The proposed total ban on CFCs is causing his clients nightmares even though they produce only minute quantities of the stuff. One of the medical uses of CFCs is in asthma inhalers. "The American Lung Association," says Gable, "is worried that the inhalers could be banned before there is an adequate alternative. It is hard to imagine banning something that does so much medical good and is safe enough to be inhaled into an asthmatic lung but not released into the atmosphere!"

Most current pollution reduction is achieved—or attempted—by the "command and control" method. All industries, whether large or small, prosperous or bankrupt, vital or stupid, are forced by law to reduce the discharge of a given pollutant by the same degree even if the amount of their current pollution is insignificant. And the EPA mandates the technology by which this must be done. Thus, every new coal-burning electric power plant in the United States was forced to install sulfur dioxide–removing "stack scrubbers." But most of those power plants could have achieved the same reduction in sulfur dioxide just by burning low-sulfur coal.

The government likes command-and-control antipollution strategy because it increases the power of government. Never mind if it works. Environmentalists like command and control because effluent fees imply a "right to pollute," and environmentalists want pollution to be evil more than they want it reduced. Even businesses like command and control. For all their free-enterprise rhetoric, businesses don't like competitors any better than the rest of us do. Mining companies with deposits of high-sulfur coal think stack scrubbers are swell.

Another method of pollution control that the people who are supposed to be controlling pollution don't care for is the exercise of plain, traditional common-law property rights. If a factory spews waste onto, into, or over your land, you sue. This is what civil court is for. Of course you have to prove harm, so you'd better have a two-headed baby ready. Tort cases★ bring environmental damage into the realm of fact and of individual action by plaintiffs, defendants, and juries. Politicians don't like facts, as any campaign speech proves. Politicians don't like individual action either. Read Lenin or Al Gore. Environmentalists don't like property rights because property rights mean we have legal control over nature, and environmentalists want it the other way around. And lefty environmentalists (or "watermelons"—green on the outside, red in the middle) don't want property even to exist.

According to Meiners and Yandle, federal courts have repeatedly ruled that interstate common-law pollution suits are superseded by federal pollution regulations. And the Clean Water Act explicitly forbids these suits. Legislative control of pollution means that we have to

---

★I probably deserve to be whipped—or, anyway, subpoenaed—for suggesting an increase in tort law cases. America's civil courts are already butt-deep in ridiculous damage suits. The City of Los Angeles had to pay Rodney King millions, but just imagine what the jury award would have been if the nightstick used to beat Rodney had proven to be radioactive. However, I'm talking about broad principles of governance here. I'm being utopian. And, in my ideal world of pollution control, frivolous lawsuits would be one of the first forms of pollution to be controlled. (Besides, this is just a book. It's not something important, like a Regis Philbin and Kathie Lee show, that's actually going to influence policy.)

concentrate on theoretical hazards rather than actual damages. The results are more complicated rules and also more pollution. "Statutes," say Meiners and Yandle, "give regulators, who have no personal incentive to bring action, rather than those harmed, primary control of the environment."

Common law has its limitations. If cars are stinking up your air, it's hard to run through traffic with a lawyer, taking down license plate numbers and handing out civil complaints. And here, as in certain other highly specific aspects of life, the government has a legitimate role. When other forms of social organization are not competent to act, government can set reasonable standards by which people may behave in order not to do significant harm to other people—unless those other people are running through traffic with lawyers, in which case you should run them over.

There are, in fact, many things government can do to make the world more verdant, lush, fresh, luxuriant, flourishing, and so on. It can encourage ecological research and provide technical assistance in measuring the effects man has upon nature. It can provide the legal framework within which Americans dispute the proper uses of that natural world. It can act as a sort of insurance company and come to the aid of individuals who are burdened with enormous unforeseen costs because of national changes in mind about the environment. But the best thing government can do is get out of here.

All that federal land should be sold. If we Americans care about the outdoors as much as we say we do, we'll help organizations like the Nature Conservancy buy it. Private environmental groups in the United States currently have combined annual revenues of less than half a billion dollars—1½ percent of the national shoe bill. We're not putting our money where our mouth is because our feet are there. But even if we're lying about our love of the planet and the sultan of Brunei ends up owning New Mexico, we'll still be better off. Think what the federal government did at Los Alamos. The sultan isn't going to explode A-bombs on his own perfectly good real estate.

National Parks should be turned over to the Sierra Club, the Audubon Society, the Izaak Walton League, and their ilk. Let the do-gooders do somebody some good. Of course, they'll have to charge for it. According to PERC, visitors' fees now cover only 7 percent of the National Park Service's operating costs. Getting into Yellowstone Park costs ten dollars per week for a whole carload of bored children and exasperated parents. It's thirty-five dollars apiece to go to Disney World. Why should Actual Real Genuine World be so much cheaper to see? The *Journal of Leisure Research* (now there's a place to get hired) has determined that the average wilderness visitor is an affluent type, something we knew already since it's hard to take a city bus to most wilderness regions. If we're worried about poor kids not getting to see enough snakes and bears, the Izaak Walton League members can visit inner-city grade schools and trade tickets to Yellowstone for 9mm pistols (or pay the kids to bump off elk).

We don't want Congress for our landlord. Try calling Pat Moynihan when your toilet overflows. Even less do we want the Environmental Protection Agency or the National Forest Service or the Food and Drug Administration as our mother. The federal bureaucracy should be relieved of all regulatory power. Congress is filled with terrible people, but at least we voted for them. The people in the federal bureaucracy are—to judge by my phone calls to them—lovely folks. But I don't recall their names on any ballots. Where'd they come from? How do we get rid of them?

Democracy means that laws can be passed only by people in that democracy or by their elected representatives. Article 1 of the Constitution says, "All legislative powers herein granted shall be vested in a Congress of the United States, which shall consist of a Senate and House of Representatives." Article 1 does not go on to say, ". . . and, we almost forgot, also vested in a bunch of other people who work for parts of the government you couldn't name on a bet and whose boss is a bozo former law partner of the president's wife."

Once we have turned ourselves into a society of private individuals living in legal equality under a voluntarily constituted system of representative government, we can take the next logical step and give Vice President Al Gore an ax, a book of matches, and a bag of trail mix and tell him to go into the woods and not come back until he's built a civilization rich enough to support 250 million people in such ease and luxury that they've got time to worry about the red cockaded woodpecker.

III

Allowing nature to be controlled by our government is bad. How much worse is allowing nature to be controlled by all the other governments in the world? That is the true meaning of "Think Globally." The United Nations—having settled Serbia's hash, put the kibosh on clan fighting in Somalia, given the bum's rush to the Khmer Rouge, and turned everybody in the Middle East into asshole buddies—will now save the planet.

In fact, consider the planet saved. The UN has held a large conference on the matter: the June 1992 UN Conference on Environment and Development, or Earth Summit, in Rio de Janeiro.

The Earth Summit had to be held in Rio for the same reason that the American Association of Hose and Nozzle Manufacturers has to hold all its important meetings in Las Vegas. Rio is, um, convenient to major air travel facilities. Holding the Earth Summit in Rio had nothing to do with Copacabana or Ipanema or Brazilian women who wear bathing suits that come out of Chinese fortune cookies. According to the Rio daily paper *Jornal do Brasil,* UN Conference on Environment and Development delegates were sending twelve hundred roses a day "to the female receptionists working at the Summit." Herewith the *Jornal*'s summary of pickup styles from around the world:

> *Arabs:* "They are the most persistent."
> *Japanese:* "They are the most prudent."

Africans: "They always want to be shown Rio by night."
Russians: "Return every day to the same place but will only
      ask for a date after the fourth or fifth day."
Americans: "Like to give little presents."
Spanish: "Like to give the 'Julio Iglesias look.'"

Not that the UNCED delegates were getting anywhere. Give the "Julio Iglesias look" as they will, UN diplomats are scrawny fellows, scrawny in a paunchy fashion, also whey-faced no matter how darkly complected. They have the kind of high foreheads that make them look bald, not intelligent. And their clothes don't fit. Jacket collars gape at the back of the neck, pants cuffs flutter above ankle bones, shoulder pads end before shoulders do. These garments are cut from nubby weaves, high-gloss twills, and other extraordinary fabrics in colors such as Miata Roadster Blue. The Earth Summit was, among other things having to do with ecology, a landfill for toxic business suits.

The government of Brazil spent thirty-three million dollars to build an ocean-side convention site for the summit. Though called "Riocentro," it was located in a beach suburb an hour's drive from downtown. That way dignitaries from places like Belize and Djibouti could ride to the summit and back in high-speed motorcades with sirens going and lights flashing and motorcycle cops all around. Many leaders of Third World countries don't get a chance to do this at home except when they're on their way to the firing squad after being deposed in a coup.

Riocentro is an example of the Self-Storage Modern school of architecture, except without any secure individual spaces. Its three big buildings are really just carports in heroic scale. Immense space-frame trusses are roofed with metal sheeting, various sides are left open to the bugs and weather, and other sides are fitted with curtain walls made of raw concrete and earwax-colored corrugated steel. Thirty thousand delegates and journalists beyond number were provided with, as far as

I could discover, four bathrooms. Obvious jokes may be inserted here.

Inside the largest of Riocentro's ghastly structures, the floor space was divided by eight-foot-high partitions forming little cubicles arranged in a rigid grid system like a maze for exceptionally stupid rats. In these cubicles were all the world's governments and the brochures thereof. Some of the cubicles (Japan's) were furnished with Spartan elegance. Some (Afghanistan's) had a folding chair and a card table. Some (Japan's) were capped off and air-conditioned. Most were simply open on top. At the edge of the cubicle labyrinth was a two-story pillar bearing no map or chart or any explanation except an inscription in English reading: YOU ARE HERE.

I stopped by the Yugoslavia cubicle. The sign painted on the door had been amended with a hand-lettered MONTENEGRO. However, there weren't any fighting people inside. There weren't any people inside at all. There weren't any people in most of the cubicles. Instead, everybody was out walking around talking into portable telephones. Thousands of portable telephones had been brought to the conference, their constant *neep-neep* and *thrip-thrip-thrip* making a background noise like New Age music. Were the delegates talking to each other? They could have stayed home and done that. Indeed, if the earth can be saved with phone calls, we can all stay home. And what were they talking about? How much they love the rhino? Maybe they were calling female receptionists. "Hello, is Ivor. Am having come same place four or five days but am only asking now for date."

IV

What the delegates were supposed to be doing was negotiating various treaties—treaties that decide the temperature of the air, treaties that make trees grow, and treaties that "let the waters bring forth abundantly the moving creature that hath life." Each of these treaties having the same approximate force in law as a note passed in study hall.

Also the delegates were composing something called the "Rio

Declaration," a manifesto to be signed by everyone on earth, more or less, and containing twenty-seven such principles as: "9. States should cooperate to strengthen endogenous capacity-building for sustainable development"—a rallying cry for the masses if ever there was one—and "24. States shall . . . respect international law providing protection for the environment in times of armed conflict." As Nelson would have said at Trafalgar if he'd been more sensitive to ecological concerns, "England expects every man to do his duty. And be careful not to hurt the dolphins."

Furthermore the delegates were drafting *Agenda 21,* which (according to *Agenda 21*) "is a comprehensive programme providing a blueprint for action in all areas relating to the sustainable development of the planet." Sort of like the first five books of the Bible and with similar textual density. Compare *Agenda 21*'s "The development transition to revitalized growth with sustainability will necessitate the innovative formulation and use of pricing policies . . ." to Exodus 29.27:1 "And thou shalt sanctify the breast of the wave offering, and the shoulder of the heave offering, which is waved, and which is heaved up . . ." However, *Agenda 21* was much longer than the first five books of the Bible, more than six hundred pages of outstretched sentences full of the Latinate nouns and polysyllabic modifiers that do to prose what the UN diplomats' tailors do to dress pants. The original of *Agenda 21* being hardly readable (or portable either) the document was boiled down to an 116-page *Guide to Agenda 21,* which proved to be just as bad in a shorter way. So the *Guide,* in turn, was condensed to a 33-page "Press Summary," which . . . The UN people could probably have just kept going, producing briefer and briefer versions of prolix incomprehensibility until they had nothing left but the prolixly incomprehensible name of the UN Secretary General himself, Mr. Boutros Boutros-Ghali.

Agenda 21 says that "developed industrialized countries . . . although comprising about one-fifth of total world population, account for about four-fifths of the consumption of fossil fuel and metal mineral resources." Of course industrialized countries do that because they're industrialized and make everything in the world. But development is bad. "The globally unsustainable use of the Earth's resources has degraded the environment and generated unmanageable amounts of waste and pollution." Yet poverty is bad, too. "Economic growth is essential to meeting basic human needs and achieving acceptable levels of personal well-being." So development is good. Or, as Secretary General Boutros Boutros-Ghali put it so plainly in his opening address to the Earth Summit, "The Earth is sick from underdevelopment and sick from excessive development."

The actual meaning of *Agenda 21* is in a kind of code or cipher, the message being contained in certain recurrent words and phrases: "global imbalances in production and consumption"; "basic reduction in debt-service charges"; "It is necessary to ensure substantial positive net resource flows to developing countries . . ." In other words, "Give me a dollar."

The Earth Summit was by no means the only cosmos-rescuing activity in Rio in June of 1992. There was the Global Forum, a gathering of ecology-minded private groups. Although private groups are not called private in UN circles. They're called "Nongovernmental Organizations," NGOs. These NGOs gathered a second time at the international NGO Forum. Here, as best I understand it, nongovernmental organizations pretended as though they were governmental after all and signed treaties with each other. Meanwhile an Earth Parliament had been convened, made up of indigenous peoples from everywhere on earth. (Maybe not *every*where; I'm an indigenous Ohioan myself and didn't notice anyone squatting amid bowling trophies.) And there was also something named the Global Forum of Spiritual and Parliamentary Leaders, doing I-don't-know-what except it brought Al Gore, the Dalai Lama, and John Denver together under one rubric.

Of these, the Global Forum proper was the largest, held on a mile-long stretch of beachfront park in the shabby Flamengo neighborhood near downtown. Some 650 NGOs hired space in little stalls made from fiberglass panels roofed with canvas-covered aluminum tubing—Bauhaus versions of carnival booths. Here the NGOs exhibited their . . . wares would be the wrong word since very little was for sale . . . opinions. The NGOs ranged from reasonable—or, at any rate, predictable—types such as the Royal Swedish Academy of Sciences, the Sierra Club Legal Defense Fund, and the World Council of Churches to oddball sorts like Eco Tibet California, International Black Women for Wages for Housework, Universidade Holistica International de Brasília, and the Institute for Fusion of Law and Science. This court finds you guilty of violating the second law of thermodynamics, and you are hereby sentenced to ten light-years in prison.

The Global Forum—bannered with its unfortunate initials in Portuguese, FAG—was surrounded by a chain-link fence. Those not professionally engaged in saving the earth were charged $10 to enter. (Brazil's minimum wage is $12.50 a week.) Inside the forum there seemed to be a great deal of paper: petitions being signed, pamphlets being handed out, bulletin boards covered with notices and schedules, three different daily tabloids devoted to forum and Earth Summit events, a "Tree of Life" covered with thousands of leaf-shaped notes and letters inscribed with pledges "to make a positive contribution to the environment," and, everywhere, paperboard containers for recycling paper. Most of the booths contained nothing but printed matter, stacks of it, plus a few rather wordy posters for décor. The Permanent Observer Mission of Palestine to the United Nations had a booklet titled, "The Impact of Jewish Settlements on the Environment." Global Energy Network International (no group at the Global Forum had an uncomplex name) presented passing journalists with an *Agenda 21*–sized and very technical press kit urging all the nations of the world to connect their electrical power lines. And the Global Forum itself issued scores of press releases, e.g.:

154. [F]amous Brazilian "King of Bossa Nova," Carlos Lira, entertained with music incorporating the sounds of whales and

wolves. On cue, the audience responded with an impassioned "howl-alluya."

93. Ashok Chaudhuri, representing the Indian branch of the International Institute for Sustainable Development, declared . . . "the problem is this bloody industrialized culture."

153. Brazilian constitution provides model for international environmental law. [Brazil's government has been overthrown seven times since independence in 1822.]

Of course, printing presses and Xerox machines weren't the only means of getting ideas across at the Global Forum. Practically everyone was wearing some important message silk-screened across his or her chest and abdomen. If Martin Luther were a modern ecologist, he would have to nail ninety-five T-shirts to the church door in Wittenberg.

The material world did occasionally intrude at the Global Forum. In a special tribal area, Amazonian Indians were selling—for three times the going rate—headdresses made from brightly colored feathers of presumably unendangered birds. The Academic Council for the International Academy of Architecture (there's a handle) had a beautifully made scale model of a thing called "Ecopolis, City of the Future." It was pyramidical in cross-section—as I believe all futuristic city designs are required to be by some United Futurists trade-union work rule—but shaped like a hula hoop when viewed from above. The whole was perched on stilts above a perfectly unharmed tropical rain forest. This presumes a city where no one throws anything over railings: a city without teenagers, a city without drunks, a city without me.

And a lovely old lady from Minneapolis or some such nearly sunless place was demonstrating a "Solar Box Cooker." It was an insulated crate with a piece of glass on top and a prop-up foil-covered reflector. This device is meant to save resources and reduce pollution in the Third World. The inside of the crate will heat up to over two hundred degrees Fahrenheit in just hours as long as you don't have any clouds or night or anything. The sun was shining in Rio. A number of people were sampling weenies that had been cooked in the Solar Box. "Why, these are really *warm*," said one young lady.

Every now and then people would gather in one of the Global Forum's large, hot, and perfectly airless tent buildings and an expert or a notable would give a peevish speech. The complaints were directed against modern life in general and, naturally, against that most modern part of it, the United States.

An overfed Bella Abzug in hundreds of dollars' worth of hat denounced liberty: "The free market is one of the driving forces behind the North's exploitation of the South."

A man from a group that loves forests claimed that America doesn't love them enough. "We've been fighting to change U.S. government policy for one hundred years," he said. A good thing that it hasn't been longer or Davy Crockett would have wound up living in Brooklyn and wearing an Irishskin cap.

And soon-to-be-Vice-President Al Gore swung for the fences. He said we moderns have been seduced by the idea "that we would be capable of building in our minds a model of the world that will allow us to completely understand it." We can't, said Gore, so kiss Stephen Hawking good-bye. The senator also said, "We have to understand the insights and understandings in traditional societies and apply these." The world is balanced on the back of a large turtle, and here's to clitorectomies for all the girls. And, said the senator, "We have to commit ourselves to freedom. But freedom also has to be sustainable freedom."

I don't know what "sustainable freedom" is, but "sustainable development" was the Earth Summit's principal catchphrase. I don't know what "sustainable development" is either. However, Dr. Jose Lutzenberger, former secretary of the environment of Brazil, addressed this question. Speaking at a meeting of the International Network of Environmental Management, Dr. Lutzenberger said, "Some even talk about sustainable growth, which is a contradiction in terms—no one can grow sustainably."

Of the people who sat inside the Global Forum's tents and listened to the gripes, about half were handsome, privileged young people groomed and dressed in that affectation of homely poverty which has been with us for more than a quarter of a century now. The other half were people my age who *still* don't have a job. All seemed confident in a sort of reverse astrology. Instead of believing that every aspect of their lives was affected by heavenly bodies, they believed that heavenly bodies were affected by every aspect of their lives.

During the whole Earth Summit I did not hear a word of dissent against environmentalism. Yet the UNCED and Global Forum participants spoke as though they were a beleaguered minority. A youngish biodiversity researcher told me, "The media is bashing environmentalism." *Time* and *Newsweek* had just printed thirty-three pages of eulogy to the events in Rio, and television networks and newspapers in the United States were paying more attention to the Earth Summit than they were paying to the rest of the earth.

"What media?" I asked the researcher.

"National Review and the *American Spectator,"* he said. "It's become the fashion to attack environmentalists."

"The fashion for whom?"

"Well, Dan Quayle."

The Earth Summit activists were also illuminati, party to knowledge the rest of us don't possess. On my first day at Riocentro there was a ball-up at the Press Center. Mobs of reporters waiting for press credentials were squashed against a counter, behind which UN employees were engaged in press-credential misplacement. An earnest female correspondent from an NGO newsletter piped up: "This is what life would be like in an overpopulated world!"

No, dear, this is what life would be like in a world run by the UN. Belief in such things as the dire consequences of population pressure, a dwindling supply of natural resources, and the fundamentally exploitative nature of trade gives people reasons to join the National Wildlife Federation. These are also the reasons Hitler gave for invading Poland and Russia. "It's a war!" an overexcited Norwegian Green Party member whom I had accidentally befriended shouted at me. He was deeply committed to the environmental cause. "I tell everyone," he said, "a nonviolent war!"

V

I wound up in a dusty and rather littered corner of the Global Forum compound, looking through the chain-link fence at Flamengo Beach. The sky was clear. The temperature was in the nineties. Trim, tan Rio de Janeirans—Cariocas, as they're called—were hopping in the surf, slapping volleyballs around, and giving the long eye to women who were wasting very few of the earth's precious resources on clothes. Here the official UNCED delegates, pestering the female receptionists, had shown themselves more culturally open than their NGO colleagues. Brazil is a country where you can look at a woman's behind and not get Anita Hill and National Public Radio camped out in your front yard for the next six months. X-rated videos are for sale in the souvenir shop at the foot of the giant statue of Christ the Redeemer.

And Brazilians, in honor of the Earth Summit, had done a wonderful job of improving this already-splendid environment. They rounded up all the street kids, homeless people, muggers, thieves, beggars, and pickpockets, and then . . . and then something. "Where are they?" I asked a woman who owns an art gallery in Copacabana.

"The government has shipped them all away," she said.

"But where?"

"Oh," she said, "very far from you." Squads of soldiers in full combat gear were guarding every intersection, bridge overpass, and public park. The Cariocas were ecstatic. "You see, I have my jewelry on," said the art dealer. "And I can wear my new gym shoes—people used to be robbed for their gym shoes."

On Friday, June 12, 1992, 110 heads of state gathered at Riocentro. They were indistinguishable in dress and deportment. Where was biodiversity when we needed it? George Bush was the goat, of course, for insisting that a global-warming treaty contain something besides hot air. That is, Bush wanted nations to present practical plans for reducing the emission of so-called greenhouse gases, something which, so far, only the United States and the Netherlands had done. Everyone else wanted the global-warming treaty to have important-sounding goals that they could solemnly swear to meet. And President Bush wouldn't sign the biodiversity treaty at all. U.S. PRESIDENT SNUBS HIS NOSE AT REST OF WORLD read the headline on one Brazilian newspaper. A Greenpeace spokesman called Bush an "environmental degenerate" and said he'd "played the role of a highway robber on the road to the Earth Summit's conclusion."

The biodiversity treaty declares that if any valuable plant, bug, germ, etc., is discovered in a developing country, the government of the country gets paid for it. By this logic every time a Russian peasant has a potato for dinner, he should send money to Peru. The biodiversity treaty also promises large amounts of environment-improving cash to developing countries and lets those countries decide how to spend it. Their idea of improving the environment may be to ship street kids into the jungle or kill Kurds or whatever. These are the countries which produce, on a fairly regular basis, such national leaders as Ferdinand Marcos, Muammar Qaddafi, Idi Amin, Pol Pot, Kim Il Sung, Saddam Hussein, Augusto Pinocet, and Fidel Castro.

Fidel Castro spoke at the Earth Summit:

Forests disappear, deserts grow, thousands of millions of tons of fertile soil end up in the oceans every year. Numerous species face extinction . . .

It is not possible to blame for this the Third World nations . . . despoiled and plundered by an unjust world economic order . . .

A better distribution of the wealth and technologies available in the world would be necessary to spare humanity such destruction . . .

Let human life be more rational. Let a just international economic order be implemented.

Poor polluted, exploited, resource-depleted, population-pressured, deforested, and desertified countries. And none of their problems are of their own making. None of their problems proceed from fatuous oligarchies, wild corruption, or whimsical economic rights; from notions of personal freedom borrowed from termite mounds; or from political systems that wouldn't pass muster in a tribe of Barbary apes. None of their problems are the result of fondness for violence or sloth or of social traditions such as treating women like dogs and treating dogs like lunch. None of their problems are caused by religious zealotry, fanatical nationalism, tribalism, xenophobia, or peculiar ideas about the nature of the world such as those held by Al Gore.

According to *Jornal do Brasil,* Castro was "the most heavily applauded" of all the world leaders. "His message," said an article in the official UNCED newspaper, *Earth Summit Times,* "was for all our tomorrows: the poor more in charge of their own destinies, and the rich with the responsibility to empower them justly." This article ran under the headline CASTRO SUPPLIES A MOMENT ELECTRIC and went on to point out that UN delegates inside the conference hall applauded Castro "all the way from the podium to his seat" and that the reaction of the rank-and-file earth-lovers, who were watching the speech outside the hall on large-screen TVs, was even more enthusiastic. "Fidel was accorded a standing ovation."

We throw these bastards out the door of human liberty and back they come through the window of ecological concern. Here is old

Busy Whiskers—puffy, aging, abandoned at the altar of Marxism, a back-number tyrant and ideological bug case who has reduced the citizens of his own country to boiling stones for soup. And now he's a friend of the earth.

7 MULTICULTURALISM

Going from Bad to Diverse

|

In Fidel Castro we see ugly politics—politics almost as ugly as I've painted them everywhere else in this book. I admit to a grudge. Politics exacerbate the problems of densely populated nations. Politics cause famine. And treating environmental ills with nothing but politics is quackery. However, politics should be useful in matters political. At least you'd think so. And the attempt of women, minorities, old people, and so forth to gain influence in political systems is certainly a political matter.

Can politics help "the unempowered" better than politics help huddled, hungry folks with smog? To find out, I thought I'd go someplace where there were lots of political ideas. Not Washington. Political schemes, political deals, political scandals—in these Washington abounds. But ideas? Instead I returned to my alma mater. When I was in college, political ideas were all over the place. Of course, most of those ideas were bad (and the worst were held by me), but that was twenty-five years ago. Maybe college students have changed. Maybe college is different. Anyway "multiculturalism" is a political idea and one that is commonly espoused on campuses. I was willing to give it a fair—okay, half-fair—hearing.

To this end I found myself steering a rental sedan through a bafflement of embowered quadrangles and Georgian brick at Miami University. No, the one in Ohio. MIAMI WAS A UNIVERSITY BEFORE FLORIDA WAS A STATE read a sweatshirt in the periphery of my disoriented vision, a sweatshirt worn by . . . gosh, the kids are baggy these days . . . worn by I don't know what.

Have college students changed? For chrissake, they're college students. No. Brief inquiry. They're in their teens and twenties. Everything is beer and the self, fluttering genitals, face time, nonplused parents. Of course they haven't changed. Their clothes are bigger.

I was lost in a fog of nostalgia. No, I was just lost. I peered through the windshield saying, "Why, right there, that's where old what's-his-name . . . him and the other guy . . . that's where they . . . did something or other." I'm not much for sentimental memories. Nothing wrong with reminiscing, except I keep forgetting to do it. If you had a great time someplace, it's not as though you can go back and get it. If you had a really great time, a warrant is probably still out. And, speaking of warrants, I wasn't entirely sober. I'd been to see a couple of old professors, men who were ancient a quarter of a century ago and who now. . . . Now they were only somewhat older than I am, however that happened. So we sipped some donnish dry sherry— tumblers of straight scotch, actually. I asked them if Miami was different. They didn't remember.

Miami didn't *seem* different.

Old Miami from thy hillcrest,
Thou hast watched the decades roll,
While thy sons have quested from thee,
Sturdy hearted, pure of soul.

Not that I recalled ever hearing the school song. I went to exactly two university-sponsored events during my undergraduate career—one freshman mixer and a Martha and the Vandellas concert. I was reading the lyrics out of the 1993–94 Student Handbook, which didn't have a campus map. The handbook made a point of mentioning that new verses had been added:

> You've embraced the generations,
> Men and women, young and old,
> Of all races, from all nations,
> And your glory will be told

Lest any nations or races of young/old men/women feel the previous verses implied they were twinky-hearted or had spiritual natures cut with baking soda. The Student Handbook was printed on recycled paper. And I was, as I said, lost.

I was supposed to be going to the president of the university's house for dinner. I can't imagine why. I wasn't a distinguished student. I'm not a prize graduate. And, as for an alumnus revisiting the halls of academe to flick the Zippo of learning with a thumb callused by reality's hard strife—I don't think they wanted that from me unless Miami has a Chair in Troglodyte Dyspepsia I don't know about.

I puttered to the curb in front of the presidential residence, which I finally recognized because I was chased off its lawn for protesting the war in Vietnam by burning a copy of the *Norton Anthology of English Literature* or something like that. The president was a terrifically nice guy. He'd gathered some folks from the university—wonderful people. We were served an excellent dinner. And the next thing I knew I was on my third bottle of wine expressing my disagreement with a dean over her support for the Clinton administration health-care reform plan by yelling that she was a political criminal. *"Advocating the expansion of the powers of the state is treason to mankind, goddamnit!"*

Miami University hasn't changed. The students haven't changed. And (Is there such a thing as ex post factor expulsion? Can one get retroactively drafted?) neither have I.

II

But maybe there's been a change in the intellectual atmosphere of academia, an ideological metamorphosis, an evolution in the moral concepts which fire the imaginations of questing young minds. Nope. In 1968 the members of the faculty and student body who were sensitive and caring (called idealistic and committed in those days) were upset about the Miami sports teams' "Redskin" nickname. Twenty-five years later Miami was still debating the matter. Seventy-two speakers had signed up to argue pro or con at an open forum held in the school's largest venue, the Miami Redskins basketball arena.

The actual Indian tribe, long ago kicked out of the region, was neutral. According to the *Dayton Daily News,* "Chief Floyd Leonard of the Miami Tribe in Oklahoma said he is not making any public comments about the issue." The Miamis probably guessed that, whether varsity squads are called Redskins or Dust Kittens, Miamis themselves would not be welcome to roam southwestern Ohio again—pitching their wigwams beside calm blue backyard swimming-pool waters, hunting and gathering midst the rich bounty of Safeway aisles, and occasionally descending upon lonely condominiums and undoing the work of Hair Club for Men.

The people arguing against *Redskin* looked like my friends and I used to look. Which seemed normal, until I thought the thing over. It was a generation ago we were dressed that way. What if I'd arrived on campus in 1965 and found the up-to-the-minute kids swooning over Bix Beiderbecke and wearing zoot suits with key chains hanging down to the ground, yard-wide fedoras, and two-toned shoes?

A perky blonde stepped to the microphone and worked herself

into a pep-filled rage. "Redskin makes me cringe!" She meant the name, of course, and was denouncing racism, not confessing to it. "Just the fact that we're here to discuss this today shows that there's something wrong with the word," she piped. The hepcats in the audience greeted her logic with enthusiasm. Indeed, through the long afternoon, they greeted every aspect of their own point of view with enthusiasm, clapping and whistling, often from a standing position. They responded to the other point of view with a recently invented little noise, something between tsk-tsk-tsk and hissing. It's the noise the kind of people who own more than one cat make when the kind of people who own more than one gun light cigarettes indoors.

A nonperky blonde in a sweater which I hope was handmade because something should be done about that machine if it wasn't said, "This country is out of control with racial unrest, and the buck stops here at Miami University." Which it doesn't much. Miami is not a hotbed of racial tension, because it's about as diverse as a Bing Crosby concert.

Only 2.6 percent of Miami's undergraduates are African-American. The school has always been stocked with the pink and well-fed progeny of Ohio osteopaths and car dealers. Not that it means to be this way. Miami welcomes minorities. Miami recruits minorities. Miami has a Department of Diversity Affairs, a Student Senate vice president of same, a Voluntary Affirmative Action Plan for Black and Other Minority Faculty and offers twenty-one courses in Black Studies and a degree in that subject. But the place is way the hell out in Rube Junction surrounded by peckerwoods and briar-hoppers, and you're not allowed to have a car at school, and the nearest city is Cincin-Marge-Schott-nati, and some members of minority groups find Bing Crosby hard to dance to.

A third speaker was dressed like the young lady on the Land O Lakes butter package, although she looked about as Indian as, say, Bing Crosby. She condemned injustices committed against Native Americans—deportation, exploitation, enslavement, disenfranchisement, genocide—and, pausing for emphasis, added what she seemed to feel was the crowning outrage, "assimilation!"

A man who was definitely an Indian, with long Indian hair, a broad Indian hat, a large Indian belt buckle, who was a member of the Lakota tribe and who came from, as it turned out, Dayton, but who was very angry anyway, said, "Go out on the reservation and see it—as much as ninety-two percent unemployment, as much as forty-seven percent alcoholism rate. Why? Because white Americans think it's good to call us 'Redskins.' "

The people arguing in favor of *Redskin* looked a bit hurt. They were stuffed suits and squares, dorks and joiners, clunks, duds, and suckers of the regular Jim and Sue type. Here they were pledging their sororities and frats, keeping their grades up, working for the old man during the summer, getting pinned and engaged, paying their taxes, lugging their way through a work-a-daddy, mind-your-mommy world. They didn't quite understand how they'd caused 92 percent unemployment and 47 percent alcoholism by rooting for the old school team.

"It's a school tradition," they said.

"We've always used Redskin in a respectful manner."

"The Miami tribe hasn't objected."

"It's a school tradition."

The clunks were insensitive. A young man (in a T-shirt bearing the name of a rock band that is very moral) presented the clunks with an admonitory scenario. He asked them to suppose a certain rival college had a hockey team named the "Englishmen." A large and exaggerated profile of Queen Elizabeth II would decorate the center ice. At halftime (something hockey games don't have, but the young man didn't look like a real hockey fan, so never mind) clownish skaters would come out wearing enormous bowler hats and carrying ridiculous, oversized umbrellas. They'd skate right across the queen and do pratfalls on her face. Then the school band would strike up a bawdy parody of "Rule, Britannia" while spectators wore fake monocles and cheered in plumy accents.

This seemed like a great idea to me. But I'm a Mick. Which brings us to the ugly, pugnacious, and probably inebriated Irishman used as a mascot by Notre Dame University. It looks exactly like my Uncle Mike.

One argument not put forth at the Redskin forum was: Resolved, spending a perfectly good Friday afternoon calibrating ethnic slurs is a huge waste of time. Though, in fact, the case was being made with some force. Miami has sixteen thousand students. About three hundred people showed up at the debate, if you count the radio, newspaper, and television reporters. And you'd better count them because the next day, when I opened the *Dayton Daily News,* there was no story headed 15,700 MIAMI STUDENTS DRINK BEER, ORDER PIZZA, PUT THE MAKE ON EACH OTHER, AND WAIT UNTIL THE LAST POSSIBLE MINUTE TO WRITE TERM PAPERS. That's not the story I'm writing either. Journalism tries to have as little as possible to do with ordinary life.

Ditto for college. I was reading that Student Handbook again. The authors of this document seem to be deeply concerned about . . . about everything. The "University Statement Asserting Respect for Human Diversity," which is printed on the inside cover where the campus map should be, says, in part:

> We will strive to educate each other on the existence and
> effects of racism, sexism, ageism, homophobia, religious
> intolerance, and other forms of invidious prejudice.
> When such prejudice results in physical or psychological
> abuse, harassment, intimidation, or violence against persons or property, we will not tolerate such behavior nor
> will we accept jest, ignorance, or substance abuse as an
> excuse, reason, or rationale for it.

Jest, ignorance, or substance abuse have been the excuse, reason, or rationale for my entire existence. That aside, we have, in this oddly titled "assertion of respect" a dog's breakfast of sanctimoniousness—intellectual offal mixed into virtue stew. Invidious prejudice results from categorizing people rather than treating them as individuals. But here people are categorized exhaustively. And all categories are prejudged to be equivalent. Racism—even the vestigial, unintended, and silly racism of calling a Polish linebacker a Redskin—is unpleasant because people do not differ according to race, not in any way that matters unless they're buying Pan-Cake makeup. But people do differ slightly—and in a way I think is swell—according to sex. This difference is necessarily important sometimes, when making babies, and not necessarily important other times, when making bond trades or dinner.

Thus, racism and sexism are not identical evils. And ageism is often not an evil at all. People differ vastly according to age. A person who failed to discriminate between a six-year-old and a twenty-six-year-old would be insane in all circumstances and jailed in some.

Homophobia (which would seem to mean, in Greek, "fear of having the same fear over again") is yet another matter. What we do when we make love is, no matter how much we want to do it, voluntary behavior. It is hard to imagine a free society that considered voluntary behavior involuntary. Therefore few systems of ethics or law—other than the Miami University Student Handbook—lump voluntary behavior together with such involuntary matters as race, gender, and religion.

And Miami isn't going to put up with any intolerance of religion either, even though all tolerance of all religions would mean picking on women and persecuting gays, these being items of faith in certain creeds.

The "University Statement Asserting Respect for Human Diversity" should read:

> Civilized behavior is expected of all Miami students, or
> we'll tell the police or your mother.

I went on a search for other evidence of lousy thinking. The bookstores in the town were much larger than they used to be, though practically bookless. Floor space was mostly given over to T-shirts, sweat suits, collegiate knickknacks, and greeting cards. I don't know if this was an intellectual minus. The books for sale were few in number but frantically multiple in point of view. A volume on the papacy seemed sure to be accompanied on its shelf by copies of *Disabled Popes, Minority Popes,* and *Single Mothers in the College of Cardinals.*

I wandered into the textbook department. Some prof had put *Invasion of the Body Snatchers* on his required reading list. Nice that the university is sensitive to the needs of every group of students, including the very stupid. In the English 101 section were heaps of an unpleasantly green-colored $22.75 paperback, *Reading Culture* by Diana George and John Trimbur. A blurb on the back cover said the authors were "leading figures in the move to introduce students to multicultural thought and cultural criticism," and, "The text encourages students to recognize that different experiences of American culture depend to a large extent on class, race, ethnicity, and gender." So the entertainment violence that influences William F. Buckley to consider mayhem normative and act out murderous impulses is Wagner's *Ring* cycle. When African-Americans vote, they vote only black votes, which are tied in a bundle and sold to Ed Rollins or given to James Carville. Harps like myself have nothing but ethnic buddy-type rights under the Constitution: the right to hang out in bars and talk sports, the right to frequent the muffler shop of our choosing, and the right to whup on our kids if we catch them listening to Wagner. And, when women make a lot of money, they get paid in women dollars, which are good only for buying Margaret Atwood novels, frozen yogurt, DKNY ensembles, and hairdos like Hillary Clinton's.

Reading Culture is a pity party, an anthology of sixty-five mostly unnoteworthy writers complaining about America: E. J. Hobsbawm crabbing about rich people, Ben Hamper whining about being poor, Michael Oreskes fretting over today's kids who don't believe in anything, David Leavitt sniveling that he's one of them, Ruth Schwartz Cowan moaning how women have to stay home and do housework, Rosalind Coward grumbling that women have to get dressed and go out, June Jordan lamenting the despotism of standard Caucasian English, the inexplicably uncapitalized bell hooks bewailing the tyranny of standard Caucasian hair, Jean Kilbourne with a beef that advertising makes women feel fat, Stuart and Elizabeth Ewen having a fit that advertising exists, Frances FitzGerald griping about retirement communities, John Fiske being a sourpuss on the subject of shopping malls, Joseph F. Trimmer carping at McDonald's, Henry Louis Gates Jr. bellyaching at how television portrays black people, Walter Shapiro in a snit over everything else on TV, Kirkpatrick Sale pissed as hell that Columbus even discovered this awful place, and—for the sake of political balance, I guess—George Will with the pants seat of his Brooks Brothers suit in a wad concerning rap lyrics. And I'll bet George can't understand one word of them no matter how loud you play your car stereo under his bedroom window at night.

Few of these authors were speaking for Americans in general, even fewer were speaking for themselves personally, and all were eager to describe the querulous, grouching, bitchy divisions into which they see—or hope to see—America splitting.

And so was my head. Please, a drink. The atmosphere in the college bars was much more collegial. In an effort to bring us together as a nation, the barmaids at one tavern had set out a beer pitcher with a sign on it: ALL TIPS WILL GO TO PAY JOHN WAYNE BOBBITT'S MEDICAL BILLS. I began doing the kind of research I am made for: Strohs all 'round. I gathered from beer-oiled undergraduate chatter that things *had* changed at Miami.

When I was in school, women students, no matter their age, were required to live in dormitories unless they were married. The dormitories had hours. Freshmen girls were locked in at ten-thirty on weeknights. Seniors had until midnight or so. Now women students can do whatever they want. What they wanted that particular week was a "Take Back the Night" march where 170 women students protested how dangerous it was to be out wandering around at night.

In my day, members of opposite sexes were not allowed to go to each other's dorm rooms. Now there's twenty-four-hour visitation. There's also a sexual harassment regulation in the Student Handbook that's forty-five hundred words long. Appendix S, sections 3.2111 through 3.2123, "Policy Prohibiting Sexual Harassment," says, among other things:

> Sexual harassment encompasses any behavior directed toward an individual that is unwelcome and that serves no defensible educational purpose. It may range from sexual innuendos, perhaps even in the guise of humor, to coerced sexual relations. Examples of verbal or physical conduct prohibited . . . include, but are not limited to:
> . . . Direct propositions of a sexual nature;
> subtle pressure for sexual activity; . . .
> comments of a sexual nature; . . .
> unwanted touching, patting, hugging, or brushing
>   against a person;
> remarks of a sexual nature about a person's clothing
>   or body;
> remarks about sexual activity or speculations about
>   previous sexual experience . . . ;
> repeated requests for a personal relationship or attention, provided that the requests would not
>   have occurred except for the gender and/or sexual orientation of the complainant

Whereby Appendix S, sections 3.2111 through 3.2123, pretty well describes dating as we knew it in the 1960s.

Drugs are now tolerated at Miami, and the school, in its

bylaws, specifically forbids itself from giving drug tests to students. But you can't smoke tobacco in the student union or any of the academic buildings. And you can't have a drink until you're twenty-one.

There used to be an Ohio law allowing eighteen-year-olds to buy beer with an alcohol content of 3.2 percent or less. Oxford, Ohio, the town where Miami is located, was reputed to have the greatest per capita consumption of 3.2 beer on the planet. You could always tell Miami alumni by their enormous bladder capacities. Every day, when classes were done, the members of the student body would rush to the High Street bars, bloat themselves with watery brew and touch, pat, hug, and brush against each other. They can't do that at eighteen anymore. But they can vote.

There's nothing I like better after a long day of multiculturalization than to go out and have myself a couple of good, stiff votes. Sometimes, on weekends, me and the guys—the persons—will do some serious voting. I mean, get political. Sometimes we'll wind up so politified, why, anybody with his baseball cap on straight, we'll sue 'em for lack of diversity. We'll boycott people for going around unoppressed, pass rules against having manners or mores without Student Senate approval, and institute a collective grading system where all undergrads get the same marks as the rest of their ethnic group, unless they're Korean or Jewish or something.

▌▌▌

Miami is not a crazy school like Antioch in nearby Yellow Springs, Ohio, which has an interpersonal-relationship policy requiring students to ask explicit verbal consent for every stage of physical intimacy, from holding hands to doing whatever it is that Antioch students do with their pierced eyebrows.

> SHE: May I involve you in an intense emotional association of mutual interdependence and personal commitment which will

lead to marriage as soon as we've graduated and thence to an increasing resentment, on your part, of the burdens of domesticity, which, combined with your regret at the loss of your youthful freedoms, will cause you, at forty, to leave me for a bimbo?

HE: Can I unhook your bra?

Antioch is where we used to go to get our dope, and it seems as though they're still plenty dopey there. Miami is a sensible, traditional, liberal arts school that—me notwithstanding—has a good academic reputation. It is white bread, perhaps, but of the warm, crusty, fresh-baked kind which at the end of Jay McInerney's *Bright Lights, Big City* saves the protagonist from a life of drugs, despair, and second-person narration. The campus is beautiful. The kids are orderly and clean. It's the kind of place you'd like to send your own whelps to college.

But they should probably go into the marines. Even at Miami there is a faint emanation of metaphysical putrescence, the slightest whiff of ideas going off, cerebral hamburger that they can't quite bring themselves to feed to the dog.

I arrived on campus during "Hunger and Homelessness Week," which was sponsored by a group of student volunteer organizations called the Miami Service Network. Members of the Service Network spent all day Wednesday squatting around campus in the pouring rain. "What we are really trying to do," said a sophomore girl quoted in the *Miami Student* newspaper, "is make the Miami students more aware of the growing homeless situation in America." In case any Miami students have spent the last ten years on the moons of Jupiter or anything. And to what purpose? According to the *Student,* the drenched sophomore "said that they were not asking for involvement from people walking by . . . just simply reading the flier would suffice." Another wet coed noted, "And it's weird how people just walk by and ignore us . . . You really get a look at the world through a completely different perspective." The perspective of an idle person engaged in moronic activity.

"The Homeless Week squatters don't qualify as members of a disadvantaged or despised group," a politically conservative student said to me. "They're not real victims. But, by spending the day out in the rain, they can achieve the status of 'associate victims.' " Miami's conservatives are, themselves, organized into a group, something I also found peculiar. That conservatives feel a need for collectivity in a place as conservative as Miami is worrying even to someone as conservative as me. It's like hearing your mother has been unionized.

The conservatives have their own newspaper, the *Miami Review,* which espouses, among other causes, retention of the Redskin moniker. The *Review* maintains that *Redskin* cannot be a bigoted term because people don't name themselves after groups they don't like. Or, as I would put it, there are no sports teams called the Miami Spics, the New York Kikes, the Detroit Niggers, the L.A. Slopes, or the Dallas Drunk White Trash (though it's an intriguing notion). "Miami students have always treated their mascot with the utmost respect," said an editorial in the *Review*.

The meaning of *Redskin,* say the conservatives, has to be understood in context. Which argument is, of course, the idea behind the dreadful *Reading Culture* textbook. "Meaning is contextual" is an axiom among left-wing nitwits. The left-wing nitwits at the Redskins forum, however, were arguing that *Redskin* has an absolute meaning. And the idea that precise and unvarying values can be conveyed by language is an axiom of right-wing peabrains. So everybody's mixed up. But, if logical consistency and intellectual clarity were in fashion, none of us would be talking about any of these things anyway.

My favorite on-campus lack of logical consistency was a calendar called "The Women of Miami." It contained photographs of a dozen bathing suit–clad female students looking, to the best of their puppyish abilities, sexy. I was told this caused a great controversy between students who thought the calendar demeaned women and students who were pretty sure the First Amendment protected medium-sized bikinis. Beneath the August pinup was a "Special Note" from the student entrepreneur who published "The Women of Miami":

> To those whom we may have offended, let me take this opportunity to apologize. . . . To those who feel that they must oppose us, please get in touch with us to help understand your point of view better. We may not always agree on certain ideas, but we do respect your criticisms. We may possibly be able to use them to produce a better product.

Perhaps a calendar containing photographs of a dozen female students wearing nothing but expressions of extreme indignation. On the last page of "The Women of Miami," surrounded by a number of additional semi-spicy photos, was a "Public Service Message" printed in first-line-of-the-eye-chart type:

> Guys,
> When a woman says NO, she means NO! It takes a "Real Man" to respect the wishes of those around him. Be Safe, Be Smart, and Be Understood!

Maybe "The Women of Miami" was meant to be aversion therapy.

Not that Miami boys spend all their time planning forced coitus and engaging in the kinds of sexual harassment that requires forty-five hundred words to describe. On a bulletin board in the History and Political Science building I saw a poster for an organization called "Men Against Rape." I was going to attend a meeting. But I didn't quite trust this group. Something to do with the name, like "Rottweilers Against Mauling Toddlers"—not that one disagrees with the sentiment, but what goes on in the rottweiler discussion group?

SPIKE: Ya know when ya run up behind a toddler real quick-like an' knock 'em down with yer paw an' ya take da whole head in yer mouth an' shake it like a dish rag . . .
BRUNO: Yeah, yeah, yeah, let's not do that!

So instead I went to a meeting of SOAP, Students Organizing against Pornography. It was held on a Saturday afternoon at the campus ministry and attracted eight students. I thought SOAP might be a Christian group, but it was people dressed like former me again. And the organization was similar in its earnestness and identical in its size to Students to Act and Education for Peace (we'd meant to spell out STEAP but got "Educate" and "Act" backwards) founded by Dusty, Sally, Earl, and myself in 1968.

The members of SOAP were nice kids, soft-spoken and not at all unwelcoming to a male grown-up with a reporter's notebook and, probably, a copy of *Behind the Green Door* in an unmarked videocassette case at the back of his sock drawer. They told me they were definitely opposed to censorship then gave me a thick package of photocopied information which contained a newspaper article about the Canadian Supreme Court ruling that pornography can be banned because it harms women. Also included was an indignant excerpt from *Against Our Will* by Susan Brownmiller:

> Liberals . . . fervidly maintain that the hatred and contempt for women that find expression in four-letter words used as expletives and in what are quaintly called "adult" or "erotic" books and movies are a valid extension of freedom of speech that must be preserved as a Constitutional right.

Much of the rest of the material was culled from *Playboy, Cosmopolitan,* and *Sports Illustrated* swimsuit issues—what used to be quaintly called "the good parts." At the end of all this was a page titled "Individual

Action," among the suggestions for which were "Read books, pamphlets, articles on the subject of pornography"; "Sit through a whole programme of rock videos, particularly the late night variety"; and "Look at pornography in all its forms and start a collection of the items which most offend you." I'm sure this was meant to be less fun than it sounded.

I asked the SOAP members if their opposition to pornography didn't put them in the same—I didn't want to say "bed with"—basket as Pat Buchanan. They looked at me with grave exasperation. "He's worried about obscenity. We're worried about *exploitation*," said a boy. "We don't see anything obscene about sexuality," he continued. "We think it would be all right to show a movie of sexual intercourse to school children—if the bodies weren't contorted, if you weren't focusing on certain body parts."

"I guess," said a girl, "one of the big differences is profit motive." True, it would be hard to get really rich showing a movie of sexual intercourse to school children, though I'm sure the kids would cough up whatever they had in the way of lunch money and bus tokens.

The main event of the SOAP meeting was showing not exactly a movie of sexual intercourse, but a video tape about prostitution. The tape had been made by a Milwaukee organization called WHISPER, a laborious acronym standing for something like "Women Having Been Involved in the System of Prostitution Engaged in Revolt." The beginning of the video was devoted to Hollywood film clips depicting prostitution as glamorous, exciting, or funny. A narrator said it wasn't. Then came prolonged interviews with ex-prostitutes who told vivid stories about the remarkable number of truly horrible things that had happened to them, none of which were their fault. Why, the narrator asked, had they become prostitutes: "It was something put on me by the dynamics of this society," said one. "Pimps taught me, society taught me, the neighborhood taught me, men in general taught me," said another. What should be done? An ex-prostitute said, "We need support systems, legal systems, health systems, education, money, housing, help with child care." And don't we all. The video ended with a plea against legalization. "All sex with prostitutes is abuse," said the narrator.

After the video there was a discussion period. One boy said, "I kind of think prostitution should be illegal because all sex with prostitutes is abuse." A girl told a story about somebody from a sorority who came to a SOAP meeting and was so upset by the way sexual exploitation turns people into commodities that the sorority member decided never to go to Chippendale's again.

Another girl said that prostitution should be illegal because prostitutes weren't really free, the same way pornography isn't really freedom of speech the way liberals say it is. (Liberal, apparently, is just as bad a word now as it was when I was in college.)

"Our whole liberal Constitution is based on individual rights," said a third girl with disgust. "Individual rights overlook a lot of social reality."

It was suggested that they send out for pizza (SOAP receives university funding). "How many are vegetarians?" asked the first girl. All eight kids raised their hands.

IV

I spent a few more days at my old school, talking to student associations, sitting in on classes, hanging around like a goof.

I went to an Introduction to Black World Studies class. In an ironic marvel resulting from Miami's lack of diversity, the class was integrated. It probably couldn't have been filled if it weren't. The students had a long conversation about poverty, all of which was deterministically described, as though poorness were a kind of prejudice exercised against poor people. There was a good deal of fumbling with racial terms, among white and nonwhite students both. No one seemed exactly sure whether or when to say "black" or "African-

American." How much better if we just called each other by our names.

Another discussion involved *Huckleberry Finn.* The book shouldn't be banned because Huck called Jim a nigger, everyone agreed about that. Everyone agreed *nigger* should be understood contextually, although everyone also agreed *Redskin* shouldn't. A hundred years is a long time. People were different back then. I guess the argument of contextuality is that anything is okay as long as it's done by people who are sufficiently unlike you. No one mentioned the passage in the book where Huck, who believes slavery is God's will, decides to spend eternity in hell rather than turn Jim in. (Not to be partisan, but Huck's combination of fearless individualism and abysmal ignorance makes this one of the great conservative Republican moments in American literature.)

I went to a government class, also. There a young man said he thought it was unfair that presidents of corporations make so much money while other workers make hardly any. Doubtless this *is* unfair. But corporations have shareholders, boards of directors, employees, unions, and customers who are free to vote, fire, quit, strike, and not buy things if they don't like the corporate pay structure. Who will take these various individual freedoms away and to whom will the collective power of deciding what's fair be given? The young man wasn't sure. "But it's unfair," he said.

At the offices of the *Miami Student,* the editors described an agonized debate among themselves as to whether to publish an advertisement from an organization that claims the Holocaust didn't happen. First the editors thought they should run the ad because this group had a right to be heard. Then the editors decided they shouldn't run the ad because other groups had the right not to be defamed. It never seemed to occur to the editors to just throw the thing away because it was a piece of shit.

In an honors program seminar a student from India told me the purpose of government is to level the inequalities between groups. He said that government power is good because it allows a larger group, the masses, to have more power than the small groups who own everything and run everything. Then he said that the socialist government of his country has been very successful in leveling these inequalities and that he had seen worse poverty in the United States than he had seen in India (in case anyone believes the innocence of youth bestows a special acuity of perception).

Was anybody, I asked, worried about an increase in government power? A member of the campus Young Republicans was. He said that making the government more powerful to increase the freedom of the individual was oxymoronic. Though he didn't finish the sentence by saying "almost as oxymoronic as 'Young Republican.' "

An African-American said government power was vital because prejudice still exists. "My parents are middle class and I come from a mixed neighborhood, and I still feel prejudice all the time." I'm sure he was telling the truth, but the U.S. government is an institution that wrote human bondage into its Constitution, enforced slavery laws until 1865, and then approved and encouraged legal descrimination according to race right up to the moment the Civil Rights Act was passed more than a century later. Yet I didn't meet a single black at Miami who was wary of legislative might. (Though, as I mentioned, there weren't exactly lots of blacks to meet.)

Said one African-American young lady who had her own highly individual talk show on the student radio station, "Maybe group power is better than no power at all."

V

That's the theory of minority empowerment. In the fall of 1992 I went to see multiculturalism in practice in former Yugoslavia. There all manner of diverse cultural groups were fully empowered—with guns.

I watched as Serbian Chetnik nationalists tried to take the village of Golubic from Bosnian-Herzegovinian Muslims. The unspellables were shooting the unpronounceables.

I was in a slit trench on a hill behind Bosnian lines. Golubic is—or, by now, perhaps, was—a trim group of tile-roofed stucco houses set in little gardens along the Una river. A rail line ran beside the riverbank, with engine and freight cars blown up on the tracks. The Una was the shade of blue that children color rivers, and its waters were speckled with rapids like dabs of white enamel. The afternoon was without wind or cloud. No leaf turned or branch swayed along Golubic's tidy lanes. The place seemed to be a miniature of itself, and the war, a war on a model-train layout and probably as meaningful.

I had a perfect view of the fighting, except there was nothing to see. High-power weapons and high-speed fire scatter modern soldiers, and camouflage and smokeless explosives render those soldiers invisible. If artists still painted pictures of battles, a battle would look like an ordinary landscape with a lot of small pockmarks and some large, charred holes. Nor is there "battle din" anymore. No trumpet calls or rallying cries or even shouts and screams could be heard in Golubic, just desultory gunfire. The putter of a machine gun would echo between the house walls. Then a pause. Then some answering thumps and pops. The Serbian artillery was a couple miles away. I could hear it go off. Later I'd hear an explosion, but usually I couldn't see where. Sometimes a shell would whistle overhead. Now and then a puff of dust would rise in the valley but with the sound of impact so delayed that cause and effect seem to have been disconnected. A few rifle shots were coming in my direction, I guess. Flying bullets don't in reality, make noise. Though once in a great while I'd hear the adventure-movie sound of a ricochet in the rocks nearby.

Golubic is in a corner of northwest Bosnia known as the "Bihać Pocket," a Muslim enclave some forty-five miles in circumference containing 320,000 people who were being shelled by Serbs. To the east and south of Bihać were the rebellious Bosnian Serbs who controlled two-thirds of Bosnia. To the west and north were the rebellious Croatian Serbs who controlled one-third of Croatia. The Muslims were surrounded. But, then, so were the Serbs. Beyond the Croatian Serbs were Croatian Croatians, and beyond the Bosnian

Serbs were more Bosnian Muslims. Thus it was across the map of ex-Yugoslavia: concentric circles of combat, murder, and rapine.

I drove to Bihać with London *Times* reporter Ed Gorman, a television reporter I'll call Tom Lamson, and a Croatian translator, Kadi, who pretended to be Serbian when we were stopped by Serbian soldiers. It was easy for Kadi to pretend to be Serbian because Serbs and Croats are so much alike that the only way they can tell each other apart is by religion. And most of them aren't religious. So the difference between Serbs and Croats is that the Serbs don't go to Eastern Orthodox services and the Croats don't attend Mass. And the difference between Serbs and Muslims is that five times a day the Muslims don't pray to Mecca.

On the fifty-mile drive from Croatian-held territory into Bihać five kinds of armies had set up seven checkpoints. In the very middle of these was the United Nations Protection Force, UNPROFOR. Most UNPROFOR troops come from nations that don't normally teach lessons in civic order to Europe—Jordan and Nigeria, for example. In this particular sector the UN soldiers were from Czechoslovakia, which at that time was itself disintegrating. The Czechoslovaks doubtless wished to be home shooting each other instead of here unable to shoot anyone. UN peacekeepers aren't allowed to fire their weapons unless they come under an attack so severe that they're probably already dead. What UNPROFOR is protecting isn't clear. Certainly not itself. The UN checkpoint was on a hillock with no cover, exposed in every direction and within a Daisy air-rifle shot of both Muslims and Serbs. The Czechs had AK-47s and a formidable-looking armored car. But their helmets were baby blue and the armored car was painted toilet-bowl white. The Czechs occupied a commedia dell'arte military outpost. They were armed harlequins and scaramouches carrying out the UN's send-in-the-clowns Yugoslavia policy.

Inside Bihać was another UN group, a six-man military observer team. The officer in charge was testy. He'd been under fire for seven weeks. "It's been quiet today," he said. There was an explosion several blocks away. "Right on cue," said the officer. We tried to ask him about the strategy of the civil war. Were the Serbs trying to occupy Bihać or neutralize it? Was the siege a bargaining ploy, something to be given up so Europe would turn a Neville Chamberlain eye on a partitioning of Bosnia? Would the Bosnians . . . "I've given up trying to figure out why. I just report," said the officer. The UN observer team's mission in Bihać was to talk to the Serbs by radio phone and arrange a cease-fire, the officer said. But the Serbs weren't returning his calls. "Sitting here, getting shelled, waiting for the phone to ring," he said, "that about sums up our situation." The observers had a logbook recording the assaults, bombings, and artillery attacks on the area. Each page was ruled in vertical columns: DATE, TIME, LOCATION, DAMAGE, CASUALTIES. The columns headed ACTION TAKEN BY THE UN were completely empty.

Bihać proper has a population of forty-five thousand, plus refugees. Farms butt against the business district, and beyond the farms is a spread of outlying villages such as Golubic, three miles away. The villages and the town have yet to grow together in the modern fibrosis of roadside commerce. Bihać looks cute to American eyes, as if built in the three-quarters scale of Disneyland's Main Street. The architecture is worth a picture postcard—vaguely antique and Palladian of aspect, though not much of it predates New York's Plaza Hotel. The atmosphere is generalized European. Bihać could be in Austria or Bavaria or Tuscany or, for that matter, in the new Euro Disney theme park in France. The mosque seemed out of place. So did the artillery damage.

The civilian response to the shelling in Bihać was appealingly civilian. All the windows in the center of town were sandbagged, but the sandbags were made from designer pillow cases in paisleys and plaids and bold geometric prints. A protective barrier around the Bihać Motel had been built out of old refrigerators filled with sand.

Bihać had been under siege since April. Casualties among

civilians had been fairly light to date: 315 dead and 1,500 wounded. The farmers in the Una valley were still getting in crops. Factories still operated. Red Cross and UN relief convoys were making it through. Everybody in Bihać said Bihać couldn't survive the winter, but nobody talked about surrendering. All the shade trees had been girdled and would be dead and ready to cut for firewood by the first snowfall. A little bit of ammunition was arriving on night flights from Croatia. Mortar shells were being manufactured in local machine shops using shotgun shells for detonators and explosives scavenged from bombs left behind by the Yugoslavian air force. The land mines looked home-made, too—rusty metal objects the shape of Mallomars and the size of hub caps with precarious spring-mounted trigger mechanisms on top. The Bosnian soldiers set rows of these across the highways and would boot them aside to let our car pass—a kind of grown-up kick-the-can, or maybe kick-the-bucket.

Gorman, Lamson, and I drove to the outskirts of Golubic. A few shells were falling, but it was hard to say how close. The locals weren't diving under things, though maybe they were fatalistic types. We had flak vests. But wearing a flak vest only makes you realize how much of a man there is besides his middle. The areas of my body that I like the best weren't covered at all. Get a flak vest, and you immediately want flak briefs and flak mittens and flak socks and flak bag to stick your head into.

A Bosnian soldier led us up a farm road to the trench above the fighting. He was wearing a Yugoslav National Army uniform with a little blue ribbon tied to his left epaulette to show he was in the Bosnian forces. The road ran along the ridge line behind a hedge row. The Serbs held the other side of the valley. Years ago TITO had been spelled out in painted rocks on the hill over there. The enormous letters were still faintly visible. The four of us trotted in a crouch—the soldier nimbly, the three reporters in the manner of circus elephants and making the trumpeting breath noises of chain smokers. Running in a flak vest is like going for a jog with your box springs. The vest weighs thirty pounds and is made of solid Kevlar plates which ring like cheap dinner dishes when you rap them with your knuckles. The vest front is formed in one smooth carapace and is not meant to be worn over a whiskey gut. I know why there are no fat turtles.

Every couple hundred yards there was a gap in the hedge, and here we'd have to run across one at a time. We'd pull up in a crowd before the opening, politely trying not to be the third or fourth to go. The theory is that snipers don't see the first couple of guys in time to shoot.

Generally it's not a good idea to wear Banana Republic–type khaki journalist clothes in a war zone. You might look too much like something that's supposed to be shot, such as a journalist. But that day, running across the hedgerow gaps in my white ducks and madras shirt, I felt almost as dumb as I looked.

Gorman, Lamson, and I spent all afternoon in the slit trench, peering through the shubbery at the indiscernible mayhem in Golubic. At one point a haystack caught fire. Later a couple of stray pigs wandered down a street. And an hour or two after that, in the middle of a fusillade, a farmer left his house and ambled over to his barn. Except for various explosions, this is all we saw. But we weren't bored. Violence is interesting. This is a great obstacle to world peace and also to more thoughtful television programming.

We spent the night at the fridge-fortified motel. It was a splendid fall evening with amber light on the horizon blending off into cobalt blue around a waning moon and air as cool as clean sheets (something the motel didn't have). We stood outside drinking the local beer, leaning against the refrigerators, and listening to the shells hit around town. The cars on the street drove by fast, keeping their lights off so as not to attract snipers. When it was dark we went into the motel bar and ate goulash by candlelight. "When there's electricity, there's no water," said the waitress, "and when there's water, there's no electricity." We commiserated. Life must be very difficult. "It's hard to make espresso," she said.

VI

Zagreb, the capital of Croatia, is even more of an ordinary European place than Bihać. The driving is just as frantic but the cars aren't being shot at. The service is mediocre but due to socialism, not siege. There is an old town of regulation charm, a hilltop cathedral inspiring the standard awe, and the usual handsome public square with a statue of a brave dead guy where you'd expect it to be.

You don't see many soldiers in Zagreb, not as many as you saw in peacetime Eastern Europe under communism, although the soldiers you do see are in combat fatigues, not dress uniforms. Some of the snapshots displayed in the instant-photo store windows are from the front—groups of men arm in arm next to something blown up. A few buildings have their windows Xed with masking tape as though some giant had won a game of tic-tac-toe solitaire. At the newsstands the gun magazines are on the front racks. Those are all the signs of war in Zagreb, and the fighting is only thirty miles away. Maybe Europeans have greater sangfroid than Americans. On the other hand, there's a lot of fighting in Detroit and things are pretty quiet in Bloomfield Hills.

In the evenings in Zagreb everyone goes to the cafés that line the steep streets near the cathedral. The cafés are chic, some are even decorated in that frenzied Parisian modernism with chairs for assymetrical, monopode life-forms and bathrooms where you can't tell the urinals from the hand dryers. Numerous young men of military age were sitting around in fancy jeans and hip, vomit-colored sweaters. I asked Kadi the translator whether these guys felt any duty to join the Croatian army. "No," she said.

It is a peculiar feature of the contemporary era that a large portion of our horrors are optional. A couple of days later I was on the Bosnian border in Slavonski Brod, a Croatian city being shelled by the Serbs. I was in the Arcade Bar drinking in the middle of the day with the twenty-six-year-old owner, Vinko. A lean-to made of timbers as thick as railroad ties shielded the front window. Vinko wore a diamond stud in his left ear and pants with enough pleats to make a concertina. Some music more current than I am was on the stereo. "War makes no sense," said Vinko.

"There's no pressure on young men to go fight," said a girl at the bar.

"I'd go fight if everyone else would go," Vinko said.

I'd talked to a soldier in Bihać, a captain in the Bosnian army who was from Serbia and not Muslim. He had been in the Yugoslav Federal Army. He said he sat out the war in Slovenia and sat out the war in Croatia and sat out the first part of the war in Bosnia "until Bosnians decided if Bosnia was just for Muslims. When they said it was for everybody who would fight, I joined." Then he told a virulently anti-gypsy joke.

As the war repels a certain number of Yugoslavs, so it attracts a certain number of foreigners. War is a great asshole magnet. *(Ipse dixit.)* The government press office in Zagreb was full of chirpy volunteers from places like Cleveland, Ohio. College-age children of Croat emigrants, they were skinny, Gap-clad, salon-tanned citizens of a 90210 planet that is in some other solar system than gory Balkan peasant feuds. Nonetheless they were willing to come back and help Yugoslavia destroy itself.

A blond Bosnian guerrilla fighter from Las Vegas seemed to live in the bar of my hotel. He wore steam-ironed battle dress with an ascot and a beret. His hair was combed into a ducktail. He told a lot of war stories, carried maps to illustrate them, and claimed he was about to lead a supply convoy into central Bosnia. He'd be leaving very soon, as quickly as possible, any day now. In the evenings I'd hear his voice above the tavern din, "Did you see me on *Good Morning America?*"

A supposed freelance journalist cornered Gorman, Lamson, and myself one night. He'd been shot in the leg. In Sarajevo. Just a few days ago. "In these very jeans." His Levi's were, indeed, torn at the knee. He'd had quite a lot of other adventures in Sarajevo. And before that he'd been in Lebanon. He'd had his throat cut and been thrown down a well there. Or was it shot and pitched off a building?

Many of the other soi-disant journalists had had no previous experience at all. I met one photographer who was just out of college and on assignment for an avant-garde Swiss art magazine named *NKKKK* or *XOX* or some such. He'd driven his daddy's car, alone, into Serbia, across Croatia, down into the middle of Bosnia, and back out again. He looked twelve, which is all I can think of to account for his not being entirely dead.

Mixed with the liars and greenhorns was the usual war-side crowd of UN bumf-shufflers, international aid agency deadwood, and other people who tangle up humanitarian assistance and get in the way of charitable help, plus the shills for peace—Greens, Buddhist monks, members of U.S. congressional fact-finding missions, and, of all things, an Iranian human-rights group.

There's another kind of person who comes to a war, though not often enough. Ed Gorman and I met him at a UN checkpoint, standing beside a tractor-trailer with vast red crosses painted on the side. His name was Mick Rhodes and he was waiting for some fighting on the highway to end so he could deliver a load of food and medical supplies to beleaguered Muslims. Rhodes was a Yorkshireman, a long-haul truck driver by trade, as wide as he was high and with a serious belly. He had any number of tattoos, hair as short as Sinéad O'Connor's, and, across the bridge of his nose, a scar shaped exactly like half a broken pint mug. Mick Rhodes looked as much like a British soccer hooligan as it's possible to look without having a throttled Juventus fan actually in your mitts. He'd been listening to BBC radio back in Yorkshire and heard an interview with a Yugoslav Red Cross official who said drivers were needed.

"They were asking for drivers to cross the lines," said Mick, "because they can't use their own guys. That's why we're all expats." He motioned to some fellow drivers, every one of whom looked like he could clear the visitor's seats at a World Cup match with a sidelong glance. Mick's company had given him six months off, and here he was. "I'm away from home ten weeks at a time normally," he said. "The only difference here is that this time I'm getting shot at as well." I asked him which was worse, that or the road traffic in Turkey. "Turkish traffic," he said. He had a wife and six kids at home. His wife was a bit nervous but "knew this was what I wanted to do." Had he ever done anything, any volunteer things, like this before? asked Gorman. Mick laughed that off. No, not him, he said, that is, not counting a few loads of donated food he'd delivered to Romanian orphans during the civil war in that country.

VII

Gorman and I went for a Sunday drive in the pokey Croatian countryside. The land north of Zagreb is hilly but well-populated, as clean as Switzerland and as dull as Idaho. Prosperous, compact, and photogenic farms cover the slopes. Heidi and her dotty granddad could have burst forth from any one of them, although nothing that exciting happened. Ed thought the towns were "eerily quiet," but Ed has never been in Boise on a Sunday. Occasionally we'd see something exotic, such as a castle, but always with a homey touch like the graffiti on the battlements of Ptuj Grad: LED ZEPPELIN, DOORS, JANIS JOPLIN.

We ran into the border of Slovenia on a two-lane country road in the middle of nothing. Here were a pair of prefabricated metal buildings of the cheaper kind, looking like they'd come from the Ikea Home Border Post store. The border guard had to lock up his kiosk and crossing gate and unlock his office and sit down and do ten minutes of paperwork and three minutes of passport stamping to give me my Slovenian visa. Meanwhile, tractors and farm wagons took an unpaved detour around the checkpoint.

Inside Slovenia everything is identical to Croatia, except that the money and flags have the Slovenian coat of arms on them, as do various posters, bumper stickers, baseball caps, and T-shirts. These appear to be manufactured by the same company which makes the sweatshirts, ashtrays, dish towels, scarves, and decorative ceramic wall plaques that have the Croatian coat of arms on them in Croatia. Ditto for Bosnia. And ditto, no doubt, for Serbia, Montenegro, Macedonia, Kosovo, and whatever other pieces this country is falling apart into. There may be a dark capitalist conspiracy behind the war in Yugoslavia but it's led by the world's tchotchke industry, not the international arms cartel.

We were back in Croatia twenty miles later and had to go through another complete set of border formalities and currency exchanges. Ed asked for imported beer at a roadside café. "Well," said the proprietor, *Slovenian* beer is imported now." Next we stopped at Kumrovec, Tito's birthplace. Kumrovec is a supposedly authentic restoration of a nineteenth-century Balkan farm village, done up in precious rusticity for the sake of Eastern-bloc and nonaligned-nation tourist visits—a Marxist peasant hero's version of Colonial Williamsburg. Nobody was there. An extremely bored tour guide rushed out and showed us around in several languages we didn't speak. The souvenir shop was closed. The guest book in the Tito homestead was nearly devoid of recent signatures. One man had printed, in large, slashed pen strokes, VUKOVAR!—the name of a Croatian city devastated by the Serbs. But whether this inscription was a message of Titoist resolve, a plea to Tito's spirit, or a curse on Tito, I couldn't tell. At any rate, ex-Yugoslavians weren't flocking to Kumrovec in gratitude for the thirty-five years that Tito spent keeping them from killing each other.

The way Tito kept Yugoslavs from killing each other was he did it for them. This is the same technique used by the Romans, Byzantines, Ottomans, Austro-Hungarians, Nazi Germans, and everyone else who's had the misfortune to rule the Balkans. (*N.B.* to UN: Nobody's had any success with wearing nursery colors and not shooting back.) The locals have to be provided with an ample supply of new grievances, otherwise old grievances come to the fore. In Tito's case, one of the old grievances was Tito.

Although Tito himself was of mixed Croat/Slovene/son-of-a-bitch background, his World War II Partisan troops were mostly Serbs. In 1946, 100,000 anti-Tito Croat refugees were handed over to Tito by the ever-admirable British. Tito's Partisans then killed something between 40,000 and all of them, with the usual number of women, children, and old people included. Of course, the Partisans didn't do this for a lark. The Croats, under raving nationalist Ante Pavelić, had established a Nazi puppet state in 1941 and killed as many as 350,000 Serbs.

Tito tried to eliminate Balkanization in the Balkans by proscribing the nationalism of Serbia, Slovenia, Croatia, Bosnia, Macedonia, and Montenegro while, at the same time, carefully apportioning the number of government and Communist Party jobs given to Serbs, Slovenes, Croats, Bosnians, Macedonians, Montenegrins, and whatever the rest of the people in these parts call themselves. Everyone was supposed to be a Yugoslavian ("South Slav") and get together and sing one national anthem, "Hej, Sloveni" ("Hey, Slavs"). This worked about as well as you'd expect a country with a national anthem called "Hey, Slavs" to work.

Now in the bookstores of ex-Yugoslavia, you can buy maps showing—with pie graphs, color lithography, and percentages worked out to the third decimal place—precisely how many people of each ethnic group live exactly where in this place that used to be a country. And in a Zagreb souvenir shop I saw an Ante Pavelić poster for sale, his portrait embellished with cartography showing the quite extensive boundaries of "Greater Croatia 1941–1945."

You mustn't ever ask the Yugoslavs why they're fighting. They'll tell you. And there's no straightening it out. If you look at a topographical map of the Balkans, you see nothing that would serve as a natural boundary and no area—no plain, valley, coastline, or mountain fastness—coherent or extensive enough to put a boundary around. It was a confused region before nations or even people existed—not big enough to be a subcontinent, too big to be a peninsula, wrinkled, creased, puckered, the cellulite thigh of Europe.

To this bad hash of terrain came a worse omelette of population. The Balkans separate Asia from the West, divide the steppes from the Mediterranean, lie athwart the road from Baltic ice and snow to Adriatic topless beaches. Most of the roving bands, nomadic tribes, pillaging hordes, and migrating populations of history have passed through the Balkans. Every time they did, they'd tell their most objectionable members to go camp around the corner. Then the band, tribe, horde, or population would sneak off.

The Christians hate the Muslims because Christians were peons under the Ottomans. The Muslims hate the Christians because Muslims were pissants under the Communists. The Croats hate the Serbs for collaborating with the Communists the same way the Serbs hate the Croats for collaborating with the Nazis, and now the Bosnians hate the Montenegrins for collaborating with the Serbs. The Serbs hate the Albanians for coming to Yugoslavia. Everybody hates the Serbs because there are more of them than anyone else to hate and because, when Yugoslavia was created in 1918 (with the help of know-it-all American President Woodrow Wilson), the Serbs grabbed control of the government and army and haven't let go yet. And everybody hates the Slovenes, too, for getting out of this civil war after only ten days.

It's hard to come back from the Balkans and not sound like a Pete Seeger song. Even those of us who are savagely opposed to pacifism are tempted to grab the Yugoslavs by their fashionably padded shoulders and give them nonviolent what-for: "Even if you win, you assholes, all you've got is *Yugoslavia!* It's not like you're invading France or something."

Yugoslavia's ethnic wounds are also, unfortunately, infected with idealism. There's a surplus of intellectuals in the region. Yugoslavia, like the rest of Eastern Europe, has more artists, writers, and teachers than it has art, literature, or schools. In the resultant mental unemployment, idealism flourishes.

Idealism is based on big ideas. And, as anybody who has ever been asked "What's the big idea?" knows, most big ideas are bad ones.

Particularly in Yugoslavia. First, there is the bad idea of nationalism; that every little group of human twerps with its own slang, haircut, and pet name for God should have a country. Then there's the bad idea of what the government of that country is supposed to do: Kill everybody whose hair looks different. And finally there is the worst idea of all, a belief common to the benighted people in underdeveloped areas everywhere from the Bosnian hills to Miami University: that nationhood is a zero-sum business. The thing that makes Croatia rich makes Serbia poor. But Japan is powerful without natural resources. Singapore is important without physical territory. And Luxembourg wields enormous influence and barely has people. Modern nations do not triumph by conquering territory or dominating strangers. War doesn't work anymore. Rape and slaughter may get Serbia on the evening news, but, from the point of view of becoming major players upon the international stage, Serbs would be better off selling Yugos.

VIII

Between Zagreb and Belgrade the Serbs and Croats fought their war on the turnpike. It's an ordinary-looking toll road with guardrails, median strips, service plazas, and long, straight lanes of pavement. The guardrails have been crushed by tanks, the median strips dug up for trenches, the service plazas reduced to ruins, and the pavement gashed with shell holes. The Croatians still give out toll tickets at one end of the road, but the tollbooths at the other have been blown to pieces. Ed Gorman and I drove ninety miles east on this thoroughfare to Slavonski Brod. There was no other traffic, just an occasional UN blue hat or Serbian Chetnik waving us over to check our papers. The highway runs down toward the Danube through the flat, open country of the Sava river valley. The scenery, except for tile roofs and Lombardy poplars, is exactly midwestern. It made me feel at home to be driving on an American-style road through an American-style landscape, and then see war damage as good as the set for any Hollywood movie.

Someday, no doubt, the various constituent parts of America will become "empowered" the way Serbia and Croatia are. Someday Aryan Nation, NOW, the VFW, Act Up, the AARP, Native Americans, Right to Life fetuses, people with Hispanic surnames, the blind, the deaf, the rest of the differently abled, Pat Buchanan, Students Organizing Against Pornography, and Spike Lee will have their dreams come true. The great thing about making the drive to Slavonski Brod is that now I know what America will look like when it happens.

Slavonski Brod is a city of seventy-five thousand on the Croatian side of the Sava river. The Bosnian Muslims were still holding a couple dozen square miles on the opposite riverbank. The Bosnian Serbs had been shelling Slavonski Brod since March. The downtown was even more boarded-up, empty, and burned-out than the downtown of an American city that size. But quieter—an intense, prickly, almost smellable silence pervaded Slavonski Brod. Until shells landed, of course. Those were loud as hell. Since the city wasn't surrounded, an unsurprisingly large number of its residents had left, and the rest stayed off the streets during artillery periods. The shells arrived mostly in the daylight and mostly on the hour. The day before we arrived, there had been eleven separate barrages—a total of 130 shells, 60 of which landed in the city and 70 in the surrounding villages. Sometimes the artillery fire was supplemented with Soviet-made Frog missiles or MIGs dropping cluster bombs.

The attacks seemed to have no particular target and no very specific purpose. The rail line and the river bridges were being ignored by the gunners or missed by remarkable margins. I suppose the Serbs were trying to frighten and demoralize the people of Slavonski Brod. And, of course, kill them. The locals were good at keeping their heads down. So far only seventy-two civilians had died, although twenty-five of those were children. As to whether they were frightened and demoralized, they couldn't make up their minds. "You want to ask us if we see the end," said a woman in the Croatian government press office, one of the few businesses still operating downtown. "We don't," she said. "There is very little hope." Then she told us morale was high.

Frightened, demoralized or not, Slavonski Brod's citizens were certainly irritated that Sarajevo was getting so much media play. "All attention is paid to Sarajevo. All the supplies and all the aid goes to Sarajevo," said the president of Slavonski Brod's Executive Council, rather pettishly. Gorman and I did our best to explain that there is a big difference, in terms of reportorial drama, between being shelled from one side and being surrounded on four. Also journalists were being shot in Sarajevo, and that is always news of the most important kind.

Outside the gates of Slavonski Brod's hospital the tree trunks were covered with black-bordered pieces of paper announcing deaths—Post-it Notes from the grave. Casualties from the fighting across the river are brought here—Croats, Bosnian Muslims, captured Serbs—some 6,500 of them in the past year, 752 of whom have died. Heavily built wooden barriers covered the hospital doors, and sandbags blocked the lower windows. All the patients and medical equipment had been moved into the basement. A few ordinary sick people were there, but most of the cases were the gory infirmities of war—young men who'd had large chunks of something blown off or blasted into them. Their beds were lined up end-to-end down the smelly, narrow basement corridors, making a kind of Lincoln Tunnel rush hour of mutilation and pain. The operating tables were in the furnace rooms with barely enough space below the pipes and ducts for the surgeons to stand upright. X-ray machines, autoclaves, and oxygen bottles were jammed hodgepodge between plumbing and electrical fixtures. Every spare corner was filled with the cots, hot plates, and hanging clothes of doctors and nurses who stay for three-day shifts. Coming and going was too dangerous to do it more often than necessary. The hospital had taken eight direct hits, and two staff members had been killed on the grounds. Most of the work—not only medical procedures but cooking and laundry—was done at night when the danger was less. And every night the hospital tried to evacuate twenty to thirty patients, driving them out of town, in the Bihać manner, at top speed in blacked-out ambulances. No one said so, but I'm sure a certain number of those patients must have wound up back at the hospital, that much the worse for a traffic accident.

The chief janitor's office had been taken over by the hospital administrator, Dr. Ivan Balen. He was in his forties and looked like an American doctor, or better, in a double-breasted glen-check suit and black polo shirt. But he also looked more tired than an American doctor and, one other difference, he smoked.

"Everything is very sad and terrible," said Dr. Balen. I looked in my notebook. Unfortunately that was the answer to every question I had meant to ask him.

IX

Tom Lamson and I thought we'd better visit Serbian territory. What with besieging Sarajevo, setting up concentration camps, shooting civilians, and engaging in "ethnic cleansing" (*raščisiti teren* in the more sinister original), the Serbs were not winning the war of publicity.

The Serbs, of course, have as many excuses and grievances as anybody does in Yugoslavia, which is to say a lot. And they are as much in the right as everybody else, which is to say they're shits. The Serbs, however, controlled the old Yugoslav National Army, the JNA, and, when Yugoslavia deconstructed, Serbia and the Croatian and Bosnian guerrilla groups that it supports wound up in control of the tanks, airplanes, and heavy artillery. "Why the dog licks his balls" is the reason Serbia has acted so viciously in this war—because it can.

We drove out the Road Warrior freeway, then turned south to Banja Luka, thirty miles inside Bosnia. Banja Luka, with two hundred thousand people, is the largest Serb-controlled city in Bosnia. Back in Zagreb we'd heard dramatic tales about the drunken, thieving, trigger-happy, rape-inclined behavior of Serb irregulars at the checkpoints. But they were pleasant enough to us. One gave me a lapful of walnuts he'd stolen off some vanished Muslim's tree.

On close inspection the Serbs *are* a little different from the Croats. The Serbs look more like John Belushi, and the Croats look more like the rest of the cast of *Animal House*. Not that either are a lot of laughs. Although we did pick up one hitchhiking Serb soldier who did a comic turn trying to get both himself and his AK-47 into our tiny backseat. Or it would have been comic if I'd been sure the thing was unloaded.

Serbian territory is also distinguishable from the rest of Yugoslavia. There's less bomb and artillery damage, since the Serbs have all the bombs and artillery. And the international embargo seemed to be working. Well, not exactly *working,* because the fighting was worse than ever, but the Serbs have been reduced to using horse carts and bicycles to save fuel. There were more cars on the road in besieged Bihać than there were here among the besiegers.

Banja Luka seemed to be about the same kind of place as Slavonski Brod except we weren't allowed to look at it. We were ushered to military headquarters and there put under escort. We told Kadi to ask if we could get a peek at some starving concentration-camp prisoners, ethnic cleansing, and murder of innocent Muslims. I trust she put the request in more diplomatic terms. The answer was, anyway, no. But the Serbs would take us to see a mosque, just to show us that it was perfectly unmolested, which—not counting the four bullet holes in the ground-floor side window—it was. It was also closed. And they let us talk in private to the local representative of the UN High Commissioner for Refugees.

The UNHCR man was a very young Greek, cleanly dressed and neatly barbered but speaking with such tired resignation that, if you closed your eyes, you could imagine he was a refugee himself. There were twenty-five or thirty thousand Muslims left in the city, he said. The Bosnian Serbs refused to recognize these people as refugees because they weren't, technically, in a war zone and because the men of military age refused to be drafted. Under the UN's bylaws, which are as simple and useful as the rules of contract bridge, there wasn't much the young Greek could do about this. The local authorities were giving him some cooperation in protecting the Muslims. "Yeah—back and forth," he said. The Serbs needed UN help because winter was coming. "They are also sick and tired of being the bad guys in the war." One hundred and twenty Muslims had been killed in Banja Luka since April, most of them in April and May. There were still incidents of beatings and so forth. The Muslims were afraid to come out of their houses. "My house has been robbed twice in the past three days," said the Greek. There was nothing there to steal. "Maybe it's intimidation." He told us the situation was "not so bad" in Banja Luka, leaving to our imaginations what the bad places were like.

Back at the military headquarters we endured an hour-long peroration from a Serb major. He was determined that the Bosnian Serbs should achieve that status of victimhood so coveted in modern politics. The wisdom of the *Reading Culture* authors has spread beyond college English classes to the world at large and now everyone wants to be oppressed. The Serb major claimed that three hundred to seven hundred rockets and artillery shells a day were being fired at Bosnian Serbs from the Croatian side of the Sava. (I had driven practically the length of this river twice and saw none.) "These attacks haven't been provoked, as we have no aspirations in Croatia." (They occupy a third of it.) "Five hundred mujahedeen from Iran are in Bihać." (Keeping a very low profile.) "We are against ethnic cleansing." With that Lamson and I could no longer contain ourselves. But the major indignantly explained that what had been reported in the international press as ethnic cleansing was just "movement of migration in some settlements."

All this was conveyed to us through a Serbian translator, a teenage girl who seemed on the point of tears at hearing this litany of Serbian travails. Or maybe she had allergies. The major presented us with a thirteen-page document, written in English and titled "Jihad Must Be Stopped." Herewith a sample of the text:

> By and order of the Islamitic fundamentalists from Sarajevo, the healthy Serbian women from 17 to 40 years

old are getting set apart and subjected to an especial
treatment. According to their sick plans of many years,
these women have to be fecundated by orthodox Islam-
itic seeds in order to make the raising generation of jani-
zaries on the spaces which from now on surely consider
as theirs/Islamitic Republic/more numerous.

The major assured us that forty thousand Serbs were being held
in Muslim concentration camps in Bosnia. "Where?" said Lamson,
because outside Sarajevo and Bihać the Muslims seemed barely to have
enough of Bosnia left to hide forty thousand of themselves. "Many
small private camps," said the major.

Somewhat to our surprise, the major was able to produce a
former prisoner. His name was Risto Dukis, a handsome kid with
bristly hair and large, light brown eyes. He was fifteen and resembled
a dirtier, healthier Ryan White. Risto seemed to be a bit startled, like
a contestant brought up on stage from a quiz-show audience. He was
from a little village called Jezero, which had been overrun by the
Bosnian military. The Muslims had held him for two months. He
didn't know where his mother and father were and had no idea what
had happened to them. He was a high school student. When he grew
up he wanted to be, he said, "a worker."

Risto said he'd been out in a field on a weekend morning
when he'd been taken prisoner by some thirty Muslim soldiers. They
questioned him, beat him, and made him dig a hole that they said
would be his grave. They stood him on a table under a tree, as if to
hang him, and shook the table. When he was properly terrified they
took him away and beat him until they got him to say he was a
Serbian scout. He was kept alone for three days in the basement of a
school, then taken to an army barracks, where he was beaten again
and forced to make another confession. He slept on a pile of old
uniforms for a month. They gave him rice or beans or soup twice a
day. Then he was sent to a camp where there was no solid food, only
soup and tea. He was beaten by Muslim refugees and forced to do

hard labor. Finally there had been a prisoner exchange, and he was released.

Risto said that he knew one of the Muslims who captured him. And this was the man who threatened his life. He was a forest worker from a neighboring village. "He knew my parents," said Risto. "He drank coffee in my house." Risto said that the man had told him, "We used to be good friends, and now you are collaborating with the Chetniks."

"Did the man believe that?" asked Tom Lamson.

Risto said he thought so.

"Had you had any unpleasant experiences with Muslims before?"

"No. I wouldn't have expected them to treat me like that."

"Do you hate them?" asked Tom.

"So I hate them," said Risto.

"What will you do now?"

"Well, if I catch them, I will do exactly the same." Tom asked him if he had any idea why all this was going on. "Muslims blame Serbs," said Risto. "I think the Serbs aren't guilty. I blame the Bosnian president." (Though I don't think Risto, any more than I, could remember that august personage's name.)

Risto seemed believable. And his story was the Yugoslavian civil war in a nutshell: past and present wrongs inspiring wrongs of the future, bigotry feeding on bigotry, violence begetting violence, and in the middle of it all the Risto Dukises—innocence defiled.

"The morning you were captured," said Lamson, "what were you doing out in that field?"

"Oh, I was scouting for the Chetniks," said Risto.

8 PLAGUE

Sick of It All

∎

Does even plague have politics? All the bad things I've written about seem to be pervaded with calculating partisanships and maneuvering special interests. Could the random awfulness of pestilence be subject to influence-peddling and wire-pulling? Do the Fates sit in a smoke-filled room? You'd think so listening to AIDS activists and seeing people wearing loops of red ribbon like campaign buttons. Are we going to elect politicians who'll decree us cured the way a governor grants clemency? Will we pass a law forbidding the Human Immune Virus to multiply?

A political reaction to disease seems absurd. Where is the Cancer Quilt? Why aren't middle-aged fat men with stressful jobs laying down in the street to raise our awareness of heart disease? When the Spanish influenza epidemic of 1918 killed twenty million people, was anyone picketing the White House asking President Wilson to stop flu?

Actually, yes. Or, rather, they were doing the WWI equivalent thereof: They were blaming the Kaiser's Huns. A story in the September 19, 1918, edition of the *Philadelphia Inquirer* quoted a government health official as saying:

> It would be quite easy for one of these German agents to turn loose Spanish influenza germs in a theatre or some other place where large numbers of persons are assembled. The Germans have started epidemics in Europe, and there is no reason why they should be particularly gentle with America.

Plague has politics. *Everything* has politics. And no matter how little we like politics and no matter how ineffective or even deleterious politics appear to be, the AIDS activists do have a point. There are political things to be done about AIDS. We can allow hypodermic needles to be sold without prescription. We can license prostitution, male and female, to put some check on this route of transmission. We can legalize any experimental medical treatment that seems reasonable to the people who want it. And we can—in fact we're doing this—allocate tax money for education, treatment, and research.

But the house of politics is always built on sand. The international relief mission to Somalia, for instance, ended in humiliation and retreat because of shifting, unstable politics in Washington as well as Mogadishu. That dune which is the electorate may drift from an attitude of compassion for AIDS victims back to the usual voter disposition of plain self-interest.

Yearly, $1.4 billion is being spent on AIDS research. In a rich nation of 250 million people, this is not much money. Even so, members of the public may begin to think, "I don't know where to get decent drugs, and not even my wife wants promiscuous sex with me. I'm never going to get AIDS. Why isn't $1.4 billion being spent on something *I* suffer from—like hemorrhoids?" Or the democratic majority may decide that other, uglier, political actions can be taken. In the United States the core group of AIDS sufferers is relatively small and not very powerful at the ballot box. And there is legal precedent for quarantine. During the Spanish influenza outbreak the District of Columbia was declared a "sanitary zone" and the U.S. Public Health Service issued an order, reading in part, "No person shall knowingly expose himself or any other persons, or if he has the power and authority to prevent, permit any other person to be exposed to infection."

A similar ruling could be used against men who might be gay. All unmarried men over thirty-five—and, whoops, that's me—could be locked up. So could all inner-city blacks and Hispanics (to the extent the American penal system isn't doing that already). You say heterosexual women are the fastest growing category of AIDS victims? They could be locked up, too. The Saudis do it.

Ergo, we must be careful when we politicize disease. But there is still a place for politics in disease control. The cause of yellow fever was discovered by a political organization—a U.S. Army commission headed by Walter Reed. The malady was suppressed by political means—laws enforcing measures to exterminate the *Aedes aegypti* mosquito. And all this was done for political ends—to build the Panama Canal.

Nearly a century later smallpox, too, would be eradicated by acts of political will with numerous governments cooperating to eliminate the disease, and they didn't even get a canal for their troubles.

Now the World Health Organization is trying to annihilate measles the same way. And although WHO is part of the UN, an institution which otherwise represents the very essence of political futility, WHO is succeeding. Seventy percent of the world's children currently receive a measles vaccination.

||

Political means could be used to prevent almost all deaths from childhood diarrhea. Diarrhea is spread by contaminated water. Public sanitation is, like personal security, national defense, and rule of law, one of the few valid reasons for politics to exist. Lowly, semicomic diarrhea kills 2,866,000 people a year worldwide, 2,474,000 of them children under the age of five. This is ten times the number of people who die from AIDS. But no one is wearing a brown ribbon on his tuxedo lapel at the Academy Awards or marching up the Mall in Washington carrying a sign reading DIARRHEA—IT CAN BE CONTAINED.

Having chosen infant diarrhea as *exemplum,* I went to the Washington headquarters of the Pan American Health Organization (PAHO), this hemisphere's branch of WHO. I talked to Christopher J. Drasbek, PAHO's "Regional Technical Officer, Expanded Program for the Control of Diarrheal Diseases." Mr. Drasbek is one of those people who—with clumsy title, on modest salary, in an office shared with two other colleagues—accomplishes the actual good in the world. He does not wallow in his virtue while accepting Hollywood prizes from fatuous hams. He does not prate in Rose Gardens to sycophantic hacks about the politics of meaning. He does not stand wreathed in television lights upon the dais of power so that the humble multitude can savor the beneficence of his every word and gesture. . . . But I've gone off on a tangent about another kind of diarrhea entirely.

Mr. Drasbek took time from the mounds of paperwork that accrue in any kind of good done in a bureaucracy (and also time, it occurred to me later, from his lunch hour) to tell me just how easily politics could rid the globe of 2,500,000 deaths.

"What would it cost," I asked, "to clean up the world's drinking-water supplies?"

"We don't even have to do that," said Mr. Drasbek. "All we need are Oral Rehydration Salts." He pulled some foil packets out of a desk drawer. "These cost eight to ten cents apiece." He explained that diarrhea kills by dehydration. The salts in the foil packet restore the body's electrolyte balance, the degree of salinity in the body's cells. Thus, the cells are able to retain fluid.

You mix one packet of the rehydration salts into a liter of clean water and get the patient to drink as much of the liquid as possible. This

Oral Rehydration Therapy, or ORT, is given for as long as the diarrhea lasts. ORT alone, with no other treatment, is enough to prevent death from diarrhea, even from cholera. "Usually, to rehydrate a child, it takes two packets," said Mr. Drasbek. In other words, between sixteen and twenty cents. So, for five hundred thousand dollars, 2,474,000 lives could be saved each year. This is about half the cost of a thirty-second Superbowl advertising spot—an apt comparison, since Gatorade is more or less a commercial version of Oral Rehydration Therapy (although the precise clinical effect of dumping it on coaches is not fully understood).

A packet of Oral Rehydration Salts contains glucose (corn sugar), which helps the small intestine absorb the salts; sodium bicarbonate, which is the same thing as baking soda; a small amount of potassium chloride, and ordinary table salt. A homemade oral rehydration solution can be prepared by mixing eight level teaspoons of sugar or honey and half a teaspoon of salt in a liter of clean water. ORT is one of the unheeded medical miracles of the twentieth century. A dozen years ago there were over 5,000,000 annual childhood deaths from diarrhea.

But that still leaves enough dead kids every year to populate Kansas (as if they hadn't been punished enough). What government is so politically screwed-up that it can't get a little boiled sugar water and a pinch of salt to sick babies? Well, close at hand, there's Haiti. According to PAHO the average Haitian child has seven episodes of diarrhea a year and only a one-in-six chance of receiving Oral Rehydration Therapy.

III

I flew to Port-au-Prince on December 22, 1993. You'd expect the Christmas decorations in Haiti to be little Santas with pins in them. It's been a long time since Saint Nick brought the Haitians much. And, in a deforested country undergoing an international oil embargo, even sticks and coal would look good in the stockings—if Haitians had socks. However, Haiti's yuletide is greeted with the usual red and green gewgaws and tinsel festoons. Christmas trees are fashioned from the branches of Norfolk pines. JOYEUX NOËL is spelled out in Mylar letters. The radio plays reggae, calypso, and merengue covers of all the noted carols. And I didn't see a doll with needle marks anywhere in the country.

Making figurines of one's enemies and torturing these playthings has nothing to do with Haiti or voodoo. It is a piece of European superstition brought to the New World by those mysterious savages, the French. Haiti has no need for such elaborate fancy goods of evil. Sturdy, utilitarian forms of wrong are readily available—the city water system, for instance.

For most Haitians the only source of water is a public well or tap. Downtown Port-au-Prince is served by one slimy concrete outdoor sink, a sort of horse trough with faucets. Here water is available only between eight P.M. and five in the morning. The women and girls carry it home in five-gallon plastic buckets. That's forty-some pounds of water balanced on the heads of people who don't weigh much more themselves. And they're carrying it through unlit streets.

These streets are heaped with trash as high as the women's bucket tops. A long mound of putrefying dreck will stretch for a block to an intersection, then turn the corner and continue for half a block more—a giant disposable traffic island. Not that it gets disposed of. According to the Pan American Health Organization, as of June 1993, Port-au-Prince had twelve garbage trucks in running condition. This to collect an estimated sixteen thousand tons of solid waste produced daily in the capital. Every now and then the locals try to burn the refuse, but the result is a parody of the North American landfill debate—biodegradability versus incineration. In Haiti's climate everything is biodegradable. And the ooze of tropical rot defeats the fires. The trash piles stay just as large, with guttering flames adding a new stench to the miasma.

I saw two of the twelve garbage trucks. One was parked down-

town, and garbagemen were behind it with shovels. The first garbageman would scoop a load of filth and dump it at the feet of the next
garbageman who would pass it to another. There was no garbage in the
truck. The Metropolitan Solid Waste Collection Service occupied a
modernistic gray and white building with expanses of tinted glass. A
long row of truck garages was attached. Here another, very clean
garbage truck was parked on a wide, smooth asphalt driveway. The
Collection Service's building was spotless, the grounds were tidy, and,
at two-fifteen on a Tuesday afternoon, nobody was there.

IV

I'd been in Haiti for about six hours when I gave up the idea of
investigating infant diarrhea or Third World sanitation or medical care
in underdeveloped nations—when I gave up the idea of writing a
chapter about plague at all. Haiti was too far gone in entropy. Investigating public health, when the public obviously didn't have any, left
me nothing but that public to investigate. If the politics of disease are
to be understood, particularly in the dreadful countries where this
understanding is most needed, then the politics of total collapse have
to be understood first. You can boil the water, but how do you boil
history, social structure, economics, and religion?

And, as it is with disease, so it is with hunger, crowding,
pollution, hatred, poverty, and so on. All these problems are knotted
and tangled together. Haiti is as good a name as any for the snarl.

I took the long list that I'd made of health experts and government officials and NGO directors I'd meant to interview and put it in
the glove compartment of my rented Jeep. My driver and translator,
Dumarsais, asked, "Who do you want to go talk to?"

"Let's just drive around," I said.

The mystery of Port-au-Prince's trash heaps is that there are so
many really immense holes in Port-au-Prince's streets. Putting one into
another would create a certain leveling, at least, if not sanitation.

The streets and roads of Haiti are so bad that they almost seem to have been made so on purpose. The mere dragging and scraping of axles and undercarriages should lower some of the great humps, and chunks of disintegrating vehicles should fill a few of the ruts. "Haitian roads are a free massage," said Dumarsais.

Maybe there are deconstructionist road crews who go out at night and wreck the macadam, gangs in the pay of the Port-au-Prince spare parts and car repair industry. But I don't think so. Several long and exceptionally dirty blocks of the capital are given over to shade-tree mechanics (minus the shade and the trees). It's difficult to tell their wares from plain scrap metal and harder to decide whether the autos they're hammering on are being put back together or beaten apart. We needed a new gas cap for the Jeep. Numerous experts came forward offering fittings ranging in size from a hubcap to a thimble, and one proffered the top of a juice bottle.

Or perhaps Haiti has guerrilla organizations so impoverished that they cannot lay hands on guns, bombs, or even knives and are reduced to terrorizing the establishment with shovels. The pavement in front of the very house of Lieutenant General Raoul Cédras, head of Haiti's military junta, had been torn up, leaving a dusty and rock-strewn gap in his suburban street. (The house was an unprepossessing stucco villa in the hills above Port-au-Prince, identifiable only by a large number of soldiers standing, decidedly not at attention, outside its gate.)

During the time I was in Haiti, Haitians were blaming such things as lousy water and roads on the international embargo. The embargo had been instituted the year before in an attempt to return elected President Jean-Bertrand Aristide to power. But, looking around Port-au-Prince, it's evident that lousiness is nothing new. The oldest buildings are wooden frame structures out of a New Orleans French Quarter attacked by termites instead of decorators. These houses are so rotted and gaping they seem to be wayward theatrical sets, held up by concealed props and guy wires. The newer buildings are random jumbles of concrete covered in battered signs: AVE MARIA DRY

CLEANERS, SKYLAB ICE CREAM, SACRED HEART ART & SNACK, SUPER MARRIAGE NUMBERS BANK. The storefronts were brightly colored once, maybe, but now are wholly grimy, like Kandinskys painted in the dirt.

The waterfront is an idle mess. Most of the docks are too rickety to hold a middle-sized reporter. The harbor is a slough of wet rubbish. The ocean itself is stained the color of tea-bag seepage. Everything is worn-out. The tap-taps, the little buses made from pickup trucks, are exuberantly so—covered with chipped decorations, dented ornaments, and scratched-up paintings and slogans. The open-air markets are woefully so—filled with more crud and dust than goods. The people are in-between—always well met and as carefully dressed and laundered as circumstances allow but tired, frayed, and thin.

Little cheerless cement houses of the lesser bourgeoisie are scattered haphazardly up the hillsides. They all have high walls with broken glass embedded in the tops or, sometimes, upended conch shells. The streets, empty lots, and open spaces of even the better neighborhoods are spread with trash.

The downtown parks are weed-grown and deeply littered, the railings knocked over, the statues of the heroes oxidized to the indistinctness of lead soldiers and dripping with pigeon muck. The only clean thing in the city center was the empty presidential palace, a mediocre beaux-arts design in the middle of ample, well-tended grounds. A single chrome kitchen chair sat unaccountably on the lawn.

Dumarsais and I went to buy fuel at the gasoline black market, which was hardly clandestine. Sales were conducted by the side of Boulevard Harry Truman down the street from the Haitian Chamber of Commerce. Gas from open hogsheads was sloshed into cans, buckets, and plastic washbasins. All purchases guaranteed filtered through a dirty cloth. It was the only place in the country where I didn't see people smoking—the fad for extreme longevity having not reached Haiti yet. One of the customers was a police officer in a squad car, and he seemed to be paying full price. In Haiti even corruption is inefficacious.

I spoke to an outbound American missionary couple at the Port-au-Prince airport, nice people from my own corner of Ohio. The wife talked about Haitian boat people. "I'd float out of here on a matchstick if that's the only chance I thought I had." She and her husband were cheerfully headed to Uganda.

V

As for plague, the whole of Haiti is a disease vector—of physical, mental, and moral illnesses.

On the night after Christmas in an alley of Cité Soleil, Port-au-Prince's largest slum, one Issa Paul was murdered, presumably by supporters of Haiti's exiled president. The next night the same alley was set afire, presumably by supporters of the junta that exiled Aristide. Paul was a member of the Front for the Advancement and Progress of Haiti, or FRAPH, pronounced like the French word for hitting somebody. FRAPH does the bidding of the Haitian military. Cité Soleil is a center of enthusiasm for Aristide. A good-sized chunk of Cité Soleil burned down.

Cité Soleil has become a squalor chestnut in the U.S. media. It is more crowded, needy, and pathetic than other places most American journalists have been, not counting singles bars in the 1970s. Whenever something awful is happening in Haiti (and something awful always is), we are given a description of this vast shantytown built on the mud flats of Port-au-Prince Bay where 150,000 people, give or take a zillion, live in a kind of poverty the news always describes as "abject." Considering America's treatment of Haitian boat people, the cliché is too appropriate: abject, from *abjectus,* Latin for "thrown out." The reporters tell us how the residents of Cité Soleil swim in mire when it rains and choke in dust when it doesn't and go hungry in either case. Then we are treated to a reflection on the irony of the place-name, "Sun City."

"Cité Soleil" is not ironic. After the ouster of dictator Jean-

Claude "Baby Doc" Duvalier, the name of the slum was changed to honor Radio Soleil, the Catholic station instrumental in Baby Doc's fall. Baby Doc's father, François "Papa Doc" Duvalier, built Cité Soleil in the 1960's and named it after his own wife: Cité Simone. That was ironic.

Cité Soleil is not the worst slum in the world. A lot of people around the globe live this way. Cité Soleil is about as bad as parts of Dhaka or Rio, better than all of Mogadishu, and, although South Central Los Angeles is more attractive looking, I have walked through Cité Soleil at three in the morning and been bothered by nothing worse than my conscience. But, in another way, all Third World slums are more terrible than the CNN videotapes can make them out to be. You can't smell television.

Cité Soleil is low, muddled, close-set, overpeopled, and made from such an oddment stew of cast-off materials that, at first, the eye registers nothing but confusion. The smells are what's clear: sweat, shit, piss, puke, rotting offal, burning rubbish, spoiled cooking oil, rancid fry-fire smoke, kerosene vapors, cheap cigarette fumes, the bad breath of diseased teeth, and the body odor of lesions and sores all underlaid with something more subtle, something with a scent reminiscent of the Madison Savings and Loan or Pentagon purchasing orders.

Even for a government project, Cité Soleil is a horror. There are no water pipes to speak of, no sewers at all, only a few electrical wires, and the oil embargo has given the military an excuse for not running electricity through them. There isn't so much as a latrine or an outhouse in Cité Soleil. When I went there a few days before the fire, the first thing I smelled was an open area in the midst of the hovels, about half an acre heaped in ordure and slime and dotted with squatting kids. "This is where people go to crap," said Dumarsais. "The children go in the daytime, the grown people at night." Goats and pigs were nibbling in the excrement as they nibble in all such piles of waste in Haiti, and it certainly moves one in a vegetarian direction when goat or pig is on the menu.

Cité Soleil was laid out with a few main roads running perpendicular to the bay. The roads are on causeways of rubble and fill. Between and below them, housing was constructed in the mud. The building material was cement block and the design inspiration was horse sheds of the less spacious kind. The old historic homes of Cité Soleil are long rows of three-walled cubicles perhaps ten feet square with no windows, doors, or chimneys, unless you count the missing fourth wall as one of each. Around these hovels, worse hovels grew up, tiny shacks made of anything that will stand or lay flat—packing-crate staves, lengths of pipe, plywood scraps, cardboard, the tin from gallon cans. The siding of one residence is the wallpaper of the next. The space between the dwellings, when there's any at all, is so narrow that walking must be done in a tango slide.

It is as though thousands and thousands of kids have all built forts on the same vacant lot—the raggediest kids ever on the worst vacant lot you can picture. And they've gotten their parents to come play, too. By which I mean, Cité Soleil, though remarkably bad, is also remarkably cheerful, noisy, and welcoming.

Haitians are not, of course, simple, happy folk who don't notice misery the way we would. But pulling a long face and railing at fate (or Americans—and the two can be hard to distinguish in these parts) isn't the fashion in Haiti. I didn't see much of it.

But at 7:30 on the morning after the fire, Cité Soleil was no longer cheerful, though still noisy. An area about the size of three football fields had burned, leaving perhaps a thousand people hovelless and an indeterminate number dead. The only thing left of the nothing these people had owned was the corrugated metal of the hut roofs. Young men were collecting the tin sheets and piling them together with a racket like a high school theater group's attempt to make thunder sound effects offstage. Two hysterical women and one crippled old lady sat in the smoldering ash. A little girl held a burned baby doll (with absolutely no pins in it). Dumarsais found me someone who could speak English.

"What happened?" I asked.

"I don't know," he, probably wisely, said.

People were picking through the debris. Some had found charred pop bottles. They might be able to get the deposits back. One woman had the very sensible idea of gathering armloads of the ruins and selling them as charcoal. I saw a burned rat. I saw two burned dogs. I don't think anybody lost his life going back for his cat.

VI

Cité Soleil is grossly flammable. The more so because the drivers of Port-au-Prince's tap-taps live there. Since the embargo, the tap-tap drivers have been squirreling supplies of gasoline in their homes. The whole slum should have burned to the ground. But, in Haiti, nothing works right.

A Port-au-Prince radio station gave a Christmas concert. The music was admirable. The staging was clever. But the cash bar didn't even have a horizontal surface. Refreshments were served circle tag–style from the middle of a crowd of thirsty audience members by a woman with a cigar box full of change, a man with a bottle, another man with several plastic cups, and a third man with a table knife and a block of ice. Whenever the woman was cornered, the man with the bottle had been tackled elsewhere. When the bottle was seized, the cups had escaped. By the time a cup had been nabbed I found myself on the extreme outskirts of the crowd and had to reenter the scrum to get back to the woman with the cigar box. I finally achieved a nearly complete drink only to be caught out by the man with the ice, a hockey puck–sized chunk of which splashed all my liquor on the ground.

Getting on my plane to Haiti in New York, the sound of "We will begin preboarding . . ." was drowned by the trampling of Haitians, all of them aware of the probable fate of checked luggage in the Port-au-Prince airport and therefore toting their complete movable possessions and some major appliances as hand baggage. More than an hour later a stewardess was still standing at the aircraft's forward bulkhead, with her hairpins come loose and her face the shade of raspberry yogurt, holding the intercom phone in a World Wrestling Federation grip and shouting repeatedly, "The-captain-cannot-take-off-until-all-carry-on-items-have-been . . ."

The grandiose Louis-Napoléon-style building of Haiti's Department of Agriculture is half burned down. Haitians—who, like most people having a hard time, are fond of the fantastic—say the army burned it to destroy records of illegal atomic-waste dumping done by foreign governments in Haiti. But a foreigner has more humdrum suspicions concerning, perhaps, fire hydrants which only work after eight P.M.

At a New Year's Eve party in the Oloffson Hotel, midnight slipped by without the band noticing.

A military attempt at propaganda sloganeering produced bumper stickers reading, HAITI—LOVE IT OR LEAVE IT. In English, at that.

And the junta's effort to win the hearts and minds of Haiti's citizens consisted of suddenly, on January 1, changing the name of Cité Soleil back to Cité Simone. Replacing the street names was more than the army could handle. But the Cité Soleil tap-taps were supposed to put Cité Simone signs on their roofs. I saw one tap-tap with a brick-shaped hole in its windshield and a "Cité Simone" placard so hastily done, the paint was still wet. I asked the driver what had happened, and he said, as the man at the fire had, that he didn't know. But another tap-tap driver claimed one of the army's plainclothes goons, or "attachés," had said—referring to Aristide or the Cité Soleil fire or maybe to everything in general—"What you like is gone, so the name is changed."

"Nothing sounds stupid here," said a left-wing French priest in a Chicago Bulls T-shirt who had just finished telling me a very stupid story about how multinational corporations choose the president of the United States and the Pentagon employs twenty million people.

The only orderly thing I saw on the Port-au-Prince streets was a neat and level line of bullet holes down the side of an automobile, and these had been also to no avail. The car was in running order and waiting in line to get gas.

In the wealthy suburb of Pétion-Ville, anti-American graffito appeared, aptly mispunctuated: FUCK U S.

Even rudeness doesn't work in Haiti. I went to the Iron Market, a city block–sized shed of steel beams and sheet metal, a tinker's and tinsmith's Carnegie Hall. It was from here that Haiti's tourists used to bring home mahogany carvings of surpassing insipidity and garish canvases showing improbable congregations of addled-looking jungle animals. The tourists were gone but plenty of people were still on hand to pester them. An insistent young man named Jesse laid hold of me. He claimed great powers as an interpreter, purchasing agent, porter, and general factotum, and he could probably cook and take Pitman shorthand. I told him to buzz off. "Be nice to me," said Jesse, with perfect frankness. "Someone else will just come along and bother you." Dozens were waiting to do so.

Jesse led me through a Minotaur's palace of handicrafts. The awful tourist stuff was there but with no one but the tourists to blame for it winding up in American dens, rec rooms, and downstairs baths. A hundred kinds of wonderful things were for sale—gross Mardi Gras masks, fine embroidery, cheerful little painted wooden boxes, large solemn polished wooden trays, beautiful tortoiseshell bracelets that U.S. Customs will confiscate, and silhouettes of strange voodoo spirits cut from the flattened sides of oil drums which will show up clearly on your baggage X rays and scare the hell out of airport security personnel. Haiti's abstract soapstone sculptures could give a refresher course to Henry Moore, if he weren't dead. Among the dross of mahogany figurines were individual pieces as well whittled as netsuke. The excellence of the palm-frond weaving made Baby Doc's old nickname, "Baskethead," seem almost a compliment. Handsome goatskin rugs were spread across the Iron Market's floor (although these were best appreciated with the ocular rather than olfactory sense). Furniture was available, too, clunky enough to be called fashionable country pine in *Elle Decor,* but better made and cheaper. For eight chairs and a dining-room table long enough to bowl duckpins on, the kickoff bargaining price was $750.

I tipped Jesse, and Dumarsais took me to a gallery owned by Issa El Saïeh, whose family, in an example of frying pan/fire emigration, had come to Haiti from Palestine. A thousand paintings were for sale in what had once been a living room, dining room, and sun porch. Issa had portraits with the wide-eyed, startled, straight-ahead impact captured usually only on driver's licenses. He had historical scenes executed with masterful but coarse technique as though the French academic school had used house-painting brushes. There were Edenic landscapes of a Haiti so unlike the real thing that it hurt worse to see them than to look at Cité Soleil. The pictures of voodoo spirits or saints, the *loas,* made surrealism so much Hallmark sympathy-card art. And the animal paintings appeared to be illustrations for fables Aesop thought it best not to tell.

Issa told me about the various painters, how one hung in New York's Metropolitan Museum, another was collected by a Rockefeller, a third had just sold out an exhibit in Switzerland. One painter seemed to have been strongly influenced by Henri Rousseau. "You know, I have to laugh when people say things like 'strongly influenced by Henri Rousseau,' " said Issa. "This is Haiti. That guy's never seen a Henri Rousseau or had a chance to. You know what influenced him? Tarzan. Go to his studio and you'll see stacks and stacks of Tarzan comics."

There was another painter I particularly liked, an impressionist who used such large blocks of pigment that the effect was almost of cubism, who had Gauguin's colors and a deft use of heavy black line like Rouault. "Oh, that's the janitor," said Issa. "Give him five bucks."

I couldn't see Issa's gallery or the Iron Market, and then think Haitians were lazy or in any way slow-thinking. Even the tap-tap buses bespoke acuity and gumption in their tags and slogans:

I WANT TO BE

I WANT TO BE FREE

BACK TO REALITY

WELCOME TO AIR

AMI DE TRAVAIL

THAT'S WONDERFUL

CRY FREEDOM

OZONE

EXODE 14:14 (referring to the Bible verse "The Lord will
   fight for you, and you need only to be still," which I
   hope is not a gloss on U.S. foreign policy)

All over the city I saw signs: COLLEGE DESCARTES, COLLEGE
PYTHAGORAS, COLLEGE ALBERT EINSTEIN, COLLEGE ISAAC NEWTON,
TWO-WAY ENGLISH SCHOOL, and COLLEGE MIXTE ALPHA—VERITABLE
CENTRE DE FORMATION INTELLECTUELLE—ORDRE DISCIPLINE
SUCCES.

Haiti is not screwed-up because Haitians are screwed-up. Haitians are courteous. "Accident do for everything," said the waiter
when I let loose an oafish gesture and knocked the sugar bowl halfway
across my hotel's dining room.

Haitians are funny. When journalists rushed to Haiti in the fall
of 1993 to cover reaction to the Governors Island Accord that was
supposed to put Aristide back in power, the staff of the Port-au-Prince
Holiday Inn took a look at the reporters and posted a sign in the lobby:
OUR EVENING DRESS CODE HAS BEEN TEMPORARILY SUSPENDED IN HONOR
OF OUR FRIENDS IN THE MEDIA.

And Haitians are law-abiding, when there is law to abide.
Along the unmarvelous sidewalks of the Rue des Miracles, dozens of
money changers stood with large wads of U.S. dollars in hand. "I'd like
to see someone try that in New York City," said Dumarsais, who once
lived in Brooklyn.

"Is there much crime in Haiti?" I asked.

"Why would we have crime in Haiti?" said Dumarsais. "We have the police and the army to do that for us."

The headquarters of that army is a modest two-storied, balconied affair sitting catercornered from the Presidential Palace. It looks colonial, which makes sense since the Haitian army is a sort of colonial occupying force, though with nothing to occupy but its own country. The parade ground consists of a parking lot, and security is provided by a few very slack sentries, or maybe these are just soldiers standing around the front door.

A public waiting room, which seemed to have a lot of wives or girlfriends in it, is separated from the offices of the high command by a glass half-wall partition less elaborate than that which protects an American liquor-store clerk. I was ushered inside by, of all things, a Canadian, Lynn Garrison, honorary consul of the Republic of Haiti.

Garrison is convinced that the military is misunderstood and that Aristide is a commie nut. Both of which may be true. Whether that means the military is any better than we think or Aristide any worse than what usually governs Haiti, I can't say. Personally, I've always thought the Haitians made a mistake not going communist. Look how well escapees from Cuba are treated by the U.S. The Haitians also made a mistake being black. Look how well escapees from British journalism are treated by the *New Yorker* and *Vanity Fair*. Anyway, it's too late now for Haiti to become part of the Red Menace.

Garrison led me upstairs to a sitting room with French windows opening to the second floor balcony. On that balcony was a crèche. Mary, Joseph, and Jesus looked American. Garrison pointed at the parking lot. "School children," he said, "come here after dark to read their textbooks under the street lamps."

Garrison made his case against Aristide, calling the little priest a symptom of the absurd expectations Haitians have about changes in government. After the fall of the Duvaliers in 1986, he claimed, there were crowds in the streets shouting, "We've had democracy for seven days—where's the food, where's the jobs?" (Which didn't sound so absurd to a reporter who's covered U.S. presidential elections.) And Garrison accused Aristide of complicity in the horrible reprisals against Duvalier supporters. This may be fair. In 1993 the *New York Review of Books,* not noted for its right-wing politics, ran three articles of Homeric length about Aristide. The author, Mark Danner, was largely praiseful but also described Aristide's constituents killing Duvalierists by necklacing them.

> Their remains were left lying in the sun to be further
> abused, or in some cases they were paraded through the
> streets like war trophies: a bloody severed head speared
> on the end of a pole; a shrunken, charred torso . . .

We need not read more. Then Danner recounted an interview with Aristide.

> "I stood and marveled at the justice of the peo-
> ple," Father Aristide told me as he sat in his church that
> March. . . . He smiled patiently at my surprise, and at the
> inevitable question: How could he, a priest, call such acts
> "justice"? . . . "One must know when to look at the acts
> of the people and judge them as a psychologist, not as a
> priest," he replied, and then, a bit more heatedly, "Our
> consciences should be clear."

I must be sure to get Father Aristide as court-appointed psychiatric expert next time I set someone on fire.

Garrison made his case for the army, calling them the "only structural element that can do anything in the country," though the single example he gave of a thing they had done was the approval of some tree planting by an international organization. Anyway, "only element that can do anything" is the excuse always given for uniformed bully boys in the Third World. Never mind that since independence

Haiti hasn't been in a real war with anyone except the Dominican
Republic and hasn't fought at all since 1855, if you don't count battling
the 1915–1934 American occupation, which was done by Haitian
peasants, not the army. But then Garrison told me something that really
was illuminating, something that explained the whole relationship
between armed might and corruption in Haiti. Full colonels in the
Haitian army are paid 5,000 gourdes a month, U.S. $417. Enlisted men
make 83 bucks.

The public moralists at Americas Watch issued a report in
February 1993 detailing rights violations by Haiti's military. In a long
list of harassments, injustices, beatings, and occasional murders, one
item caught the eye as painfully typical. It seems that most of Haiti's
pigs had to be slaughtered in the early nineteen-eighties because of an
outbreak of African swine fever. Various international aid agencies
have been trying to rebuild the ham population ever since—teaching
pork-chop husbandry, providing adopt-a-piglet services for rural co-
operatives, and so forth. Said Americas Watch: "Soldiers . . . took
advantage of their new power after the coup to steal pigs from peasant
groups. . . . In [the town of "X"], a soldier [named "Y"] was the worst
offender. . . . he came home from the capital a few days after the coup
firing his gun into the air. He got some friends together and they stole
a pig to feast upon. In the following days [Y] and his group stole more
than 60 pigs in [X]. This encouraged other military supporters to steal
pigs."

I was in X myself and the area did seem pigless, also politicized.
The head of an aid agency in Port-au-Prince had told me pig distribution was being broken up by the military, lest it somehow lead to rural
insurrection. "Every time they see a pig," said the agency head, "they
think there is a group of peasant organizers near." An aid worker in X
confirmed this, saying, "Whenever anyone is working directly with
peasants he or she is suspected by the authorities." Not that those
suspects weren't pretty far gone in political paranoia themselves. Someone else in X told me the whole swine-fever episode had been a plot
by American pig monopolies.

VII

Haitians aren't screwed-up, but everything political, intellectual, and material around them is. Even so, some Haitians have molded comfort and success from this poor clay. I was surprised to see a Jaguar sedan in Port-au-Prince, surprised because most of Haiti's rich drive Range Rovers, the roads being what they are. Enough of these rich exist to people a fancy suburb called Pétion-Ville five miles into the mountains from downtown. A reasonably fancy suburb, anyway; there's still plenty of garbage around. And, while some of the houses are very large, none could be said to be distinguished. And none could be said to be attached to a sewage system either.

They are the typical pastel residences of the prosperous in warm climates, faintly modern, vaguely Mediterranean. Pétion-Ville looks like the Hollywood Hills during a strike by Mexican gardeners. And there is the same grand vista, sufficiently distant to make even Los Angeles or Port-au-Prince look good.

But the bars on the windows of the houses in Pétion-Ville are more decorative than those in Hollywood. The grilles and gratings protecting the property of Pétion-Ville take the form of elaborate scrollwork lattices. Similar filigrees, called *vèvè,* are used in voodoo ceremonies to represent the *loas*. The designs are drawn on the floor of the voodoo temple with flour, coffee, ashes, or even gunpowder to invoke a *loa*'s power. Some scholars of voodoo trace the *vèvès* back to the Dahomey, or to the Arawak tribes who occupied pre-Columbian Haiti. Others claim the *vèvès* derive from eighteenth-century French embroidery motifs, china patterns, and wrought iron. So, whether the barred windows of Pétion-Ville draw upon the symbolic power of voodoo, or whether voodoo draws upon the symbolic power of window bars remains an open question.

The rich of Haiti are as cosmopolitan as rich people anywhere, more so than the roasted-chicken franchise magnates and software slob billionaires of the United States. Posh Haitians speak at least three languages. No one affects Brooks Brothers sack-o'-responsibility or Ralph Lauren hairdresser-to-the-Wild-West looks. My hotel was a redoubt of flower gardens, tennis courts, and airy shaded terraces. Built in 1947, its architecture was a nod to the less lithium-deficient designs of Frank Lloyd Wright. And pay no mind to the little snake in the pool, the rat that ran through the bar every night, and the guard with a shotgun at the gate to the grounds. I put on a necktie and crashed one of the several wedding parties held over the Christmas holidays. There were Parisian hors d'oeuvres, Jamaican barbecue entrées, Westchester ice sculptures, and Beethoven's Ninth for the bridal march. And prettier than most rich brides she was.

Haiti has a history of race warfare, not between blacks and whites—because the whites all fled or were killed at independence—but between blacks and mulattoes. Under French rule many mulattoes were freedmen, often rich and educated. The mulattoes owned slaves themselves, and blacks haven't forgotten it. Since Haiti became a free country mulattoes have dominated the nation's economy and often pulled its political wires, and blacks haven't forgotten this either. Meanwhile Haiti's only sustained contact with whites was an invasion by marines and an even more devastating—through the introduction of AIDS alone—invasion by tourists and charity givers. Yet Haiti is integrated in a way not seen in the United States except in soft-drink television commercials.

At the radio station Christmas party, every skin shade possible was represented from sable to much lighter than my purple Irish sunburn. And the music was multicultural enough to baffle David Byrne. Wispy little French cabaret songs were sung in a big American way by someone who looked like Nat King Cole. "White Christmas" and "Silent Night" were crooned in the Gaulic manner by Maurice Chevalier's double. Then came RAM, a Haitian voodoo rock band led by an American, Richard Morse, who owns the Oloffson Hotel. RAM is so diverse, it has a song on the *Philadelphia* movie soundtrack.

The New Year's Eve party at the Oloffson was more eclectic yet. Mulatto businessmen and industrialists came with their pale-skinned wives; so did members of the black elite, whose families rose to wealth through the government and armed forces. There were embassy personnel in the crowd, aid workers, journalists, wandering hipsters, artists, musicians, regular and irregular Haitians of all kinds, even an absurdly dressed group of French holidaymakers, the seeming victims of a very shady travel agency.

Since Graham Greene set his novel of Papa Doc terror, *The Comedians,* there in 1966, the Oloffson has been an emblem of everything that is strange, gothic, incomprehensible, and outré about Haiti, although nothing else in the country resembles it. The Oloffson is a meandering white folly of Victorian gimcrack covered in hundreds of layers of paint, all the paint missing from everything else in Port-au-Prince. It's built into the side of a hill, so that the back of its ballroom is the face of a cliff. The names of various famous people who have stayed there are inscribed on the hotel room doors: IRVING STONE, LILLIAN HELLMAN, ANNE BANCROFT, and, too rightly, CHARLES ADDAMS.

RAM, of course, performed again. Richard Morse was dressed in khaki with a military officer's cap and a big cigar. Except for his ponytail and normally shaped face, Morse looked a good deal like Raoul Cédras. RAM played a song that has caused the band political trouble. One radio station was shut down for broadcasting it. "You're just playing this same song over and over," the soldiers told the station manager (a kind of armed playlist criticism with which Top 40 listeners can, in a way, sympathize). Translated from the Creole, the offending lyrics are: "I only have one son / And he's been forced to leave the country." At the back of the crowd a natty gentleman in a very good suit was standing on a chair, digging the tune. Dumarsais told me this was the richest man in Haiti.

VIII

I'm glad I didn't see Haiti's disparity in material goods when I was still a member of STAEP and a caring and committed young fellow. I'd probably be in the mountains of Peru or the hills of Chiapas state babbling Maoist nonsense to this day. Are Haiti's wealthy the cause of its disease and anguish? Are they just bloodsuckers, sweat jobbers, and bums on the plush? Doubtless some are. And maybe some are only making a living. Are they in cahoots with the military? As if they have a choice. Armed partnership negotiation is at least as effective as armed music reviewing. Anyway, sharing the wealth is not going to solve Haiti's problems. With a $370 annual per capita GNP, every Haitian would wind up with . . . $370.

Maybe Haiti is really not screwed-up at all. If we take the longest possible view of human existence—which, like the view from Pétion-Ville or Mulholland Drive, allows us to ignore such unpleasant details as life and death—Haiti is normal. Haitians live the way the great majority of people have lived throughout history, like the cattle of stronger men. Haiti has an unwritten Bill of Rights (no matter, since only 35 percent of Haitians can read) to the effect of "Who can, may." The government exists solely to benefit the governors. The enforcement of law consists of force only. The elite is divorced from its fellow countrymen and feels the same responsibility toward the other party that, after a divorce, most of us feel. In a society where commonweal does not exist, there are no duties, only exactations to be avoided, and no freedoms, only privileges to be grabbed. There can be no such thing as "public services" because nothing in the country is truly public. Everything is somebody's fief. And every fief must be exploited if the exploiter cares to survive. Haiti is so dangerous and unstable that loyalties to clan and alliances for power have to take precedence over civic virtue. Anyway, how can civic virtue exist without *civis?* The votes of Haitians count for nothing. Their labors go for naught. And the entire business of their nation, from colonial times to the present, has been conducted in French, a language 90 percent of Haitians don't understand. Haitians are no more citizens in their own country than Anglo-Saxons in Norman England, helots in Sparta, or Republicans in Chicago.

So how did Haiti get to be so normal? The French settled on the western end of Hispaniola in 1641 in an attempt to quell—or get in on—Caribbean pirate activity. The French soon discovered that Saint Dominque, as they called their colony, was better suited to sugarcane growing than plank walking. By the late eighteenth-century Saint Dominque was exporting 177 million pounds of sugar a year. Its commerce with the mother country made up a third of all French foreign trade and provided the single greatest source of French government revenue. Saint Dominque was counted the richest colonial possession in the world.

The trouble was that sugar plantations required large numbers of unhappy people. Growing sugarcane is miserable labor done in a wretched climate. Tending, carting, and pressing the cane, boiling down the molasses, and refining the sugar are all hard work. And harvesting the cane is a nightmare business of stooping through a tropical marsh swinging a machete and making snakes and rats mad.

To harvest enough sugarcane to make a few bottles of rum, the way the *ribereños* do in the Amazon, is one thing. But to harvest enough to make 177 million pounds of sugar, and for someone else's profit, is another matter entirely. No one in his right mind wants to work on a sugar plantation. The SDS types who joined the Venceremos Brigades to help Castro with his cane harvests in the 1960s are living testimony. Thus slaves were imported to Haiti, and a lot of them. By the time of the French Revolution, Saint Dominque was estimated to have a population of 32,000 white people; 24,000 freedmen, mostly mulattoes; and 480,000 slaves. This was as many slaves as there were in the entire thirteen colonies during our own Revolution, and in a country the size of Maryland.

For Saint Dominque, the first steps on the road to liberty were not exactly a freedom march. In 1789, after the Declaration of the Rights of Man, the white planters grew frightened that the new National Assembly in France might grant the vote to mulattoes or even abolish slavery. They convened a Colonial Assembly in order to declare themselves to have no political rights whatsoever. They claimed to be under direct rule of the king. This set off a slave rebellion, which set off another rebellion by mulattoes, who claimed loyalty to the National Assembly. The mulattoes fought both the Colonial Assembly and the slaves.

In 1792 the government of France sent a civil commission to Saint Dominque to straighten out this mess. One of the commission members was a Jacobin named Sonthonax who dismissed the Colonial Assembly, quarreled with the National Assembly loyalists, infuriated the governor general, got on the wrong side of the army garrison, and ended up siding with the rebel slaves.

Sonthonax, in a good move, considering who his allies were, announced the end of slavery. The blacks left the plantations. The whites left the country. And such chaos ensued that even some of the slave rebellion's leaders, among them Toussaint l'Ouverture, deserted to the Spanish troops who had invaded from the other side of the island. Then the British invaded, too. And at this point—though I have been back and forth through Haitian histories a number of times—I lose count of how many people were fighting each other.

In 1794 Toussaint l'Ouverture redeserted to the French governor general's side. Toussaint was a freed slave of minor education and unimposing looks, but he possessed that military genius which seems to come to men sometimes out of nowhere, as it did to Spartacus and Sam Nunn. Toussaint chased away the Spanish immediately, expelled the last of the British in 1798, and used political maneuver to rid himself of Sonthonax and the remaining powerful whites. He then defeated the mulattoes, killing some of their leaders and exiling the rest. By 1801 Toussaint was in complete control of Haiti.

And he didn't know what to do.

Given Haiti's economy and the lack of skills and sophistications among its inhabitants, the only recourse seemed to be to put people back to work on the plantations. This Toussaint did by means of forced labor, although now the workers were supposed to be entitled to a share of estate proceeds, and they were, of course, theoretically free.

Perhaps this policy would have created stability and prosperity sufficient to allow Haiti to evolve into a veritable Arkansas of the Antilles. But the world's other resident military genius from out of nowhere, Napoléon, decided on reconquest in 1802.

The commander of the French invasion, General Leclerc, brought along his wife, Napoléon's extremely annoying sister Pauline. Leclerc was thus eager to spend as much time as possible out campaigning. He overran Haiti in a few months and nabbed Toussaint. Then Napoléon made the mistake of reinstituting slavery in Guadeloupe and Martinique. Haitians could take a hint. All hell broke loose.

By December 1803 the French had been driven from the country. Of the forty-three thousand troops Napoléon sent to Haiti, thirty-five thousand had died, most, including Leclerc, from—speaking of the political aspects of disease—yellow fever or malaria. Toussaint was also killed, in a tropics-to-temperate-zone exchange of ills, by pneumonia in a French prison cell. Independence was declared on New Year's Day, 1804, by Toussaint's lieutenant, Jean-Jacques Dessalines. He stood on the beach at Gonaïves and tore the white stripe out of the French tricolor and had the remaining sections sewn together to create the Haitian flag. Then he massacred the French whites who had been dumb enough to remain in Haiti during all of the foregoing.

Dessalines, like Toussaint before him, could think of nothing to do with Haiti but return it to the plantation system. Haitians were not pleased with Dessalines's decision. An enlisted man shot him.

In 1807 Haiti was divided between an illiterate ex-slave military commander, Henri Christophe—who crowned himself Emperor Henri I in the north—and a French-educated mulatto, Alexandre Pétion—who made himself the president of a republic in the south. Christophe continued the tradition of absolute rule and plantation service. Pétion had liberal ideas about franchise rights, land reform, and teaching agricultural methods by example. Here was an experiment to see which system of government would best benefit the Haitian people.

Neither.

Christophe invented a nobility for his fellow army officers—Comte de Limonade and Duc de la Marmelade among the titles. Everybody else got to live under the feudal peonage that Europe had just spent a thousand years getting rid of. Christophe grew nasty, paranoid, and self-indulgent, as those who possess an excess of power and notice invariably seem to do. He became Roseanne Arnold with infantry. Those Haitians who could, fled to the more lenient regime of Pétion. Meanwhile Christophe spent the wealth from the plantations of his little empire on knee breeches, gilt furniture, and royal carriages from Europe; on the huge, carelessly named Sans Souci palace; and on a string of cyclopean fortifications. The largest still stands, the Citadel of La Ferrière. It's on the top of one of Haiti's tallest mountains. The walls are 140 feet high and 30 feet thick. This stronghold once mounted 365 cannon and cost, the Haitians say, twenty thousand peasant lives in the building. It was meant to repel foreign enemies. They never came. The enemies were right at home.

By 1820 the North was in rebellion. Then Christophe had a stroke that left him paralyzed from the waist down. The gleeful army mutinied. In Haiti, being a defeated political figure does not result in fat lecture fees and large publishing advances, at least it didn't before Aristide. Christophe shot himself.

Things didn't go much better for Pétion. He and his fellow mulattoes had what contemporary meddlers in poverty would call "high self-esteem" and "good workplace communication skills," et cetera. But the mulattoes had favored slavery and therefore possessed no moral standing with the majority of their countrymen. That majority had been through half a generation of war mingled with repression almost as onerous as what they'd suffered during bondage. The mood of most Haitians under Pétion was akin to the mood of boys just out of school in June. Going back to cutting cane, even their own cane, must have seemed as bad an idea as mowing the lawn once seemed—really, still seems—to me. Also, Christophe, angered by the desertions of his populace and hopping with megalomania, kept threatening to invade the South. The wherewithal of the Pétion government had to be spent on defense. The republic went broke. Pétion worried himself sick. He wasted away in 1818 saying he was sick of life.

Jean Pierre Boyer was elected to replace Pétion and took over the whole country when Christophe died. He signed a stupid treaty with France agreeing, in return for international recognition, to pay Haiti's ex-landowners huge reparations. When the bill for this came due, Haitians, yet again, were sent to the plantations by force. They rebelled. Boyer resigned and sailed for Jamaica in 1843.

Major Charles Herard replaced Boyer. According to *Black Democracy: The Story of Haiti* by H. P. Davis, Herard "entered the capital on March 21st amid an extraordinary demonstration of popular approval." He promptly invaded the Dominican Republic, lost the war, blew his popularity, and in April 1844 "sailed for Jamaica."

Three presidents followed in the next three years until General Faustin Soulouque was elected in 1847, supposedly because he was too idiotic to bother anybody. Soulouque crowned himself "Emperor Faustin I," named 624 princes, dukes, and other nobles, and initiated a court etiquette so elaborate that after a joke the chamberlain would announce, "His majesty is laughing. Gentlemen, you are invited to laugh also." Soulouque sailed for Jamaica in 1859.

Then came General Fabre Geffrard, who sailed for Jamaica in 1867. And Major Sylvain Salnave, who was tried and shot in 1869. And Nissage-Sagent, who actually served out his constitutionally mandated term and left office peacefully. This so confused the nation that there was a coup d'état anyway. General Michel Domingue sailed for Jamaica in 1876.

The next president, Boisrond-Canal, sailed for parts unknown. (Jamaica being, apparently, full to the brim with ex-leaders of Haiti.) J. N. Leger, in *Haiti, Her History and Her Detractors,* says the people showed great sympathy for Boisrond-Canal and "cheered him as he left the wharf."

So it went for Haiti through another eleven chief executives, only one of whom gave up power on purpose, until we arrive at the case of Guillaume Sam. "General" Sam was "elected" "president" in

1915, that date being the only thing in his career which doesn't require quotation marks. Once Sam was installed, the usual rebellion got under way outside Port-au-Prince, and the usual political opponents were locked in the national prison. Revolutions in Haiti don't normally involve much fighting. The standard procedure is for the leader of the rebellion, when he feels stong enough, to send a small force of men into the capital. The rebels attack various government buildings, and the government troops either fight back or don't according to whether they think the revolution is likely to succeed. Sam, however, committed a rules-book violation and had all his political prisoners slaughtered. The public was wroth. Sam had to hide in the French legation. A mob gathered there. In the words of H. P. Davis:

> The mob remained without the gates, but a small body of well-known citizens, after courteously explaining to the French minister that the people were no longer to be baulked of their revenge, entered the house and, finding Sam under a bed in a spare room on an upper floor, pulled him down the stairs, dragged him along a driveway, and threw him over an iron gate to the mob.

Sam was torn to pieces.

It was then that the United States bowed to the kinds of pressure that the United States is forever being pressured to bow to—in Kuwait, Somalia, Bosnia, and Haiti right now, for instance—and intervened. The U.S. Marines were sent to straighten things out in short order. They stayed nineteen years. And everything in Haiti has been hunky-dory ever since.

IX

Washington Irving called Haiti "one of the most beautiful islands in the world" (although he went on to say "and doomed to be one of the most unfortunate"). As recently as 1936 Alec Waugh said that the country was "of extraordinary natural beauty, which might almost have inspired Rousseau's dreams of the ideal state of nature." (Waugh was talking about Jean-Jacques Rousseau, rather than Henri, but "Tarzan" was still what he meant.) Haiti doesn't look like that anymore. In the hills the deforestation is complete, as though the geography had been sanded. What green is left is down in the cracks and crevices of the landscape awaiting some cook-fire-building or charcoal-making equivalent of Zip-Strip. On the plains a few big trees are left, looking like amputee veterans of a botanical war. The Haitians cut off one limb at a time to keep their fuel supply growing as long as possible.

There are no zombies working the fields in Haiti. No one's working the fields at all. It is impossible to tell a Haitian farm from a brush patch, although there is a shortage of cultivatable land in Haiti and all those brush patches are, in fact, farms. A few banana trees will appear in a chicken-infested thicket of weeds with, here and there, a patch of cassava, sorghum, sweet potatoes, chickpeas, or corn, and, in the mountains, maybe a half-wild coffee bush or two. Why aspire to agricultural surplus when soldiers will just steal your pigs? And most of the farmers don't own their land or don't have clear title to it. A title would, anyway, be under the power of those august local officials— mayors, army officers, and government-appointed *chefs de section*—who can read and write. And the document would be in French besides.

Dumarsais and I traveled to the Haitian countryside, driving north from Port-au-Prince on a road known as "the goat path." This climbs the quite-dry Montagnes Trou d'Eau and the once green Montagnes Noires to Haiti's central plateau. The initial ascent is steeper than college tuition and made via zigzags like a Washington polygraph. At no point is the road wide enough for two vehicles to pass safely, and at some points nothing at all can pass without mortal risk. There are two brief sections of guardrail, thought-provokingly dented. What has gone on at the curves that don't have guard rails?

Beggars appeared along the roads of the central plateau, also soldiers. I saw many more soldiers in the middle of the country than I saw at the border. Going into the mountains we were stopped at three military checkpoints and questioned at each, the information on our passports and press cards laboriously copied by officers who held the pencil stubs as though they were large power tools.

The soldiers were nice enough. I was headed for the outhouse at the army garrison in Mirebalais when a private motioned for me to stop. He ran back into the barracks. I could see him through the unglazed, unscreened window as he opened a large vinyl suitcase. He returned with a precious commodity he'd brought from home, toilet paper.

It was hours after dark when we arrived in the town of "X." I'll call it "Pignon," which is a real town elsewhere in Haiti, as are Bombardopolis, Ditty, Mme Joie, Marché Canard, and Moron. We'd been delayed when a truck ahead of us went into a rut so deep that it fell over on its side.

The army barracks in Pignon were completely unlit. A soldier came out of the moon shadows and motioned us into a large, dusty room empty except for three straight chairs and a table. Eventually another soldier arrived with a candle. He was followed by a wide man in a loud sport shirt. This was the lieutenant. He wore a huge gold watch of elaborate design. And what a great rogue of a pig thief he must have been, if this was real, which it wasn't.

The lieutenant, with the aid of the candle, my flashlight, and a Bic, solemnly read every entry and exit stamp in my passport. I wish I knew what he thought. As the result of a busy reportorial weekend in the aftermath of the opening of the Berlin Wall, I have something like fifteen East German visas in there. "I'm in Haiti to cover the terrible health effects of the U.S. embargo," I ventured.

"Thousands of children are dying," said the lieutenant, his tone indicating even an East German spy could understand that.

X

I wouldn't, I hoped, see any dying children. But I did want to see the Pignon town clinic that treated them. We went there to wash up by

Eveready light. The clinic had all the normal plumbing fixtures, but running water came from only one tap sticking out of a wall in a rear supply room. I stood in the shower and sluiced myself with a bucket.

We slept in a small house that the clinic owned. A broken exercise bicycle stood in the corner of my mud room. What CARE flub, Peace Corps mix-up, or kink in charitable intentions had put it here? Hundreds of international aid agencies are working in Haiti and doing needful things. But I went off to sleep wondering what it must be like to be the object of so many ministrations. The middle-class American equivalent would be what? Having Martha Stewart move right into your home? Or—I blinked at the exercise bike—Richard Simmons?

In the morning the porch of the clinic was full of patients, mostly women and children, all dressed in their best clothes because not much happens in Pignon. Getting sick is an occasion. Thirty-five to forty people a day are usually treated. The clinic is run by one of those international aid agencies that had haunted my sleep. The agency works in cooperation with Haiti's Ministry of Health. In what should perhaps be a warning to Ira Magaziner, the Ministry of Health is one of this unhealthy nation's largest employers. About one-fifth of the country's civil servants, some eighty-nine hundred people, are on its payroll. And 62 percent are in administrative positions. I suspect the Haitian Ministry of Health's principal contribution to health in Haiti is providing nice, healthy jobs to those Haitians with the connections to get them.

The Pignon clinic, however, couldn't be called a patronage plum. It was a humble structure, superior to its surroundings only by virtue of a poured-concrete floor. The dispensary was untidy, with medical supplies stacked wherever space could be found. The examining rooms were not very clean. A refrigerator was used only to keep things from getting lost or rat-eaten. There'd been no electricity since the international embargo began.

The clinic had a little laboratory, not much more complicated than my boyhood chemistry set. But twenty-five tests could be performed, including cancer biopsies and Pap smears. There was a gas oven to sterilize the equipment for simple operations such as cleaning and suturing tropical country life's endemic machete wounds. There was a delivery room, its walls decorated with sexy posters promoting breast-feeding. Only very difficult births took place here, maybe three a month. Midwives attended the rest. The clinic staff had made friends with the midwives, convincing them to wash their hands and so forth. The midwives had even been enlisted to sell safe water for infant formula to the mothers for a penny or two a jug.

One of the midwives came up and gave me a kiss. She was a very old woman with no teeth but real gold earrings and a face that was a Montagnes Noires of smile lines. Her fame seemed to rest on having had triplets. She also had a swell scar all along her leg. This she showed everyone. I'm not sure if the scar was supposed to have any relation to midwiving skills.

The clinic even had a dental chair. Treatment was all by extraction as far as I could tell by observing the locals. A dentist, a volunteer from France, came by every so often to yank the really difficult teeth.

The Pignon clinic had no doctor and only moderate hopes of getting a nurse. Until then, the clinic was run by a nurse's aide. The aide did not know how many people lived in the area his clinic served. Haiti does not yet suffer from information overload. But the Pan American Health Organization estimates that the population of the central plateau is over 473,000 and says there are just forty-four health centers, mostly the doctorless kind. The hospital nearest Pignon (and hospital is stretching the term) is several hours away over worse roads than we had come in on.

But Haitians don't die of the fancy hospitalized maladies which afflict the sanitized and healthy. They don't live long enough. Life expectancy is fifty-five years. And the mortality rate among children under five is 13.5 percent. These kids expire from the most prosaic causes—a cough, the runs. And here the nurse's aide was able to perform the kind of wonders practitioners at Mayo can only pray for.

He could clear lungs with decongestants and cure most respiratory infections with cheap antibiotics. And he had reduced diarrhea cases to less than three a week.

"How?" I asked.

"Safe water."

"But how do you get safe water?"

"Chlorine."

"Where can you get chlorine?"

"Five drops of Clorox in a gallon," said the nurse's aide. "That's all."

The nurse's aide said foreign donations were down. Dumarsais blamed it on the embargo. He said people were mixed up about what they should or shouldn't do for Haiti. But I think people are mixed up about Haiti, period. We like to give to hopeful or heroic causes. Note how few charitable campaigns are targeted at "Muddling Through," "The Bumbling Masses," or "Ain't Life the Pits?"

The clinic used to provide medicine for free but now sometimes had to sell it. "What if people can't pay?" I asked.

"We open a line of credit," said the nurse's aide.

"And what if people can't pay off the credit line?"

The aide seemed puzzled by my question. "Those who can," he said, "pay back. Others just can't." A nurse's aide in Haiti has come up with an eight-word national health-care-coverage program. The plan the Clinton administration presented to the Congress was fourteen hundred pages long.

The Pignon clinic has been operating since 1978. Before that the only medical treatment in the area was from—as the nurse's aide put it—"a not-trained woman who gave injections." The success of the little clinic, all the things it accomplished with facilities and skills that wouldn't do to treat an American for a hangover, was wonderful. But this is a sad kind of wonder. It should be this easy to save the millions of other dying kids, kids so unfortunate they don't even have the luck to live in Pignon.

Pignon had no stores or shops. The only thing that marked it as a town was a town square. An aberrant bit of government attention had been paid to this plot of land. The bare earth was overlain with a maze of cement curbings and walkways to make a formal garden without the garden. And cement benches had been placed around it as though Haiti lacked spots to sit and do nothing.

There was nothing with any charm in Pignon, except every one of its residents. They waved each time they saw us, inquired after our well-being and comfort, and insisted that I wear an absurd straw hat while I wandered around in the sun—lest, I suppose, my weird red skin pop like a weenie's on a grill. Not that they had any weenies. Or grills either.

When we had a flat on our Jeep, two chairs were brought out so Dumarsais and I could sit in the road while half of the town's men went to work repairing the tire with scraps of rubber and a vulcanizing oven improvised from an old piston head.

No one begged or stared. Only one kid could have been labeled pesky, and he was cute about it. The very pariah dogs were friendly. Or maybe they'd given up even the hope of having anything to bite.

XI

Of course, the humans in Haiti have hope. They hope to leave. Back in Port-au-Prince, I asked Dumarsais to take me to the wharf in Cité Soleil where boat people embark. I stood on one of the dock's few missing planks and looked at a wooden sloop that seemed to have been built with a hammer and a pocket knife. The vessel was maybe thirty feet long with a shallow draft and an awkwardly wide beam. The hull looked soggy with age. The sails appeared to have been sewn from grain sacks. There was no cabin or shelter of any kind. "Put a couple of hundred people on board," I said, "and it's going to be an unpleasant cruise to Florida."

"Ha!" said Dumarsais. "It's for fishing. The refugees don't use those." He turned me around and faced me toward the shore. A couple of twelve- or fifteen-foot lorries were sitting swaybacked on a mud bank. Their hulls had been eaten by rot. I could see daylight through their sides. *"That,"* said Dumarsais, "is what people go to Florida in."

And for those who cannot get to Florida, there is heaven or, anyway, voodoo.

Someone at the bar at the Oloffson Hotel had said to me, "You'll never understand Haiti if you don't understand voodoo."

"Can you explain it to me?" I asked.

"You wouldn't understand."

Dumarsais took me to a voodoo temple, or *hounfò,* a few blocks from the pier. This was a room about thirty feet by thirty feet, a grand space for Cité Soleil, and decorated in a manner that owed something to the sacramental and something to party time. The ceiling was covered with small paper flags, crêpe bunting, and inflated beach balls. The walls were painted putt-putt golf green and arrayed with *vèvè* symbols and with pictures of the *loas* the *vèvès* represent.

Loas, though descended from African pantheons, are identified with Catholic saints. Saint John the Baptist is Jan Batis Trasetonm, the Virgin Mary is Metrès Ezili, Saint George is Ogou Chango, and the Three Kings are Simbi Boua, Simbi Nandezo, and the rap-group-sounding Simbi 3 Kafou. The saintly *loas* were depicted here in a carnival-booth art style, and combined with the cagelike *vèvès,* they gave the *hounfò* the look of a canonized sideshow menagerie.

In the center of the room was a pillar of stepped-back, ziggurat design like a Sunday-school illustration of the Tower of Babel. This was the *potomitan,* the ladder by which *loas'* spirits descend into the *hounfò.* Most of a voodoo ceremony's rituals and dances center upon it. It was decorated with ribbons and with drawings of eyes and other symbols. There's a hint of the maypole in the *potomitan,* though May is not the season when nature awakes from a long sleep in Haiti. Nature may not ever do that in Haiti again.

The members of this *hounfò* were adherents of Bizango, one of a number of voodoo organizations in Haiti. They are called "secret societies," but the secret is only that they have some private ceremonies and passwords, as do the Free and Accepted Masons, which, if you think about it, are no more strangely named.

The *houngan,* or priest, wore a shirt and tie and looked as if he might *be* a Mason, a thoughtful small businessman, the kind who does a lot of volunteer work. Indeed, his title in this Bizango chapter was the unexotic one of president. He asked me if I would like to see the altar. It was actually a room, no bigger than a kitchen pantry, lit only by a few small oil lamps. A confusion of sacrifices were in here, pieces of velvet and satin, items of clothing, vases, pottery cups, flags, artificial flowers, foodstuffs, bottles of rum, and, in the center of these, a cross swathed in dark-colored draperies. It was as though, in collecting these sacred objects, the worshipers had tried to touch upon every aspect of existence, including reality—a number of long and nasty-looking knives were thrust into the dirt floor in front of the cross.

I'm not of mystical inclination. Aside from the occasional prayer-in-time-of-medical-tests, I am rooted in the profane. Nevertheless, I was affected by the reliquary. Voodoo is a syncretic religion. All its myriad labors of inclusion and reconciliation were enshrined here. If it was just a closet in a slum, it was a closet with a story. People from dozens of Africans societies, with their hundreds of deities, had been seized and taken to a place that might as well have been another planet. Here—like the fantasies of John E. Mack's *Abduction* made real—they were subjected to the worst indignities by people the color of grubs and slugs. These pasty tyrants claimed that the son of their own god said everybody was equal. This god and his kid and the kid's mother were all filled with infinite mercy and love, but, if you didn't convert, they baked you in an oven when you died.

Whatever the African words for "bullshit" are, slaves in Haiti must have spoken them frequently. And yet those slaves studied Christianity, and they studied all their own various creeds. From this metaphysical slumgullion they created something upon which they could agree, just as they created a language, Creole, in which they could agree they agreed. Thus a measure of comfort, hope, and social structure arose in conditions that would have driven less decent and intelligent people—me, for instance—into atheistic rage. What voodoo's nameless apostles accomplished makes the labors of the early church fathers at the First Council of Nicaea seem a mere keeping of minutes at a PTA meeting.

I said something to this effect to the *hounfò's* president. He opened a narrow door next to the altar room. "I don't think any outsider has ever seen this," said Dumarsais. There was a small space inside, little more than a cupboard. This was the sanctum sanctorum of the chapter. I confess that to me it looked like more of the same spiritual jumble sale. But an electric charge of reverence ran through Dumarsais. And the president himself seemed awed. I had to be satisfied with feeling honored.

Dumarsais said there was a meeting of the chapter that night, a ceremony only for the initiates, but the president said we could come. And so at nine o'clock we returned. The street was empty except for our Jeep. No one and nothing stirred aboard in Cité Soleil.

The *hounfò* was lit by a single lantern. About forty-five people were inside. They ranged in age from early twenties to the indeterminate venerabilty that comes so early to Haitians. The men wore identical gray smocks trimmed in crimson, the peasant smocks of eighteenth-century France but in dress-parade version. The women wore archaic peasant dresses in the same colors. Everyone had a red kerchief tied at the neck, and one was loaned to me.

People sat around the margins of the room, smoking cigarettes and talking. An old woman swept the packed-earth floor. Branches from some aromatic plant had been piled around the *potomitan,* like a combination room freshener and preparation for an auto-da-fé. I couldn't tell exactly when the ceremony began. The president, now wearing the sequined shirt of a salsa bandleader, came in. And three men began to play on a graduated set of congas. But the president didn't burst into song. He spoke in conversational tones. A young man moved through the crowd anointing the congregation with something like Aqua Velva, pouring so much of it on our hands and heads that the room smelled like one giant fourteen-year-old boy learning to shave. Someone else had a censer on a chain, incense fumes pouring out, and he used it very differently than in a Catholic Mass, swinging the vessel between the legs of the men and under the skirts of the women.

Candles were distributed and lit. The president, punctuating his remarks with a gourd rattle, made one general prayer to the *Gran Mèt,* the Big God. Voodoo is, at its heart, monotheistic. But God is conceived—quite reasonably, given Haitian experience—as remote. He is too la-de-da for daily affairs. Once obeisance had been made to the *Gran Mèt,* all further invocation was aimed at the more workaday *loas.* We prayed to the *loas* represented on the walls, the *loas* to which this particular chapter of Bizango was consecrated. Dumarsais prompted me as to when to kneel, turn, stand, or shut up. Some dancing started. First the men, then the women, then everyone but me circled the *potomitan* in a desultory fashion.

It was a hour and a half before the ceremony took on form. Several people seemed to have been appointed as ritual police. They nudged the others to do the correct thing at the correct time the way Dumarsais nudged me. Late in the evening, the enforcers would also wake those who dozed. A choir was nudged into song. And two angry-acting men entered the dance, one carrying a noose and the other swinging a hide whip.

Voodoo societies had been founded, Dumarsais told me later, for mutual protection in the anarchistic slave communities. The rope and the lash had nothing to do, as I would have thought, with the slave masters. Rather, the whip was a token of self-discipline and the noose stood for catching thieves. The slave masters did not need to be dealt with symbolically, they'd been dealt with in an actual manner in 1804.

The dances grew more practiced and complex—bows and side-slip steps, thigh slaps and arm-waving salutes, turns and bobs and genuflections. If country line dancing were done for some serious purpose to better music by people more coordinated than Houston suburbanites, it would look like this.

And, then again, no it wouldn't. The women rushed into the altar room and came out waving knives. They picked up the branches from the base of the *potomitan* and put them on their heads like laurel wreathes. The drumming quickened. The singing rose in pitch. And a weaving, flailing, cantering dash around the center post began. The speed increased until centrifugal force should have sent the dancers slamming into the *hounfò*'s walls. The man with the whip, a huge person with a shaved head like an artillery shell, stood snapping the plait at the dancer's feet and taking mouthfuls of cane liquor and spraying these over the celebrants. An awful keening chant arose. The frenzy in the darkened room seemed more primordial than Haiti's African heritage. The great kingdoms of west Africa date only from the fourth century A.D. Maybe this is what the Greek mystery cults did on their lodge nights. Dionysus, that city-state yuppie, only invented wine, not rum, but just such Dionysian furors were described in 408 B.C. in *The Bacchae* by Euripides. I had no more than thought so when a woman dancer spun out of the crowd straight at me, sweeping her knife through the air and looking perfectly like one of the maenads about to tear her sacrificial victim to pieces. There was the fate of Guillaume Sam to be considered.

But the woman meant me no harm. She didn't even see me. She was possessed, being "ridden by her *loa*," as it is sometimes described. Then another woman was possessed. Then half a dozen women were describing dervish circles and groaning to heaven. One fell on the ground and made pig noises. Some shook and convulsed. Others lost control of arms and legs, and these limbs would then propel them about the room in spastic flips and tosses. They began to speak in tongues. But this was not so impressive. I have a born-again sister who does that. And my own French probably sounds like glossolalia.

Whoever was closest to a possessed woman would (myself

excepted) brave the knife blade, run in and catch hold of the ecstatic, and clutch her until the *loa* jumped off or lost interest or whatever. I remember this sort of thing from LSD in the 1960s. And, as with LSD, it was hard to tell whether possession was terrifying or superb. A bit of both, if memory serves.

For the next couple of hours, dancing waxed and waned and raptures came and went. Then, on some cue I did not see, the crowd faded back to the walls. A delegation of officers and officials went to the small door next to the altar room, the entrance to the holy of holies, and there performed a number of Masonic rituals. My father and all my uncles were Shriners. I know the drill. My instincts about the Bizango president had been right. Later, reading the Haitian voodoo scholar Gérard Alphonse Férère, I discovered that one more thing voodoo had drawn upon was the abandoned Free Masonry of the dead and exiled French slaveowners.

When the salutes and incantations were finished, the door of the tabernacle was opened and a cross and three coffins brought out. I'd just looked in there that afternoon. There wasn't space inside for these. The coffins were for an infant, a child, and an adult. The man with the shaved skull raised his rum bottle and took hold of a machete. A woman picked up the cross, and the two of them performed a dance of menace and confrontation—the eternal verities versus Saturday-night fun. The fun seemed to triumph. Another woman put the baby's coffin on her head, and the dance was repeated. She too was vanquished, as was a third woman who danced with the larger, child-sized casket precariously balanced aloft. Finally, four male pallbearers took hold of the biggest coffin, drew daggers from their waistbands, and chased the machete-wielding drunkard around the *potomitan*. Death holds trumps. The cross and all the caskets were waltzed through a macabre cotillion, a Busby Berkeley eschatology.

In the end the coffins were stacked crisscross fashion with daggers and candles arrayed in front of them and a crucifix drawn on the earth in flaming rum. Each member of the congregation came forward to make elaborate gestures of respect, to knock several times on the lids of the coffins and place a cash offering on the polished wood. "The grave is just one more thing we have to go through," said Dumarsais. And, considering what Haitians have been through already, I could see his point.

The last act of the ceremony was for the coffins to be run up and down the streets of Cité Soleil. Whether this was to exhibit Bizango's victory over death or just to scare the neighborhood, I couldn't tell. But Dumarsais said to me, "There is no real protection in Haiti without voodoo."

When the coffins had been brought home—carried backwards into the *hounfò* and backwards through the sanctuary door—the members all embraced each other. Each of them hugged me and clasped my hand. Then, though it was two in the morning, it was time to talk. A voodoo society is also a social club and a mutual aid organization and even a community bank. Everyone had his say. They asked me to speak, too.

All I could manage was "Thank you." But what I really wanted to tell the voodoo celebrants was "I wish all of you could come to the United States and live there. You're an immense improvement on the other people who go to Florida. And, if Americans are worried that immigration will cause overpopulation, ecological problems, and such, then we could arrange a trade. You sail north. And we'll get a bunch of crabby families in Winnebagos, drug smugglers, Disney executives, Palm Beach divorce lawyers, 2 Live Crew, Burt and Loni, time-share condo salesmen, Don Johnson, Miami Beach aerobics instructors, William Kennedy Smith, kvetching retirees, teenage gang members, and wounded German tourists, and we'll send them back to Haiti on the same boat."

9 ECONOMIC JUSTICE

The Hell with Everything, Let's Get Rich

There are better ways to solve life's problems than by holding voodoo ceremonies or shooting your neighbors or sending twits-of-all-nations to Rio. Politics won't do it. And politicians surely won't. The best method of existential improvement is making money.

It is precisely this that is being done in—of all places—the People's Republic of Vietnam. But don't tell them. Shhh, they think they won the war.

The old Communists who run Vietnam actually believe they defeated decadent Western capitalism. So where did the little girl in Hoan Kiem Park, in the middle of downtown Hanoi, get a hula hoop? Why did every house in the city have a workshop, store, or tea parlor in the front room? Whence the hundreds of tiny factories? Wherefore the hawkers, barkers, jobbers, and drummers shouting their wares in the streets? How come foreign investors packed the haute cuisine restaurants? How come there was haute cuisine? And what was that eminently capitalist organization, British Petroleum, doing signing a co-venture agreement with the state-owned Vietnamese oil company in the lobby of my hotel? With an open bar?

After the signing, pyrotechnics were ignited to drive away evil spirits. Twenty-foot strings of firecrackers hung from the hotel balcony. The explosions were forceful. I kept thinking about all the effort I put into dodging the draft. Now I was going to die in Vietnam anyway, twenty years later, from a stray cherry bomb.

When that famous last helicopter left the roof of the American embassy in Saigon in 1975, we were—capitalistically speaking—just going out for a beer. We're back. Meanwhile the locals have let go of Karl Marx with both hands.

I traveled to Vietnam in 1992 with my photojournalist friend John Giannini, the man who had played eighteen holes on the "most in-your-face golf course in the world" in Bangladesh. Giannini speaks Vietnamese and has been in and out of the country for most of a generation. He served two combat tours with the U.S. Army, returned as a reporter, lived in pre-communist Saigon, got wounded during the Khmer Rouge takeover of Cambodia, and—John being as persistent as Rambo sequels—came back to Vietnam again after the fall of the South. He'd been in Hanoi last in 1990 and warned me that, although so-called Ho Chi Minh City was coming to life, the North remained a typical People's Republic locale—short on everything except lines to stand in, dull, gray, glum, "a big slab of drab."

But Hanoi had changed. On first impression it seemed like sixties America—not pot, war, and hirsute-aggravation sixties America, but the madras-clad, record-hop, beach-bunny nation of my high school days. Of course Hanoi, with its crumbling tropical seventh-arrondissement architecture and dilapidated boulevards shaded by enormous tamarind trees, couldn't look less like midwestern suburbia. And everyone was working instead of doing the Hully-Gully. Nevertheless there was a *doo-ron-ron* in the air. Hanoi is a young city. More than half the people in Vietnam are under twenty and cheerful with the infinite possibilities of baby-boom cheer. These kids wear jeans. They

wear T-shirts with catchphrases in English (sort of in English—DAR-
LING PIGEON/MY PEACEFUL MIND and A LIFE'S BEACH). And they ride
Honda 50s. The coffee-can exhaust note, the two-cycle gas smell, the
windup-toy gear racket are exactly the same as they were in Ohio the
summer "Little Honda" was a Top 40 hit.

The streets of Hanoi were thronged with hundreds of these
motorbikes and thousands of pedal-operated *cyclo* rickshaws and tens of
thousands of bicycles, all preposterously overloaded. I saw four school-
girls on one Honda seat, a hundred cartons of something lashed to a
single bicycle, and ten adults and children—I counted twice—packed
into and hanging off of a *cyclo*.

Everyone seemed to be making, selling, or accomplishing
something or hurrying someplace to do so. The most modest resources
sufficed to start a business. At every intersection old ladies hunkered
next to bicycle pumps, selling tire air. There weren't many black
pajamas to be seen, and some that I did see I suspect were Armanis.
There were no long Bolshevik files of people either. The only lines I
saw were lines of *cyclo* drivers waiting for fares outside restaurants and
hotels. Gasoline was readily available (this unheard of in a Marxist
country); 93-octane unleaded sold for $1.04 a gallon. It even seemed
to be a buyer's market at the Ho Chi Minh Mausoleum with short,
fast-moving queues to see the old dead guy.

A wealth of construction was under way, mostly private
houses. These were only one room wide but as much as sixty feet deep
and three or four stories high. They were built of fired-clay blocks or
of rubble framed between poured concrete uprights. Exteriors were
bright-painted stucco with mosaic decorations. Porticos, balusters, cor-
nices, and roof crestings were given shapes as fantastic and modern as
the simple building materials allowed. The effect was Lego deco.

Our government translator and guide, a young foreign service
officer I'll call Pham, said property was expensive in central Hanoi.
Pham had no idea what the city's many "Heroic Workers" and "People's Victory" monuments commemorated. He had to go up and read

the plaques like anyone else. But he knew to the penny—or, rather, to the carat—what real estate costs: one ounce' of pure gold per square meter, payment in bullion only.

A government department store, the Universal State Shop, still existed, but "steerers" hovered at every counter. These were young men who told you how you could find better, cheaper merchandise—in the private shops which paid them to stand there. The steerer in the bicycle department said, quite loudly, that bikes made by the Vietnamese state monopoly cost too much, thirty to thirty-five dollars. He could get us a smuggled Chinese bicycle for half that price.

The private vendors in the vast, glazed-roof, trainless train-station central market had spices, vegetables, fruits, poultry, and fish in profusion. I stumbled over a yard-wide wire basket filled with a python. "God, what's that?" I said.

"Food," said Pham.

But a large part of the Hanoi market—and of every other market in Vietnam—was given over to tools. Pipe threaders, die cutters, soldering irons, calipers, and micrometers were for sale along with the usual Third World hoe blades and ax heads. Plus there were all kinds of motor parts and bits of electrical and even electronic hardware. The marketplace was devoted not just to things but to things that make things. It was an industrial revolution in its nonage, like seeing young James Watt stare at a boiling kettle or watching an infant Thomas Alva Edison get a shock after petting the cat.

Plenty of consumer goods were being sold, too—clothes, shoes, clocks, thermos bottles, dishes, kitchen utensils—cheap but serviceable products of mainland China. Giannini said the pot and pans used to be made by hand in Hanoi. He wondered if Chinese imports had put people out of work. We drove a few blocks to Hang Thiec, "Tin Street," but found everyone fully employed. The tinsmiths were spread out across the sidewalks and had laid sheets of corrugated metal in the road to be flattened by passing cars and trucks. Men banged on various objects with a noise like a thousand skateboarders on the roof of a Quonset hut. One fellow was hammering out a medium-sized rectangular thing, the purpose of which escaped us. "What's that?" asked Giannini.

"Ice-cube tray!" said the artisan.

▌▐

We don't know what causes poverty. Poverty isn't caused by over-crowding. Hong Kong is a moosh pit plus an airport. Poverty isn't caused by a shortage of resources. Belgium has none at all if you don't count Brussels sprouts. And poverty isn't caused by sloth. I speak as an American prone on the sofa with the video remote.

We don't know what causes wealth either. Obviously, we don't. If we did, I'd be too rich to be writing and you'd be too rich to be reading. We'd be drinking on our yachts. All we can really do in the study of poverty and wealth is watch carefully when one is turning into the other.

Vietnam wouldn't seem to be a promising subject for such research. In 1990 Vietnam's annual per capita income was estimated by the World Bank to be $230—$140 less than Haiti's. Only 22 percent of Vietnam's land is farmable, and nearly all of its 69 million people live in the arable regions. Thus Vietnam is, in effect, more densely popu-lated than Bangladesh. Vietnam endured a civil war as bitter—and more protracted (thanks to some help from us)—as those in Somalia and ex-Yugoslavia. And, in the course of that war, Vietnam suffered terrible ecological damage. But the other Third World countries writ-ten about in this book were awful, and Vietnam wasn't. In fact, almost all of the places I've traveled for the past two and a half years—my old college campus included—were depressing, yet Vietnam was full of good cheer.

What do the Vietnamese have going for them? Family? Tradi-tion? Culture? Maybe. People say so. I don't know. The Vietnamese seemed pretty much like regular folks to me, as did everyone else I met in my peregrinations. Bangladeshis, Californians, Somalis, marines, Yagua Indians, coeds, Czechs, environmentalists, Bosnians, Serbs, Haitians—each was about as likely as another to be swell or a jerk. Okay, the environmentalists and the Somalis were total assholes. But in a dozen years of being a foreign correspondent I've yet to meet a person who wasn't an easily identifiable member of my own species or who was any worse than some of the people I hung out with in high school. I doubt the Vietnamese are fundamentally different from the rest of us.

But Vietnam does have an advantage over the grimmer regions I've described. The Vietnamese have acquired—or reacquired—the one freedom upon which all other prerogatives, privileges, activities, understandings, and creations are based. "A power over a man's subsistence amounts to a power over his will," wrote Alexander Hamilton in the *Federalist Papers*.

Of course Vietnam is still a dictatorship. Economic freedom is a precondition of individual rights, not a guarantee that you'll get any. You can do more or less what you want to do in Vietnam. You are not, however, supposed to have opinions about doing it. But Vietnam is a poor country and most Vietnamese can't afford a subscription to the *New Republic* and are too busy working to watch *Crossfire,* so there aren't that many opinions around.

And it's too late for opinions anyway, at least for Marxist ones. The day after the British Petroleum signing, John and I were leaving our hotel when the foreign minister of China walked into the lobby. He was fresh from a first-ever meeting with his Vietnamese counterpart, and the two were giving a press conference in the banquet room. We peeked through the doorway. Everybody in there was Chinese or Vietnamese, but the press conference was being translated into English. English is the language of nations with prospects (and, let us not forget, also the language of nations with freedoms).

That night, listening to the BBC World Service on shortwave, we heard Vietnam was sending food aid to the former Soviet Union.

And two weeks later in Saigon—which no one pretended to

call Ho Chi Minh City—I watched a young man make model airplanes out of beer cans. He folded the aluminum into carefully detailed barroom origami: C-130 transports, F-4 Phantoms, Cobra helicopters, and one triangle-shaped jet with a star embossed on each wing. "Soviet?" I said.

"No, no Soviet," he said. But it looked like a MIG-21.

"Soviet?" I repeated.

And he pulled out a much-fingered U.S. military plane–spotter's guide, older than he was, and pointed to a picture of this plane, a General Dynamics F-106 Delta Dagger. "No Soviet," he said. "All American. Soviet no good."

III

Material progress in Vietnam was not limited to the big city as it had been in the Czech Republic. A pleasant flurry of economics spread from Hanoi all through the fields of the Hong River valley. Every garden plot was tended with the minute care Westerners wouldn't give a bonsai tree. This paid, to judge by the Hondas in the farm yards. And gaudy, perpendicular Hanoi-style houses rose from the middle of rice paddies like misplaced cubism exhibits.

We drove east to Ha Long Bay on the Gulf of Tonkin. The Hong River delta has only a few bridges. The Soviets and the Chinese collaborated to build an enormous one, but they built it where there wasn't traffic. We crossed a Hong tributary, the Peaceful Time River, on a listing barge. Our car was surrounded with peasants, all of them spitting something—sugarcane pulp, sunflower-seed hulls, betel-nut juice—like two hundred high school juniors making their first try at dipping snuff. The barge was nudged across by a Chinese tugboat. The tug looked to have been sunk and raised several times. Running it was a position of social consequence. The captain dressed in a three-piece suit and fedora and flew a large red flag made of painted burlap.

At Bai Chay town on Ha Long Bay the mountains rose immediately from the riverine plain without prelude of uplands or foothills. These dolomite and limestone promontories were eroded into whimsical towers, looking like the mountains on Chinese scroll paintings, as well they might, since they served as models for many of those paintings.

The mountains continued directly into the sea, giving Ha Long Bay some three thousand islands, which were in fact the tips of mountain peaks. Waves had further eroded the limestone so that each island was wider above the high-tide mark than it was at water level. Many of the islands were named after the strange resulting shapes: Teapot Island, Head Island, Turtle Island. And you could go on naming them yourself: Large Order of Fries with a Burger Island, Overturned-Car Island, Tip of My Dick in the Bathtub Island, etc.

We hired a wooden boat, some thirty feet long and powered by a Chinese diesel engine with a single cylinder the size of a wastepaper basket and rpms so low that you could hear each stinking detonation in the combustion chamber. We motored at dog-walking speed into a flat and misty ocean. Wooden junks with their fish-fin sails were becalmed in the distance, and all around us were woven-basket boats, coracles, hardly bigger than front-hall rugs. Fishing families live in these year-round, going to bed under a roof of bowed matting and coming ashore only to sell their catch and get fresh water.

"They have lots of children," said Pham. "Not much else to do." But I didn't see more than two children in any basket boat, so maybe they lose a lot of children overboard, too.

The little islands, few of them more than ten acres, were covered in gnarls of vegetation. Every island seemed to have a cove and a sea arch, a little beach and a cave. One cave opened at the waterline like a whale sneer, stalactite-toothed and deep enough to hide everybody in a Scout troop who wanted to sneak a smoke.

Three thousand oriental Neverlands. It was a scene of incredible beauty and, hence, completely off the subject of economics, which this chapter is supposed to be about. On the other hand, what's money for? An old woman skulling a coracle came along side and sold us ten quarts of Chinese beer. We puttered for hours, wholly content, returning to shore only in the last moments of an immense red-gold sunset so beautiful that it rendered fiscal punditry mute.

Back in Hanoi, Pham dutifully took us to Ho Chi Minh's home, a simple, open, tile-roof affair built in mountain-tribesman style. It was little more than a gazebo, really, with two small rooms surrounded by a veranda upstairs and with nothing but a patio underneath. On the patio was a conference table with three telephones, and here Ho used to sit and run the whole Vietnam war. Ho Chi Minh adopted this spartan style of life in order to devote all his energy to Marxist/Leninist revolution. It made me think better of Imelda Marcos.

Ho's house, Ho's tomb, and a Ho museum were all contained in a large park, a sort of Six Flags Over Ho with several nice ponds but no water slides into them.

The museum was supposed to be a monument to world socialism. It was designed by an East-bloc architect working with ferroconcrete in the prepostmodernist style—all needless parabolas, ramps to nowhere, and soaring spaces that didn't contain anything.

The gift shop had a display of stuffed carcasses of various animals that were nearing extinction in Vietnam. These were "for sale to benefit endangered species."

The museum exhibits were confusing, too. One seemed to detail the history of man from the Neolithic age until the time when countries all over the world—Albania, Cuba, Laos, Mongolia, Peru, and Ceylon—sent souvenir gifts to Ho Chi Minh.

The American Communist Party had sent Ho a wristwatch, a gold "Jules Jurgensen" on a leather strap. Back in the States I asked a jeweler about this brand. He said, "It's the kind of thing you see in a catalogue. You know—'$795 list price. Discount price $395. This week only, $285.'"

Another exhibit contained a Coca-Cola sign, a blown-up photograph of a dead U.S. Marine, a Marilyn Monroe poster, and a plaster sculpture of an Edsel grille. This was, I think, supposed to be a mixed-media presentation about the failure of bourgeois materialism, but I couldn't tell for sure because the lights and sound system were broken.

No bourgeois materialism was evident at our hotel—a government guest house, actually. The place had been built and decorated in a purely Soviet spirit. The exterior walls were made of preformed concrete. The interior walls were painted a Bulgarian green, and each room was lit by a single six-foot fluorescent tube so that we felt like cheap merchandise in a display case, Jules Jurgensen wristwatches perhaps. But there were non-communist touches: hot water, a new bar of soap, *two* towels. And when Giannini came down with some kind of malarial frisson the room boy gave him a massage and rubbed Tiger Balm on his eyelids.

The morning meal was served in traditional socialist fashion—very slowly, with the courses out of order so that the jelly arrived half an hour after the toast and the coffee didn't come until we'd called for the check. However, it was hard to be angry at a place that had ice cream, beer, and cigarettes on its breakfast menu. And the cooking was good.

Everywhere else in Hanoi the cooking was even better. Also, cheap. Dinner for two at the best restaurant was six dollars. Vietnamese food is like Chinese food prepared by a great French chef. No. That would mean frog fried rice and trying to get snails out of their shells with chopsticks. Vietnamese food is like French food with wonderful Chinese. . . . That isn't it either. There's no moo shu pork in sauce béchamel. Though some odd things did turn up on the bill of fare:

> Vaporize Sea Fish
> Volcano in Raw Mixture
> Fried Beep in Minute
> Fish-Sound with Chicken

Tortle in Rose Souse
Creamable Eggs
Spaghetti Soup with Chicken

The last being an accurate description of the dish. But it was delicious. It was all delicious. And every meal came with perfectly baked baguettes, the only decent bread in Asia, and cups of *café filtre,* the only drinkable coffee east of Peshawar.

Not that Giannini and I were drinking much coffee, not with Johnnie Walker Red (listed on the menu as "Scotland Whiskey Wine") available at $17 a quart and with 750 ml. bottles of Stolichnaya for only $1.75. After plenty of that and some surprisingly drinkable Singapore cognac, we would be pedaled to the guest house in a pair of *cyclos,* rolling through the pitch-dark but still-bustling streets of Hanoi, lolling around in our chairs like participants in an Alzheimer's Olympics.

IV

We drove out of Hanoi again, heading south on Highway 1, the old colonial road to Saigon. Every bridgehead, rail crossing, and flood dyke was marked by a squat, crumbling, mold-blackened French pillbox. In the Indo-Chinese War the French managed, by means of these pillboxes, to control all the pillboxes in the Indo-Chinese War.

In Japan people drive on the left. In China people drive on the right. In Vietnam it doesn't matter. Highway 1 was a no-lane road. The Vietnamese public sector was—public sector–like—not performing with the constructive vigor of Vietnamese private citizens. There was no more infrastructure in the country than there'd been in Haiti. There were no sewers. Electricity was a sometimes thing. The tap water was an instant weight-loss plan—one tablespoon with every meal and eat what you want. The pavement on Highway 1 was so bad that we would have made better time if we'd driven off it and sunk to our hubs in the rice paddies. But Vietnam has private property now, and we couldn't do that.

We were traveling in an old Toyota Land Cruiser with solid axles and a leaf-spring front end, a vehicle designed to dispel any notion of the Japanese as automotive design geniuses. Our driver, whom I'll call Vo, had been a convoy trucker on the Ho Chi Minh Trail during the war. And we could have used some U.S. air strikes on Highway 1's bicycles, water buffalos, motorcycles, jeepney buses, tractors, goats, dogs, children, oxcarts, flocks of ducks, private automobiles, and genuine Vietnamese potbellied pigs, the kind fashionable Americans have for pets and we had for dinner. Vo was good—able to drive around (or over) all these at forty miles per hour on road surfaces barely fit for walking. But an hour out of Hanoi he suddenly pulled to the side. "We have a serious problem," he said. "We can go no further."

"What?" we said.

"The horn is broken."

Vo sorted through scavenged car parts at a roadside repair shed while farmers tried to sell wives to Giannini and me. Used wives. A crowd of children collected around us.

"Lien Xo! Lien Xo!" ("Soviet"), the children said.

"Nguoi My! Nguoi My!" ("American"), said John.

The children pondered that. We looked pretty scruffy. John was obviously wrong. *"Lien Xo! Lien Xo! Lien Xo!"*

This—plus one souvenir store at China Beach with a faded sign in Russian—was all that remained of Soviet presence. "Americans without money" is what the Vietnamese call their erstwhile allies from the ex-USSR.

Vo jury-rigged something that made enough noise to get us south. Away from Hanoi the farms were still rich but the farmers not so much so. Houses were made from woven sticks or straw thatch or, sometimes, brick. The Three Little Pigs seemed to be the senior partners in the local architecture firm. Here and there tall bamboo poles rose with television antennas lashed to the tops.

As we neared the coast, the land became hilly and dotted with limestone formations, chimneylike cousins of the towers in Ha Long Bay. The locals were breaking up these with picks and shovels— chipping away at the sights to make gravel for roads, but anyone who's been on the roads in Vietnam would rather have pavement than scenery.

The country people really do wear conical hats, called *non la*. Peering down from the highway at the open-air markets in the villages, all I could see were hundreds of these bobbing, weaving, swaying bonnets—the dancing mushrooms from *Fantasia*. Once that thought had entered my head, I could never look out the car window in Vietnam again without hearing Tchaikovsky's *Nutcracker Suite*.

We reached Vinh, about 170 miles from Hanoi, after ten hours of travel. We checked into another government rest house, like the last one but with cockroaches the size of bronzed baby shoes. GUESTS ARE REQUESTED TO DRESS IN A REGULAR WAY IN HOTEL RESTAURANT AND BAR read a sign in English over my bed. Vinh had been the great staging point for the Ho Chi Minh Trail, the route by which the guerrillas and NVA regulars fighting in the south were supplied. But the only evidence of this was a weed-grown freight yard where a single watchman was keeping an eye on abandoned railcar undercarriages.

Below Vinh is the neck of Vietnam, where the Indochinese cordillera, the Chaîne Annamitique, runs in close parallel to the sea. At its narrowest point, the country is only thirty miles wide. The Ho Chi Minh Trail wasn't a communist invention. It was the old trade route through Laos and Cambodia to Saigon. The North Vietnamese either had to use the trail or come down the middle of Highway 1 like a St. Patrick's Day parade.

This has always been the poorest part of Vietnam, and, as the poorest parts of so many places do, it has the best views. At one spot near the Giang River the landscape fell in multicolored bands like a fancy after-dinner drink—a layer of sea, a layer of dunes, a layer each of grass shacks and gardens, a layer of bamboo-shaded road, another of rice paddies, and a final layer of thick, dark mountains—a pousse-café of beauty.

The mountains were covered in enormous growths of tropical hardwoods. Though not for long, to judge by the number of trucks we saw carrying logs the size of trailer homes. This was all government timbering, a communist version of the U.S. Forestry Service. Excuse the redundancy.

A high lump in the coastal plain marked the DMZ, the "Demilitarized Zone" that used to exist between North and South Vietnam. A cow was scratching herself against a barely legible sign commemorating the "Vietnamese People's Victory over the McNamara Line." This, if anyone remembers, was a system of highly sophisticated electronic sensors devised by JFK's secretary of defense and planted in the DMZ to detect North Vietnamese infiltration, infiltration that would have been as hard to miss as ten thousand Irishmen with bagpipes and the mayor.

The food got even better, improving in proportion to the filth of the restaurants along the road. The best meal we had in Vietnam was served in a sagging, cobwebbed, three-walled shack in Dong Hoi where rats were running along the rafters and I had to step over a pig to get to the bathroom. Not that there was anything on the other side of the pig except a hole in the dirt floor.

Here they brought us *cha gio,* miniature spring rolls; chicken *pho,* the "spaghetti soup" that was on the menu in Hanoi; another soup called *bun bo hue,* made from beef and noodles and, I think, 500 chili peppers; still another soup, *canh chua dau ca,* "sour fish soup" (the Vietnamese will turn anything into a soup, just as Americans will turn anything into a sandwich); plus pork balls and grilled shrimp and sticky rice and regular rice and beer and tea and mineral water, all for a buck apiece.

Food is eaten by holding a bowl under your nose and pretending to use chopsticks while sucking food into your mouth with loud slurping noises. Holding your chopsticks too close to the tips is considered uncouth but belching, smoking, picking the teeth, and spitting on the floor are fine. It takes a while for table manners to return to normal after a visit to Vietnam.

Most of the food is dipped in, and all of the food is flavored with, *nuoc mam*. *Nuoc mam* is made by squeezing the juice out of fish and letting it rot in a large clay vat. The resulting liqueur is diluted with water and vinegar and set in a shallow dish on every table—the salt, pepper, mustard, ketchup, and A.1. Sauce of Vietnam. *Nuoc mam* is an acquired taste, a taste you'd better acquire quickly if you don't want to vomit.

We did not have—so far as I know—the other local delicacy, which is dog. It is disturbing to Western sensibilities to see a wire cage full of puppies on the way to the abattoir or, in the market, to brush against a hanging hindquarter of Rover. There is that little tail, which did so lately wag at master. "Sit!" "Fetch!" "Shake hands!" "Now jump in the frying pan!" "Good dog!"

V

We arrived in Hue, on the Perfume River, at sunset. Hue was the imperial capital of Vietnam, famous for its two-square-mile fortress, the Citadel. This was built by the emperor Gia Long in 1804 but never saw any actual fortress use until the 1968 Tet Offensive, and then the Vietcong attackers got on the wrong side of the walls and held out in there for twenty-four days.

Inside the Citadel is the impressive Palace of Supreme Harmony. Though what impressed me, really, was the unfamiliarity of the decorations—the dragon tangles carved into the woodwork, the Parcheesi-board patterns in the screens and railings, and the old-shoe-in-the-closet turned-up tips of the roof corners. Once I'd looked at it awhile I realized that the Palace of Supreme Harmony was squatty and dank and not a patch on the average Grand Hyatt.

Hue is also famous for beautiful women, though all of Vietnam has them and not just singular enchantresses but huge aggregate percentages of sirens and belles. Any random group of thirty Vietnamese women will contain a dozen who make Julia Roberts look like Lyle Lovett. In the early evening in Hue the girls from the secondary schools come home from classes, fleets of them bicycling through the streets, all dressed in white *oa dai*, trim shirt-dresses worn over loose-fitting trousers. Not for nothing do the remaining Catholic churches ring the Angelus this time of day. I wondered if it changes the nature of a society for beauty to be so common. Maybe in Vietnam "She has a wonderful personality" really means something. But I couldn't figure out a polite way to ask.

We left for Da Nang at dawn. Driving in the dark is impossible in Vietnam, so we had reverted to the visceral body clock of the medieval serf—passed out in the vermin by nine and up before five. Thirty-five miles south of Hue we drove up an astounding set of switchbacks, unguardrailed and rapidly coming unpaved, our precarious roadbed crossing and recrossing the equally precarious roadbed of Vietnam's single railway line. Then Vo wheeled us down at a startling angle onto a coast of little shining harbors and cheddar-colored beaches arrayed in quarter moons and trefoils between rocky headlands. Thatch villages sat in palm groves between the ocean and the road; emerald gardens opened out to the west. Either Eden looked like this or Eve was right to back the snake.

Now I understood how the United States got involved in Vietnam. We fell in love. Maybe the grunts didn't. They had to look at too much incoming and too many other grunts. But the big shots we sent here—the suits, the brass hats, the striped-pants cookie pushers, the CIA white-shoe boys, and special-envoy face cards—they swooned for the place. Everybody, from the first advisors Ike sent in 1955 to Henry Kissinger at the Paris peace talks, had a mad crush on Vietnam.

It broke their hearts. They kept calling and sending flowers. They just couldn't believe this was good-bye.

It's been twenty-one years now. U.S. newspapers, magazines, and television programs weren't, in 1966, filled with agonizing reappraisals of World War II. Let me be the first American to write something about Vietnam without having kittens. I wasn't in the war. I didn't lose my youth and innocence here. (I lost them the regular way, with a calendar.) I don't feel guilty about dodging the draft. Well, I do, but I'm forty-seven years old, and by now I've done a lot of things to feel guilty about. Ducking conscription into a dubious military venture is somewhere down the list. Yes, I had friends who died here. But I had friends who died from cocaine, and I don't get all weird every time I see a glass-topped coffee table.

Qua roi, "past enough," is what the Vietnamese say when you ask them about the war. Our battles in Vietnam are as remote in time for the majority of Vietnamese as our battles in Korea are for me (if Korea had taken place on my block, of course). To look at Vietnam, you'd never know there'd been a war. Giannini said the farmers used to use bomb craters to raise catfish. But since price controls on rice were lifted, the craters have been filled and smoothed into the surrounding paddies. I heard that damage from the defoliant Agent Orange lingered in some places, though how to tell it from government lumbering, I don't know. U.S. air bases stood fenced-off and unused in Da Nang and Tuy Hoa, the rocket-proof hangars looking like upside-down poker-chip trays. The great strategic jackpot of Southeast Asia, Cam Ranh Bay, contained exactly one freighter, rusting and locally registered. On a scrap heap south of Hue I saw two empty napalm pods stenciled USAF. I saw a MIG fighter-plane kiddie carousel in Vinh. In Haiphong a ruined street has been preserved to commemorate the 1972 "Christmas Bombing," which President Nixon launched to remind the North Vietnamese to pay attention at the negotiating table. But when Pham and Vo asked, nobody in Haiphong could recall where the street was.

John and I had gone to the War Museum in Hanoi. Its main courtyard was filled by a ziggurat of American plane wreckage—a Hellcat supplied to the French in the fifties, some kind of pilotless drone from 1965, an F-111 shot down in 1972, and large sections of a B-52 intercepted that same year. Perched on top, all in one piece, was a North Vietnamese MIG-21. This was supposed to be a triumphal display, but it only succeeded in looking like the pile of waste it was.

Inside the museum just a few of the galleries were dedicated to what we think of as the war in Vietnam. Displays were arranged chronologically. The first exhibit concerned Trung Trac and Trung Nhi, sisters who led a rebellion against Chinese colonialists in 40 A.D. Thus the Vietnamese had 1,923 more years of experience in guerrilla warfare than the U.S. Army did. The largest exhibit was a scale model of the valley at Dien Bien Phu, a miniature landscape as big as a tennis court showing, in precise detail, just how dumb were the French.

In the rooms devoted to the American era there were huge photos of U.S. college students protesting the war policies of President "Gion Xon." I couldn't actually find my face in any of the pictures, but I saw plenty of similar dweeby mugs. This was embarrassing: It's one thing for me to be nostalgic about hippie days and something else for commie dictators to celebrate my past.

And then the museum just kept going—fall of the South Vietnamese government in 1975, expulsion of Pol Pot from Phnom Penh in 1978, border clashes with the Chinese in 1979. "When," I asked Pham, "was the last period of sustained peace in Vietnam?"

"Oh, seventeenth, eighteenth century," he said.

One night at dinner Vo and Giannini discovered they'd been on opposite sides of the same series of battles along the Cambodian border in the early seventies—something they both seemed to think was very amusing. A large number of toasts were drunk. Pham, who was too young to have fought Americans, and I, who'd been a longhaired peace creep, were left out. John and Vo filled their glasses first with beer, then with scotch, then with a terrifying rice whiskey called *ba xi de*. "One hundred percent!" Vo would shout, the Vietnamese call for a chugalug. *"Di di mau!"* John would shout, which means "Get the hell out of here." And they'd drain their drinks in a gulp. They got quite merry. And so did the restaurant owners, happily totaling the check.

VI

It was the first full moon of the lunar new year when we arrived in Da Nang, an auspicious day. New fishing boats were being launched into the harbor with so many good-luck fireworks going off that these boats would never sink—they'd explode. We went down the coast a few miles to the old port town of Hoi An, a center of Vietnam's ethnic Chinese, or Hoa. They number 1.3 million, or did before 1975 when many became "boat people," Haitians of the Far East. The Hoa were merchants and manufacturers. They were very successful and thus, according to the logic of Marxism (and the Clinton tax hike), responsible for society's failures.

The Hoa suffered the same fate as the pizza-parlor owner in Spike Lee's *Do the Right Thing,* except at the hands of the world's fourth largest army instead of a small, petulant movie director.

But most Hoa stuck it out. On this day they'd come to Hoi An's pagodas to pay respects to their ancestors. We saw our first civilian Mercedes-Benz here and several Honda Accords. New clothes and big jewelry abounded. We visited a house on the quay along the Thu Bon River, built in the eighteenth century and occupied by the same family of Hoa merchants for seven generations. These tradesmen had survived the radical leveling of the 1771 Tay Son Rebellion (slogan: "Seize the property of the rich and distribute it to the poor"), the ridiculous taxes of the subsequent Nguyen dynasty, the thefts and depredations of French colonialism, the worse thefts and greater depredations of Japanese occupation, the amazing corruption of the Ngo Dinh Diem regime, the drunkenness and diddlings of American soldiers, and the all-of-the-aboves of communism.

The long, dark interior of the house was dense with ornament, its walls carved and lacquered like an inside-out reliquary. The exterior looked—wisely enough—like nothing much.

Vo had to go back to Hanoi. We got a second, and very bad, driver to take us on to Saigon. We went along the coast, past the fabulous expanse of China Beach where there was no trace of Americans, not even any actress litter such as wadded-up divorce rulings or leftover nose jobs. A quack doctor was giving a show by the roadside. He held forth with the wide gestures and speedy cadences universal to his type. But humbug is improved by ignorance of the language. "Relieves Marxist/Leninism!" perhaps the quack was saying. "Purges collectivist thinking! Alleviates central planning! An unfailing antidote and panacea—it will even cure health-care reform!"

South of Da Nang the villages were small—grass shacks on the beaches with terraced fields cut out of the hills on the other side of the highway. Despite the heavy traffic, the farmers left sliced sweet potatoes on the road to dry in the sun—sweet potatoes in a light asphalt sauce finished with truck tire. The good land in Vietnam is so well-peopled and thoroughly farmed that there was no place else to put the crop. This absence of wasted space was also a problem when I wanted privacy for certain body functions.

Traveling in the Third World entails an extraordinary amount of needing to go to the bathroom. And right now. I've read a lot of travel writing and never seen this mentioned. T. E. Lawrence did touch on bowel movements in *Seven Pillars of Wisdom,* but that was war reporting and, anyway, he was constipated, which hardly counts. The irresistible food and unmentionable hygiene of Vietnam made a particularly bad combination. And no amount of Lomotil, Pepto-Bismol, Oral Rehydration Salts, or quick trips over the top of restaurant pigs seemed to do any good. Between Da Nang and Nha Trang I actually found a gas station with a decent john. It was a Turkish, squatter-style toilet in a dark, damp room. But it didn't smell, and it had toilet paper instead of the usual small jug of water. I dropped my jeans and was just hunkering down when I spied movement. I stood up and lit a match. The toilet was full to the brim with crawling insects, uncountable numbers of them, each as big as a Bic lighter.

Even when I didn't have to go to the bathroom, I felt as if I did. My kidneys were swinging around like twin tetherballs during the fourteen hours a day of jolting in the Land Cruiser, and my prostate was swollen to the size of a paperback book. Actually this was a welcome distraction from back pain. My spine felt like a stack of broken china. But, since we were getting up at five, no discomfort was too severe to keep me from dozing off. Then the car would drop into an abysmal pothole and my sleeping face would be sent on a long arc into the dashboard.

Fortunately Giannini and I were adhering to the two key rules of Third World travel:

1. Never run out of whiskey.
2. Never run out of whiskey.

We were also calling frequent halts so we could make notes or take pictures. We were willing to do anything, even our jobs, to get out of the car.

We stopped in a village called Xuan Tho where the men were all building a wooden boat, like the one we'd used in Ha Long Bay. The timber had been cut locally. The keel, transom, gunwales, and other specifically named pieces of boat wood were being shaped by hand. A man squatted by a whetstone doing nothing all day but sharpening adzes and chisels. There was one power tool, an electric drill hooked up to the village's small generator. Bolts, washers, and nuts were the only machine-made parts in the hull, and there were only a few of these. The rest of the boat was being put together with wedges and pegs. The whole, including cabin and fittings, would cost about two thousand dollars, but then they'd have to pay thirty-five hundred for a Chinese diesel engine. It won't be long before they hear about outboards. By the time I get back to Vietnam they'll be skiing behind this boat.

We stopped at another village to watch a fight. The long wooden yokes used to carry coolie baskets turn out to double as quarter staffs—in case anyone wants to do multicultural casting of Little John in the next *Robin Hood* remake.

We stopped at another village to look at circus posters. Most of the acts seemed to involve severed heads or girls in tight clothing being pierced by knives, plus some levitation and swallowing of razor blades. The circus posters were propped against a wall, obscuring a communist propaganda mural. The figures in the mural—a worker, a peasant, a soldier, and so forth—were staring off into the distance. People in communist art are always staring off into the distance. Did they just cut one?

Giannini tried to talk to everybody we met so we wouldn't have to get back in the Land Cruiser. But he didn't have much success. John speaks with a Saigon accent and Vietnamese regional pronunciation varies greatly. I had a little book called, tellingly, *Vietnamese So Easy!* I didn't even try. Vietnamese is tonal, so that meaning varies not only according to the sound you make but according to whether you make that sound as a tenor or a baritone. *Cho, cho,* and *cho* mean, with tonal variations of the vowel, "market," "dog," and "to give." The rest of the language is just as phonetically subtle. *Com* (cooked rice), *khong* (no), *cam* (orange), *ca'm* (not allowed), and *kem* (ice cream) are all pronounced, to the American ear, "kum." Thus you can ask somebody to give you ice cream and wind up in the market with a forbidden orange dog.

We turned inland at Phan Thiet. The hills, at the end of the dry season, were sere and almost Mexican-looking. Old American and European cars began to appear on the road. The mile markers all read

SAIGON now instead of being painted over with the abbreviation for Ho Chi Minh City. Churches were open, and I saw a new Catholic church being built. Buddhist monks wandered around with their begging bowls—almost as many as in Boulder, Colorado.

Saigon didn't begin at any particular place. It just oozed out of the surrounding country until we realized the farms were gone and we were circled by industrial litter. Billboards advertised Taiwanese electronics and Japanese cameras. And motor traffic was heavy enough to cause the first true traffic jams we'd seen. There were four stoplights in the 1,050 miles between Hanoi and Saigon, and only the one in Saigon was being obeyed and only because the intersection was blocked. Here, finally, was something other than a beauty spot. Saigon has none of rural poverty's loveliness, none of manual labor's charm. Saigon is like all the other great modern cities of the world. It's the mess left from people getting rich.

VII

Rich is, of course, what we must be if we're going to fix the world.

A rich Bangladesh wouldn't be an overcrowded hell hole. It would be a suburb, albeit a suburb with bad basement flooding problems.

The rich don't die of hunger. No famine has been known to sweep through the yachts of Monaco or decimate Connecticut's suburbs. If the Somalis were rich, the clan warfare that has caused the famine in their country would turn into the kind of family fights we're all familiar with from holiday dinners. Cousin Mohammed is out of it on qat again. Dad's livid because Rashid's second wife is fasting to protest female circumcision. Granny's getting deaf and doesn't realize everyone could hear her when she said Mom's goat roast tasted like camel flop.

Rich Yagua in the Amazon would become eco-tourists, and

after two weeks they'd leave. The rain forest would be pristine forever, and America would have an interesting new ethnic group armed with blowguns—very good for the crime rate, if they can hit anything.

The millions of rich people in the Czech Republic could burn money instead of soft coal.

The hundreds of rich nations gathered in Rio to fret about ecology could actually fret about ecology instead of panhandling the United States. The fretting would still be a waste of time but it would get Al Gore out of our hair.

In ex-Yugoslavia, everybody would be rich enough to go to college. All their violent impulses would be exhausted in long, acrimonious debates about what to call the University of Ex-Yugoslavia's team mascot. (My suggestion: "Dead.")

And money won't buy health, but it sure will pay doctor bills. The residents of Cité Soleil would be in the pink (in a dark brown way) if Haitians were all rich. Plus they could buy guns and shoot their government.

Money unsaddles the Four Horsemen of the Apocalypse or, anyway, mounts them on donkeys. Famine, Plague, Destruction, and Death become Heart Disease, Cancer, Car Wrecks, and Accidents in the Home.

The Vietnamese understand all this and—damn the years of communist indoctrination—never has there been such a pure, unconcealed, all-hogs-to-the-trough rush into capitalism among the citizens of a supposedly collectivist society. (Never, that is, if you don't count the drug and tie-dye bazaars in the parking lots outside Grateful Dead concerts.)

The Vietnamese government had been edging toward economic reform since the late seventies. But nothing seemed to work. Whatever the government tried, the country remained a socialist skid row. Then, in mid-1990, the Commies just gave up. They took the price controls off everything, put privacy back into private property, and told everybody to go make a living. Faced with a choice between leading and following, the Vietnamese government got out of the way.

And the Vietnamese people aren't Russians. They didn't just stand there with their dong in their hands. (Dong is, no joke, what the money's called. U.S. $1 equaled 11,500 dong at the time of my visit. Claudia Rosset, editorial page editor of the *Asia Wall Street Journal,* pointed out that the first thing the Vietnamese had to do, if they were serious about becoming a credible part of the world economy, was change the name of their currency.)

The economic situation in Vietnam was so interesting that I was interested in talking to economists. I interviewed Do Duc Dinh, whose business card read, "Head of Developing Countries Economic Study Department, Institute of World Economy, National Center for Social Sciences of Viet Nam"—a title almost as long as one of those articles in the *Nation* excusing the failure of Marxism. Speaking of which, Mr. Do was firmly against central planning. The people who generate central planning's abstract theories were no longer important, he said. "You may think of sky," said Mr. Do, "and not know sky. You may think earth looks like sky."

Where this left the Institute of World Economy and its Developing Countries Economic Study Department, I didn't have the heart to ask. But wasn't Mr. Do—as a nominal Marxist, or employee of nominal Marxists, or, anyway, public official in a country with a famous dead Marxist stuffed and exhibited for veneration—worried about capitalist exploitation of the masses? "People were afraid if the window was opened, flys and mosquitoes would come in," said Mr. Do. "But with money we can buy mosquito repellant or screens."

Next I interviewed Le Dang Doanh, deputy director of the Central Institute for Economic Management. He was even more emphatically against economic management being centralized in things like institutes. He told me a story about a fisherman who was a Communist Party member and the head of a local fishing cooperative. The government-set price for fish was less than the cost of catching them. The other fishermen sold their fish on the black market and made a living. But the party member felt the dignity of his office and couldn't bring himself to break the law. He lost money every time he went to sea. Finally he cut off his thumb so he'd never have to fish again.

Mr. Le said that in 1989 state-controlled markets were selling rice for fifty dong a kilo. When price restrictions were lifted the price increased by more than 1200 percent. For a moment I thought Mr. Le was describing the other side of the coin, that I was going to hear another story, this time about someone who cut off his thumb for food. But no. "In one year rice production increased by one million metric tons," said Mr. Le. Vietnam, which had formerly needed to import 500,000 metric tons of rice a year, was now exporting 1.4 million. "Production increased and consumption fell," said Mr. Le. But, I asked, does that mean people are going hungry? "Ha!" said Mr. Le. "They used to stand in line to buy rice for pigs. It was cheaper than pig food."

Mr. Le—who is sometimes called, for his rhetorical style, "Mr. I-would-like-to-say"—then lectured me on the benefits of the free market. He lectured *me*, a New Hampshire tax refugee and unreconstructed Republican. Le Dang Doanh was educated in East Germany. Le Dang Doanh was an economic advisor to Truong Chinh, the hard-line former secretary general of the Vietnamese Communist Party. And Le Dang Doanh wanted to make sure *I* understood economic liberty.

Of course, maybe Mr. Le had a point. I am an American voter and look at what American voters have done to free enterprise lately. Now that Vietnam and the United States have diplomatic relations again, I hope Mr. I-would-like-to-say will give his sermon to Bill Clinton.

On the other hand, Le Dang Doanh and Do Duc Dinh sounded a bit like Bill Clinton themselves. Their free-market gab was all mixed with calls for government programs. In fact, they and Bill Clinton were calling for government programs from the same government—ours. Mr. Le and Mr. Do wanted U.S. aid in the form of IMF and World Bank loans to the Vietnamese state.

Mr. Le and Mr. Do saw nothing contradictory about pursuing economic liberty while increasing totalitarian wherewithal. Nor did a third economist, Dr. Nguyen Xuan Oanh. Dr. Nguyen went to Harvard and was once an official in the South Vietnamese government. He was sent to a reeducation camp after the fall of Saigon but had been rehabilitated and was now a member of the National Assembly.

Imagine the coals-to-Newcastle problem of turning a Harvard graduate into a socialist. Not that Dr. Nguyen was a socialist anymore. "If you keep on being socialist, the only way you go is down," he said. Nonetheless he was full of ideas for social engineering. He proposed mandating "weaker beer" to alleviate the social chaos that might result from capitalism.

"Isn't it dangerous," I asked, "to mix the unlimited economic power of an unregulated market with the infinite political power of an undemocratic state? Isn't this a recipe for corruption on a truly Dan Rostenkowski scale?"

Dr. Nguyen disagreed. "I don't think it would cost much to corrupt *our* politicians—they wouldn't know what to do with large amounts of money."

Le Dang Doanh had told me that in Vietnam "the taxation system is quite weak." He seemed to think this was a problem. "The state is poor but people are rich," he'd said. Consider the glorious prospect of Bill and Hillary living in a trailer on their Whitewater parcel. Imagine senators forced to panhandle for legislation. "Spare fifty billion for a five-year Omnibus Farm Bill?" This would be worth some crummy infrastructure. Picture the U.S. attorney general moonlighting as a mall cop and the secretary of housing and urban development living in the projects. Think about Ted Kennedy trying to cash food stamps at a liquor store. Envision, if you will, 435 mem-

bers of the House of Representatives on Constitution Avenue squee-
geeing windshields.

VIII

Saigon looked like it was governed by bums already. People were
sleeping in doorways. Laundry hung in the guard towers of the former
U.S. embassy. The old architecture had long gone to seed and hadn't
been much to begin with, a product of fifties aesthetics and sixties
communal violence—bunker modern.

Gnat packs of little kids followed me down the sidewalks
shouting, "Where you from! Hello! You give me money!" The ped-
dlers and shopkeepers shouted at me, too, "You buy here! Where you
from! Where you from!" I waved them all away trying to say "No! No!
No!" in Vietnamese and probably saying "Ice cream! Cooked rice!
Orange!"

Saigon was still mostly a two-wheeled city, but motorized and
not just with little Honda engines. Young idiots hardballed down the
avenues on 500cc café racers. Even bicycles were ridden with attitude.
Traffic was like a bad dog. It wasn't important to look both ways when
crossing the street; it was important to not show fear.

There were many more cars here than in Hanoi. Some were
new and Japanese, but there were also Citroëns and Peugeots from the
fifties, Mustangs and Mercedes from the sixties, and giant Chevrolets
from the early seventies. The older cars were well preserved. In 1975
the citizens of Saigon drove their automobiles through the French
doors into the front parlors of their homes, turned the locks, pulled the
blinds, and waited until Vietnam got over communism.

John and I visited a little garage the size of a home workshop
and not much better equipped. The mechanics had one drill press, one
lathe, a paint sprayer, and an acetylene torch. With these, a dozen cars
from Saigon's unintentional time capsule were being restored: a 1971
Peugeot 404 convertible, a little A-2 U.S. Army jeep, a 1972 Toyota

800 sports car, and so on. They were collector's items now and would all be reexported to foreign buyers. An exquisite 1958 Citroën Traction—the getaway car of choice in twenty years of French bank-robber movies—had just been sold to someone in Italy for six thousand U.S. dollars.

This was one of myriad plans and schemes, projects and plots. In the rest of Vietnam people were trying to get rich. In Saigon they were succeeding. Restaurants were opening by the score, none as good as the Dong Hoi roadside shack with the pig in the toilet but all with concessions to international taste such as forks, hamburgers, sit-down commodes, and huge prices. It was like being in the Vietnam Pavilion at Epcot Center. There was even a bar called Apocalypse Now, decorated with war memorabilia. And plenty of American Vietnam vets were back on vacation, reeling around in shock at discovering their teenage girlfriends had turned forty. An international marathon had just been run in Saigon, although the Vietnamese are inexperienced in these matters and didn't think to block traffic. And the locals were so intrigued by people running without being chased that they swarmed onto the course, asking, "Where you from!"

The apartment where the narrator in Graham Greene's *The Quiet American* smoked his opium had been torn down to make way for a six-hundred-room hotel financed by Taiwanese. A floating hotel—which had gone into Chapter 11 on the Great Barrier Reef because Aussies prefer a drunk in the room to a room in the drink—had been towed up the Saigon River. I was schmoozed by a woman in the bar there. I assumed she was a call girl. Worse than that, she sold real estate.

"Joint venture!" was—after "Where you from!"—the most-heard phrase in Saigon. Government and private citizens alike were trying to get in on them, though the government was doing so with typical communist confusion. I visited the gigantic state textile company, Legamex, which wanted to turn itself into a publicly held corporation. "The problem now," an executive told me, "is how to evaluate our fixed assets," a value of what people would pay apparently not having occurred to him.

The government had also reopened Phu Tho racetrack. The grandstands hadn't been painted, or swept, since Saigon fell, and the groundskeepers seemed to belong to some littering advocacy group, but Phu Tho was filled with punters. God knows what their handicap method was. The horses were ponies, the jockeys were children, and neither seem to be trained for anything particular. Just getting the kids mounted was no sure bet. They were supposed to be sixteen years old but I doubt most were twelve, and some looked as young as eight. I watched one trainer hold a tyke in racing silks aloft with both hands and chase a rearing horse around the paddock, trying to slam-dunk his jockey into the saddle. In the first race only one kid had his feet placed properly in the stirrups, and he ran second to last.

When the starting gate opened, the horses ran down the track any old way, like mice let out of a paper sack. Jockeys were launched in every direction. A riderless horse placed third in one race. The moment the jockeys crossed the finish line—or came to in the in-field—they had to run back to the tack room and strip. Somebody else needed the jersey for the next race.

Di choi, "go for fun," the atmosphere in Saigon is called. Giannini and I tried to have some at the Super Star Disco. Unfortunately, Asia is the continent rhythm forgot. At best Asian music is off-brand American pop, like Sonny Bono in a karaoke bar. At worst Asian music sounds as if a truck full of wind chimes collided with a stack of empty oil drums during a birdcall contest. The locals boogied away regardless, dancing in the style of parents at a Bar Mitzvah.

Out on the streets the prostitutes were cruising; prostitutes on motor scooters who wore tight jeans, a pound of makeup, and elbow-length blue gloves; prostitutes being pedaled around in *cyclos* by their combination pimp/rickshaw-driver boyfriends; and prostitutes who stood outside hotel lobbies. "Where you from! Where you from! Where you from!" There were heroin addicts, too. They couldn't get needles, so they slashed their legs with razor blades and rubbed heroin into the wounds. They were bandaged and hobbling on crutches like victims of pathetic accidents except for the slow and dreamy way they limped.

"How is this different from Saigon before it fell?" I asked Giannini.

"It isn't."

IX

Money is preferable to politics. It is the difference between being free to be anybody you want and being free to vote for anybody you want. And money is more effective than politics both in solving problems and in providing individual independence. To rid ourselves of all the trouble in the world we need to make money. And to make money we need to be free. But, oh, the trouble caused by freedom and money.

So, in the end, Vietnam was a bit depressing, too. Hard to believe that the thrilling idea of human liberty always results in people acting so . . . human. Like Americans or something. (Ho Chi Minh called himself "the George Washington of Vietnam.") Is it possible what the great philosophers have told us through the ages is true? That money isn't everything? Sure, they'd tell us this. Because how much does being a great philosopher pay? How many times have you heard about a rich person who "inherited an old logical positivist fortune"? And yet even vast amounts of cash in small, unmarked bills cannot release us from the human condition.

I'd like to end this book with a clarion call to all the peoples of the earth. . . . Is a clarion some kind of very large clarinet? I don't know. And how would clarinet music solve our problems? I'd like to end this book a lot of ways. Except I don't have any answers. Use your common sense. Be nice. This is the best I can do. All the trouble in the world is human trouble. Well, that's not true. But when cancer cells run amok and burst out of the prostate and take over the liver and lymph glands and end up killing everything in the body including themselves, they certainly are acting like some humans we know. All the trouble *in this book* is human trouble. We can fix it all and we'll still be humans and causing trouble.

Maybe this *isn't* such a hopeful moment in history. Really, it's something of a disappointment to know that when mankind—through noble struggles, grim sacrifices (and a lot of money-making)—does achieve such things as property rights, rule of law, responsible government, and universal education, the fruit borne of these splendid accomplishments is, um, me.

And for the future—(but I write this reeling,

Having got drunk exceedingly today,

So that I seem to stand upon the ceiling)

I say—the future is a serious matter—

And so—for God's sake—hock and soda water!

—Lord Byron